Cold War
Almanac

8/04

Cold War
Almanac

Volume 1

Sharon M. Hanes
and Richard C. Hanes

Lawrence W. Baker,
Project Editor

REF
909.825
HAN

Detroit • New York • San Diego • San Francisco • Cleveland • New Haven, Conn. • Waterville, Maine • London • Munich

THOMSON
— ✦ — ™
GALE

Cold War: Almanac

Sharon M. Hanes and Richard C. Hanes

Project Editor
Lawrence W. Baker

Editorial
Sarah Hermsen, Matthew May, Allison McNeill, Diane Sawinski

Permissions
Margaret Chamberlain, Shalice Shah-Caldwell

Imaging and Multimedia
Mary Grimes, Lezlie Light, Mike Logusz, Kelly A. Quin

Product Design
Pamela A. E. Galbreath, Jennifer Wahi

Composition
Evi Seoud

Manufacturing
Rita Wimberley

Library of Congress Control Card Number: 2003019223

ISBN 0-7876-9089-9 (2-volume set); 0-7876-7662-4 (volume 1); 0-7876-9087-2 (volume 2)

Printed in the United States of America
10 9 8 7 6 5 4 3 2 1

Contents

Introduction vii

Reader's Guide. xi

Words to Know xv

People to Know xxix

Cold War Timeline. xxxv

Research and Activity Ideas xlix

Volume 1

Chapter 1: Origins of the Cold War 1

Chapter 2: Conflict Builds 27

Chapter 3: Germany and Berlin. 55

Chapter 4: Dawning of the Nuclear Age. 79

Chapter 5: Homeland Insecurities. 99

Chapter 6: Espionage in the Cold War 125

Chapter 7: A Worldwide Cold War 167

Volume 2

Chapter 8: Renewed Tensions 191

Chapter 9: Cuban Missile Crisis 213

Chapter 10: Mutual Assured Destruction 233

Chapter 11: An Unsettled World 251

Chapter 12: Home Front Turmoil: The 1960s 275

Chapter 13: Détente: A Lessening of Tensions 297

Chapter 14: A Freeze in Relations 319

Chapter 15: End of the Cold War 347

Where to Learn More lix

Index lxiii

Introduction

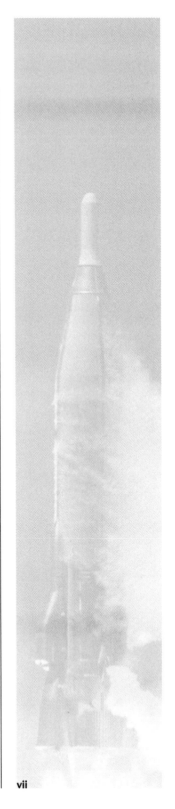

Sometimes single events alter the course of history; other times, a chain reaction of seemingly lesser occurrences changes the path of nations. The intense rivalry between the United States and the Soviet Union that emerged immediately after World War II (1939–45) followed the second pattern. Known as the Cold War, the rivalry grew out of mutual distrust between two starkly different societies: communist Soviet Union and the democratic West, which was led by the United States and included Western Europe. Communism is a political and economic system in which the Communist Party controls all aspects of citizens' lives and private ownership of property is banned. It is not compatible with America's democratic way of life. Democracy is a political system consisting of several political parties whose members are elected to various government offices by vote of the people. The rapidly growing rivalry between the two emerging post–World War II superpowers in 1945 would dominate world politics until 1991. Throughout much of the time, the Cold War was more a war of ideas than one of battlefield combat. Yet for generations, the Cold War affected almost every aspect of American life and those who lived in numerous other countries around the world.

The global rivalry was characterized by many things. Perhaps the most dramatic was the cost in lives and public funds. Millions of military personnel and civilians were killed in conflicts often set in Third World countries. This toll includes tens of thousands of American soldiers in the Korean War (1950–53) and Vietnam War (1954–75) and thousands of Soviet soldiers in Afghanistan. National budgets were stretched to support the nuclear arms races, military buildups, localized wars, and aid to friendly nations. On the international front, the United States often supported oppressive but strongly anti-communist military dictatorships. On the other hand, the Soviets frequently supported revolutionary movements seeking to overthrow established governments. Internal political developments within nations around the world were interpreted by the two superpowers—the Soviet Union and the United States—in terms of the Cold War rivalry. In many nations, including the Soviet-dominated Eastern European countries, basic human freedoms were lost. New international military and peacekeeping alliances were also formed, such as the United Nations (UN), the North Atlantic Treaty Organization (NATO), the Organization of American States (OAS), and the Warsaw Pact.

Effects of the Cold War were extensive on the home front, too. The U.S. government became more responsive to national security needs, including the sharpened efforts of the Federal Bureau of Investigation (FBI). Created were the Central Intelligence Agency (CIA), the National Security Council (NSC), and the Department of Defense. Suspicion of communist influences within the United States built some individual careers and destroyed others. The national education priorities of public schools were changed to emphasize science and engineering after the Soviets launched the satellite *Sputnik,* which itself launched the space race.

What would cause such a situation to develop and last for so long? One major factor was mistrust for each other. The communists were generally shunned by other nations, including the United States, since they gained power in Russia in 1917 then organized that country into the Soviet Union. The Soviets' insecurities loomed large. They feared another invasion from the West through Poland, as had happened through the centuries. On the other hand, the West was highly suspicious of the harsh closed society of Soviet communism. As a result, a move by one nation would bring a response by the other. Hard-liners on both sides believed long-term coexistence was not feasible.

A second major factor was that the U.S. and Soviet ideologies were dramatically at odds. The political, social, and economic systems of democratic United States and communist Soviet Union were essentially incompatible. Before the communist (or Bolshevik) revolution in 1917, the United States and Russia competed as they both sought to expand into the Pacific Northwest. In addition, Americans had a strong disdain for Russian oppression under their monarchy of the tsars. Otherwise, contact between the two growing powers was almost nonexistent until thrown together as allies in a common cause to defeat Germany and Japan in World War II.

It was during the meetings of the allied leaders in Yalta and Potsdam in 1945 when peaceful postwar cooperation was being sought that the collision course of the two new superpowers started becoming more evident. The end of World War II had brought the U.S. and Soviet armies face-to-face in central Europe in victory over the Germans. Yet the old mistrusts between communists and capitalists quickly dominated diplomatic relations. Capitalism is an economic system in which property and businesses are privately owned. Prices, production, and distribution of goods are determined by competition in a market relatively free of government intervention. A peace treaty ending World War II in Europe was blocked as the Soviets and the U.S.-led West carved out spheres of influence. Western Europe and Great Britain aligned with the United States and collectively was referred to as the "West"; Eastern Europe would be controlled by the Soviet Communist Party. The Soviet Union and its Eastern European satellite countries were collectively referred to as the "East." The two powers tested the resolve of each other in Germany, Iran, Turkey, and Greece in the late 1940s.

In 1949, the Soviets successfully tested an atomic bomb and Chinese communist forces overthrew the National Chinese government, and U.S. officials and American citizens feared a sweeping massive communist movement was overtaking the world. A "red scare" spread through America. The term "red" referred to communists, especially the Soviets. The public began to suspect that communists or communist sympathizers lurked in every corner of the nation.

Meanwhile, the superpower confrontations spread from Europe to other global areas: Asia, Africa, the Middle East, and Latin America. Most dramatic were the Korean and Vietnam wars, the Cuban Missile Crisis, and the military standoffs in Berlin, Germany. However, bloody conflicts erupted in many other areas as the United States and Soviet Union sought to expand their influence by supporting or opposing various movements.

In addition, a costly arms race lasted decades despite sporadic efforts at arms control agreements. The score card for the Cold War was kept in terms of how many nuclear weapons one country had aimed at the other. Finally, in the 1970s and 1980s, the Soviet Union could no longer keep up with the changing world economic trends. Its tightly controlled and highly inefficient industrial and agricultural systems could not compete in world markets while the government was still focusing its wealth on Cold War confrontations and the arms race. Developments in telecommunications also made it more difficult to maintain a closed society. Ideas were increasingly being exchanged despite longstanding political barriers. The door was finally cracked open in the communist European nations to more freedoms in the late 1980s through efforts at economic and social reform. Seizing the moment, the long suppressed populations of communist Eastern European nations and fifteen Soviet republics demanded political and economic freedom.

Through 1989, the various Eastern European nations replaced long-time communist leaders with noncommunist officials. By the end of 1991, the Soviet Communist Party had been banned from various Soviet republics, and the Soviet Union itself ceased to exist. After a decades-long rivalry, the end to the Cold War came swiftly and unexpectedly.

A new world order dawned in 1992 with a single superpower, the United States, and a vastly changed political landscape around much of the globe. Communism remained in China and Cuba, but Cold War legacies remained elsewhere. In the early 1990s, the United States was economically burdened with a massive national debt, the former Soviet republics were attempting a very difficult economic transition to a more capitalistic open market system, and Europe, starkly divided by the Cold War, was reunited once again and sought to establish a new union including both Eastern and Western European nations.

Reader's Guide

Cold War: Almanac presents a comprehensive overview of the Cold War, the period in history from 1945 until 1991 that was dominated by the rivalry between the world's superpowers, the United States and the Soviet Union. The *Almanac* covers the origins of the Cold War, including the fierce divisions created by the differences between American democracy and capitalism and Soviet communism; the key programs and treaties, such as the Marshall Plan, Berlin Airlift, and Strategic Defense Initiative (SDI); how the general public coped with the rivalry and consequent nuclear buildup; government changes designed to make society feel more secure; the end of the Cold War, brought about by the fall of communism in Eastern Europe and the dissolution of the Soviet Union; and the aftereffects of the Cold War, still felt in the twenty-first century.

Coverage and features

Cold War: Almanac is divided into fifteen chapters, each focusing on a particular topic or time period, such as the origins of the Cold War, the beginning of the nuclear age, the arms race, espionage, anticommunist campaigns and political purges on the home fronts, détente, the Cuban Missile Crisis, the Berlin Airlift and the Berlin Wall, the Korean and Vietnam wars, and the ending of the Cold War. Each chapter contains three types of sidebars: "Words to Know" and "People to Know" boxes, which define important terms and individuals discussed in the chapter; and boxes that describe people, events, and facts of special interest. Each chapter concludes with a list of additional sources students can go to for more information. More than 140 black-and-white photographs and maps help illustrate the material.

Each volume of *Cold War: Almanac* begins with a timeline of important events in the history of the Cold War; "Words to Know" and "People to Know" sections that feature important terms and people from the entire Cold War era; and a "Research and Activity Ideas" section with suggestions for study questions, group projects, and oral and dramatic presentations. The two volumes conclude with a general bibliography and a subject index so students can easily find the people, places, and events discussed throughout *Cold War: Almanac*.

U•X•L Cold War Reference Library

Cold War: Almanac is only one component of the three-part U•X•L Cold War Reference Library. The other two titles in this set are:

- *Cold War: Biographies* (two volumes) presents the life stories of fifty individuals who played key roles in the Cold War superpower rivalry. Though primarily a competition between the United States and the Soviet Union, the Cold War is a story of individual personalities that critically influenced the direction of the rivalry at various crossroads and in different regions of the world. Profiled are well-known figures such as Joseph Stalin, Harry Truman, Nikita Khrushchev, Henry Kissinger, John F. Kennedy, Mao Zedong, and Mikhail Gorbachev, as well as lesser-known individuals such as physicist and father of the Soviet atomic bomb Igor Kurchatov, British foreign minister Ernest Bevin, and longtime U.S. foreign policy analyst George F. Kennan.

- *Cold War: Primary Sources* (one volume) this book tells the story of the Cold War in the words of the people who lived and shaped it. Thirty-one excerpted documents provide a wide range of perspectives on this period of history. Included are excerpts from presidential press conferences; addresses to U.S. Congress and Soviet Communist Party meetings; public speeches; telegrams; magazine articles; radio and television addresses; and later reflections by key government leaders.

- A cumulative index of all three titles in the U•X•L Cold War Reference Library is also available.

Acknowledgments

Special thanks to Catherine Filip, who typed much of the manuscript. Much appreciation also goes to copyeditor Jane Woychick, proofreader Wyn Hilty, indexer Dan Brannen, and typesetter Marco Di Vita of the Graphix Group for their fine work.

Dedication

To Aaron and Kara Hanes, that their children may learn about the events and ideas that shaped the world through the latter half of the twentieth century.

Comments and suggestions

We welcome your comments on *Cold War: Almanac* and suggestions for other topics to consider. Please write: Editors, *Cold War: Almanac,* U•X•L, 27500 Drake Rd., Farmington Hills, Michigan 48331-3535; call toll free: 1-800-877-4253; fax to 248-699-8097; or send e-mail via http://www.gale.com.

Words to Know

A

Alliance for Progress: A program designed to block the spread of communism by improving the overall quality of life for Latin Americans. The Alliance attempted to reduce disease, increase literacy, and ease poverty throughout Latin America.

Allied Control Council: An organization of military governors from each of the four zones of Germany.

Allies: Alliances of countries in military opposition to another group of nations. In World War II, the Allied powers included Great Britain, the United States, and the Soviet Union.

Annihilation: Complete destruction.

Armistice: A temporary agreement to end fighting in a war; a cease-fire.

Arms race: A key aspect of superpower rivalry in which one superpower amasses weapons, particularly nuclear weapons, to keep up with another superpower or to gain an edge.

Asymmetrical response: The potentially much harsher retaliation of a nation already attacked.

Atomic bomb: An explosive device that releases nuclear energy (energy that comes from an atom's core). All previous explosive devices were powered by rapid burning or decomposition of a chemical compound; they only released energy from the outermost electrons of an atom. Nuclear explosives are energized by splitting an atom, a process called fission.

Atomic Energy Commission (AEC): A unit established by Congress in July 1946 that managed the nuclear research facilities in Oak Ridge, Tennessee; Hanford, Washington; and Los Alamos, New Mexico.

Authoritarian: A political system in which authority is centered in a ruling party that demands complete obedience of its citizens and is not legally accountable to the people.

B

Bay of Pigs: The failed U.S.-backed invasion of Cuba at the Bay of Pigs by fifteen hundred Cuban exiles opposed to Fidel Castro, on April 17, 1961.

Berlin airlift: Massive shipments of food and goods, airlifted into the Western sector of Berlin, organized by the Western powers, after the Soviets halted all shipments of supplies and food from the eastern zone into West Berlin. The Americans nicknamed the airlift Operation Vittles, while the British dubbed the effort Operation Plain Fare.

Berlin blockade: A ten-and-a-half-month stoppage by the Soviets of shipments of supplies and food through East Germany into West Berlin. The Soviets also cut all coal-generated electricity supplied from East Germany to Berlin's western sectors, and land and water routes from West Germany into Berlin were closed.

Berlin Wall: A wall dividing the Soviet-controlled sector of Berlin from the three Western-controlled zones, built in an attempt to stem the tide of refugees seeking asylum in the West.

Big Three: The trio of U.S. president Franklin D. Roosevelt, British prime minister Winston Churchill, and Soviet leader Joseph Stalin; also refers to the countries of the United States, Great Britain, and the Soviet Union.

Blacklisting: Denying employment to anyone found connected to a group that in any way had anything to do with subversive activities, real or imagined.

Bolshevik: A member of the revolutionary political party of Russian workers and peasants that became the Communist Party after the Russian Revolution of 1917; the terms Bolshevik and communist became interchangeable, with communist eventually becoming more common.

Brinkmanship: An increased reliance on nuclear weapons as a deterrent to threats of communist expansion in the world; an international game played between the Soviet Union and the United States of who had the highest number of and the most powerful weapons with which to threaten the enemy.

Bugs: Listening devices planted in such places as telephones and in walls to allow eavesdropping on conversations.

C

Capitalism: An economic system in which property and businesses are privately owned. Prices, production, and distribution of goods are determined by competition in a market relatively free of government intervention.

Central committee: The important administrative body in the Communist Party overseeing day-to-day party activities.

Cold War: A prolonged conflict for world dominance from 1945 to 1991 between the two superpowers—the democratic, capitalist United States and the communist Soviet Union. The weapons of conflict were commonly words of propaganda and threats.

Collectivism: A system that combines many local holdings, such as farms or industry, into a single unit that is supervised by the government.

Colonialism: An economic system in which Western European nations controlled various underdeveloped countries located around the world.

Communism: A system of government in which the nation's leaders are selected by a single political party that controls all aspects of society. Private ownership of property is eliminated and government directs all economic production. The goods produced and accumulated wealth are, in theory, shared relatively equally by all. All religious practices are banned.

Containment: A key U.S. Cold War policy to restrict the territorial growth of communist rule.

Counterculture: A rebellion of Americans, mostly youth, against the established U.S. social values largely spawned by opposition to the Vietnam War.

Counterinsurgency: A military strategy to fight guerilla forces rising against established governments.

Coup d'état: The violent and forceful act of changing a government's leadership.

Covert: Secret.

Cryptosystems: Secret code systems that protect countries' communications; also called cipher; a cryptonologist "deciphered" the secret codes.

Cuban Missile Crisis: A showdown in October 1962 that brought the Soviet Union and the United States close to war over the existence of Soviet nuclear missiles in Cuba.

D

Decolonization: When a country's people subjected to rule by a foreign power seek to overturn that rule and gain national independence.

Deficit spending: When a government spends more money than the revenue coming in; a key feature of the Cold War arms race with high military expenses.

Democracy: A system of government that allows multiple political parties. Their members are elected to various government offices by popular vote of the people.

Destalinization: Soviet leader Nikita Khrushchev's effort to introduce social reforms to the Soviet Union by providing greater personal freedoms, lessening the powers of the secret police, closing concentration and hard-labor camps, and restoring certain legal processes.

Détente: A lessening of tensions between nations.

Deterrence: An attempt to discourage another nation from initiating hostile activity by threatening severe retaliation such as nuclear war.

Dictatorship: A form of government in which a person wields absolute power and control over the people.

Disarmament: The reduction of weapons and armed forces of a nation.

Dissidents: Those who actively disagree with the ruling authority.

Doctrine: A particular idea or policy embraced by a state or group.

Domino theory: The belief that if one country falls to communism then nearby nations will be taken over one after another.

E

Eisenhower Doctrine: A doctrine giving the U.S. president the right to use force in the Middle East against any form of communist aggression.

Espionage: The act of spying on others to discover military or political secrets.

Expansionism: The policy of a nation to gain more territory by taking over control of other countries.

F

Fascism: A dictatorship based on strong nationalism and often racism.

Fifth Amendment: An amendment to the U.S. Constitution that protects people from having to testify against themselves in formal hearings.

Fission: A process in which the nucleus of an atom of a heavy element is split into two nuclei, resulting in lighter elements releasing a substantial amount of energy; the process utilized in atomic bombs such as that dropped on Hiroshima, Japan, in 1945.

Flexible response: The military strategy to maintain both sufficient conventional and nuclear weapons so that hostile actions by another nation may be met with a similar level of force.

Fusion: The joining together of atomic nuclei of the element hydrogen, generating an incredible amount of heat; the process utilized in hydrogen bombs.

G

Glasnost: A plan for greater freedom of expression put into place by Soviet president Mikhail Gorbachev in the mid-1980s.

H

Hollywood Ten: Ten producers, directors, and screenwriters from Hollywood who were called before the House Un-American Activities Committee (HUAC) to explain their politics and reveal what organizations they were part of. Eight of the ten had communist affiliations.

House Un-American Activities Committee (HUAC): A congressional group established to investigate and root out any communist influences within the United States.

Human rights: A broad notion that all people, simply by being human, deserve certain economic and political freedoms of opportunity such as freedom from various kinds of deprivations including freedom from oppression, unlawful imprisonment and execution, torture, persecution, and exploitation.

Hydrogen bomb: A bomb more powerful than the atomic bomb that derives its explosive energy from a nuclear fusion reaction.

I

Ideology: A body of beliefs.

Imperialism: A policy of expanding the rule of one nation over foreign countries.

Industrialization: A large-scale introduction of industry into an area, normally replacing agriculture to some degree.

Intercontinental ballistic missile: A missile that has a range of over 3,500 nautical miles.

Intermediate-range ballistic missile: A missile that has a range of between 800 and 1,500 nautical miles.

Internationalist: A person who promotes cooperation among nations.

Isolationism: A policy of avoiding official agreements with other nations in order to remain neutral.

J

Junta: A group of military leaders in political control.

K

Kiloton: Approximately equal to the amount of explosive force (energy released) of 1,000 tons of TNT, a conventional (non-nuclear) explosive.

Korean War (1950–53): A conflict that began when North Korean communist troops crossed the thirty-eighth parallel into South Korea.

L

Land reform: A common feature of nationalist movements that often involves taking away large land holdings owned by foreigners and parceling them out to its citizens for small farming operations.

M

Manhattan Project: A project begun in 1942—during World War II (1939–45)—with the goal of building an atomic weapon before scientists in Germany or Japan did.

Marketplace: The world of commerce operating relatively free of government interventions where demand and availability of goods and materials determine prices, distribution, and production levels.

Marshall Plan: A massive U.S. plan to promote Europe's economic recovery from the war; officially known as the European Recovery Program for Western Europe, it was made available to all nations, though the communist regime rejected it.

McCarthyism: A term used to describe a person who makes accusations of disloyalty supported by doubtful evidence; it originated during the 1950s anticommunism campaign of U.S. senator Joseph R. McCarthy of Wisconsin.

Megaton: Approximately equals the explosive force of 1,000,000 tons of TNT.

Military industrial complex: A politically powerful alliance of the military services and industry that provides materials to the military.

Moles: Spies who betray the agency they worked for by quietly funneling top secret information to the enemy.

Molotov Plan: A Soviet series of trade agreements—made after the rejection of the Marshall Plan—designed to provide economic assistance to eastern European countries.

Most-favored-nation status: An economic and political program that lowers taxes on goods exported by a foreign nation to the United States, making it much easier to sell goods to the U.S. public and businesses.

Mutual assured destruction (MAD): A military strategy in which the threat of catastrophic damages by a nuclear counterstrike would deter any launch of a first-strike attack.

N

Nation building: Installing friendly governments wherever feasible around the world by the United States and the Soviet Union.

National Security Act: An act that created the National Security Council, which advises the president on national security policy.

National Security Agency (NSA): The United States' prime intelligence organization that listens to and analyzes foreign communications.

National Security Council Document 68, or NSC-68: A plan for keeping Soviet influence contained within its existing areas; the strategy required dramatic increases in U.S. military spending.

Nationalism: A strong loyalty to one's own nation and the quest to be independent from other nations.

Nationalize: To place land or industry under ownership of the state.

Ninjas: Highly skilled spies who can move in and out of buildings without keys, find entrance into forbidden places, or easily slip in and out of personal relationships.

Nonproliferation: The halt of the spread of nuclear weapons to previously non-nuclear countries.

Normalization: Improved relations between two countries to more usual diplomatic conditions.

North Atlantic Treaty Organization (NATO): A peacetime alliance of the United States and eleven other nations, and a key factor in the attempt to contain communism; the pact meant that the United States became the undisputed global military leader.

O

Overt: Open; not secret.

P

Parity: The act of maintaining an equal amount of something, such as similar levels of nuclear weapons between the two superpowers.

Peace Corps: A U.S. program designed to promote world peace and friendship by having citizens travel abroad and assist developing nations.

Peaceful coexistence: A state of living peacefully and accepting other ideologies that widely differ; with regard to military competition, the United States and the Soviet Union sought to coexist peacefully.

Perestroika: A 1980s Soviet plan for recovery by restructuring the Soviet Union's economic and social systems.

Philosophies: Certain principles or bodies of knowledge that are followed by a group.

Plutonium: A radioactive element capable of explosive fission.

Politburo: The important policy making body of the Communist Party.

Prague Spring: A brief thaw in Cold War communist policies when in 1968 Czechoslovakia's Communist Party leader, Alexander Dubcek, sought to modernize communism with certain democratic reforms, including greater freedom of the press.

Propaganda: The spread of information or ideas to promote a certain organization or cause.

Purge: To remove undesirable persons from a group, such as mass executions of Communist Party members by Soviet leadership.

R

Red scare: A great fear among U.S. citizens in the late 1940s and early 1950s that communist influences were infiltrating U.S. society and government and could eventually lead to the overthrow of the American democratic system.

Reparations: Payments made by a defeated nation for war damages it inflicted on the winning nations.

Resistance movement: Underground forces within a nation organized to defeat an occupying force.

Revolutionaries: Those seeking change by forceful overthrow of the existing government.

S

Sabotage: An illegal interference of work or industrial production such as by enemy agents or employees.

Satellite: A country under domination by another; also, a man-made object that is launched into orbit around Earth.

Second strike capability: A military strategy in which a sufficiently large nuclear arsenal would ensure enough U.S. missiles would survive a Soviet first strike to effectively destroy the Soviet Union in an automatic second strike.

Silent majority: The segment of society in the 1970s that quietly supported the nation's war efforts in Vietnam as opposed to the more visible anti-war protesters.

Southeast Asia Treaty Organization (SEATO): An alliance of nations created to combat the expansion of communism in the Southeast Asian region, specifically Vietnam, Cambodia, and Laos. Member nations included the United States, Great Britain, France, New Zealand, Thailand, Australia, Pakistan, and the Philippines.

Space race: A key feature of the Cold War rivalry between the two superpowers in their quest to gain dominance in space technology and achievements.

Sphere of influence: An area over which a nation holds domination over other nations, such as the United States and Soviet Union during the Cold War holding influence over major areas of the world.

Strategic Air Command (SAC): A unit established by the U.S. military with the goal of identifying targets in the Soviet Union and being ready to deliver nuclear weapons to those targets.

Strategic arms: Military weapons key to the strategy of making the enemy incapable of conducting war; generally refers to long-ranging weapons.

Strategic Triad: The United States' trio of weapons aimed at the Soviet Union; the arsenal consisted of long- and intermediate-range missiles fitted with nuclear warheads, long-range bombers carrying nuclear weapons, and nuclear-powered submarines with onboard nuclear-tipped missiles.

Subversive: An individual who attempts to overthrow or destroy an established political system.

Superpowers: Nations capable of influencing the acts or policies of other nations; during the Cold War, the United States and Soviet Union were considered the superpowers.

T

Tactical arms: Military weapons that allow flexibility and skillful maneuverability in combat; generally referring to short-range weapons.

Thermonuclear: A nuclear fusion reaction releasing tremendous heat and energy as utilized in the hydrogen bomb.

Third World: Poor underdeveloped or economically developing nations in Africa, Asia, and Latin America. Many were seeking independence from political control of Western European nations.

Totalitarianism: A highly centralized form of government that has total control over the population.

Tradecraft: The tricks and techniques used by spies in their covert, or secret, operations.

Treaty: A formal agreement between two nations relating to peace or trade.

Truman Doctrine: A Cold War–era program designed by President Harry S. Truman that sent aid to anticommunist forces in Turkey and Greece. The Soviet Union had naval stations in Turkey, and nearby Greece was fighting a civil war with communist-dominated rebels.

U

United Nations: An international organization, comprised of most of the nations of the world, created to preserve world peace and security.

Uranium: A metallic natural element used primarily in atomic bombs and in nuclear power plants.

V

Vietcong: Vietnamese communists engaged in warfare against the government and people of South Vietnam.

W

Warsaw Pact: A mutual military alliance between the Soviet Union and the Eastern European nations under Soviet influence, including East Germany.

Y

Yalta Conference: A 1944 meeting between Allied leaders Joseph Stalin, Winston Churchill, and Franklin D. Roosevelt in anticipation of an Allied victory in Europe over Adolf Hitler and Germany's Nazi Party. The leaders discussed how to manage lands conquered by Germany, and Roosevelt and Churchill urged Stalin to enter the Soviet Union in the war against Japan.

People to Know

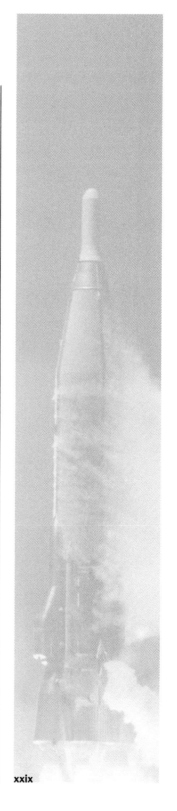

A

Jacobo Arbenz Guzmán (1913–1971): Guatemalan president, 1950–54.

Clement R. Attlee (1883–1967): British prime minister, 1945–51.

B

Fulgencio Batista y Zaldívar (1901–1973): Cuban dictatorial leader, 1933–44, 1952–59.

Lavrenty Beria (1899–1953): Leader of the Soviet secret police (KGB) and manager of the Soviet bomb project.

Anthony F. Blunt (1907–1983): One of the KGB's famed Cambridge Spies.

Willy Brandt (1913–1992): West German chancellor, 1969–74.

Leonid Brezhnev (1906–1982): Leader of the Soviet Union Communist Party, 1964–82.

Zbigniew Brzezinski (1928–): U.S. national security advisor, 1977–81.

Guy Burgess (1910–1963): One of the KGB's famed Cambridge Spies.

George Bush (1924–): Forty-first U.S. president, 1989–93.

James F. Byrnes (1879–1972): U.S. secretary of state, 1945–47.

C

Jimmy Carter (1924–): Thirty-ninth U.S. president, 1977–81.

Carlos Castillo Armas (1914–1957): Guatemalan president, 1954–57.

Fidel Castro (1926–): Cuban premier/president, 1959–.

Whittaker Chambers (1901–1961): A journalist who admitted at the House Un-American Activities Committee (HUAC) hearings that he had once been a communist but had later denounced communism; he named Alger Hiss as a communist.

Chiang Kai-shek (1887–1975): Ruler of China's Nationalist (Kuomintang) party, 1943–49.

Winston Churchill (1874–1965): British prime minister, 1940–45, 1951–55.

D

Charles de Gaulle (1890–1970): French president, 1958–69.

Deng Xiaoping (1905–1997): Leader of Communist China, 1976–90.

Martin Dies (1900–1972): U.S. representative from Texas, 1931–44, 1953–58; chairman of the House Un-American Activities Committee (HUAC), often called the Dies Committee.

Anatoly Dobrynin (1919–): Soviet ambassador to the United States, 1962–86.

Alexander Dubcek (1921–1992): Czechoslovakian Communist Party leader, 1968.

John Foster Dulles (1888–1959): U.S. secretary of state, 1953–59.

E

Dwight D. Eisenhower (1890–1969): Thirty-fourth U.S. president, 1953–61.

F

Gerald R. Ford (1913–): Thirty-eighth U.S. president, 1974–77.

Klaus Fuchs (1911–1988): British scientist who worked on the U.S. Manhattan Project and began passing detailed notes to the Soviets about the work being done on the development of a nuclear bomb.

G

Mikhail Gorbachev (1931–): Soviet president, 1985–91.

Andrey Gromyko (1909–1989): Soviet foreign minister, 1957–85.

Leslie R. Groves (1896–1970): U.S. Army officer in charge of the Manhattan Project.

H

Alger Hiss (1904–1996): U.S. State Department official who was accused of being a communist; he served three years and eight months in prison after being convicted of perjury.

Adolf Hitler (1889–1945): Nazi party president, 1921–45; German leader, 1933–45.

J

Lyndon B. Johnson (1908–1973): Thirty-sixth U.S. president, 1963–69.

K

John F. Kennedy (1917–1963): Thirty-fifth U.S. president, 1961–63.

Robert F. Kennedy (1925–1968): U.S. attorney general, 1961–64.

Nikita Khrushchev (1894–1971): Soviet premier, 1958–64.

Martin Luther King Jr. (1929–1968): African American civil rights leader.

Henry Kissinger (1923–): U.S. national security advisor, 1969–75; secretary of state, 1973–77.

Igor Kurchatov (1903–1960): The Soviet Union's premier nuclear physicist who led the building of the Soviet's atomic bomb in 1948.

L

Vladimir I. Lenin (1870–1924): Leader of the Bolshevik Revolution, 1917; head of the Soviet government, 1918–24; founder of the Communist Party in Russia, 1919.

Patrice Lumumba (1925–1961): Congolese nationalist movement activist; prime minister, 1960.

M

Douglas MacArthur (1880–1964): Supreme commander of occupational forces in Japan, 1945–51, and UN forces in Korea, 1950–51.

Donald Maclean (1913–1983): One of the KGB's famed Cambridge Spies.

Georgy M. Malenkov (1902–1988): Soviet premier, 1953–55.

Mao Zedong (1893–1976): Chairman of the People's Republic of China and its Communist party, 1949–76.

George C. Marshall (1880–1959): U.S. secretary of state, 1947–49; secretary of defense, 1950–51.

Joseph R. McCarthy (1908–1957): U.S. senator from Wisconsin, 1947–57; for four years, he sought to expose American communists by manipulating the public's fear of communism and by making false accusations and claims that a massive communist conspiracy threatened to take over the country.

Mohammad Mosaddeq (1880–1967): Iranian premier, 1951–53.

N

Gamal Abdel Nasser (1918–1970): Egyptian president, 1958–70.

Ngo Dinh Diem (1901–1963): Republic of Vietnam president, 1954–63.

Richard M. Nixon (1913–1994): Republican congressman from California, 1947–50; member of the House Un-American Activities Committee (HUAC), and closely involved with the investigation of accused communist Alger Hiss; U.S. senator from California, 1950–53; vice president, 1953–61; and thirty-seventh U.S. president, 1969–74.

O

J. Robert Oppenheimer (1904–1967): A theoretical physicist who led the building of the U.S. atomic bomb during World War II.

P

Kim Philby (1911–1988): One of the KGB's famed Cambridge Spies.

R

Ronald Reagan (1911–): Fortieth U.S. president, 1981–89.

Franklin D. Roosevelt (1882–1945): Thirty-second U.S. president, 1933–45.

S

Eduard Shevardnadze (1928–): Soviet foreign minister, 1985–90.

Joseph Stalin (1879–1953): Dictatorial Russian/Soviet leader, 1924–53.

T

Harry S. Truman (1884–1972): Thirty-third U.S. president, 1945–53.

U

Walter Ulbricht (1893–1973): Head of the East German government, 1949–71.

V

Cyrus Vance (1917–2001): U.S. secretary of state, 1977–80.

Y

Boris Yeltsin (1931–): Russian president, 1989–99.

Cold War Timeline

September 1, 1939 Germany invades Poland, beginning World War II.

June 30, 1941 Germany invades the Soviet Union, drawing the Soviets into World War II.

December 7, 1941 Japan launches a surprise air attack on U.S. military installations at Pearl Harbor, Hawaii, drawing the United States into World War II.

November 1943 U.S. president Franklin D. Roosevelt, British prime minister Winston Churchill, and Soviet premier Joseph Stalin meet in Tehran, Iran, to discuss war strategies against Germany and Italy.

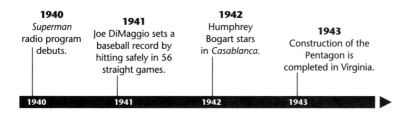

1940 *Superman* radio program debuts.

1941 Joe DiMaggio sets a baseball record by hitting safely in 56 straight games.

1942 Humphrey Bogart stars in *Casablanca.*

1943 Construction of the Pentagon is completed in Virginia.

1940   1941   1942   1943

August-October 1944 An international conference held at Dumbarton Oaks in Washington, D.C., creates the beginning of the United Nations.

February 1945 The Yalta Conference is held in the Crimean region of the Soviet Union among the three key allied leaders, U.S. president Franklin D. Roosevelt, British prime minister Winston Churchill, and Soviet premier Joseph Stalin to discuss German surrender terms, a Soviet attack against Japanese forces, and the future of Eastern Europe.

April-June 1945 Fifty nations meet in San Francisco to write the UN charter.

May 7, 1945 Germany surrenders to allied forces, leaving Germany and its capital of Berlin divided into four military occupation zones with American, British, French, and Soviet forces.

July 16, 1945 The first successful U.S. atomic bomb test occurs in Alamogardo, New Mexico.

July-August 1945 U.S. president Harry S. Truman, Soviet premier Joseph Stalin, and British prime minister Winston Churchill meet in Potsdam, Germany, to discuss postwar conditions of Germany.

August 14, 1945 Japan surrenders, ending World War II, after the United States drops two atomic bombs on the cities of Hiroshima and Nagasaki.

December 2, 1946 The United States, Great Britain, and France merge their German occupation zones to create what would become West Germany.

March 12, 1947 U.S. president Harry S. Truman announces the Truman Doctrine, which says the United States

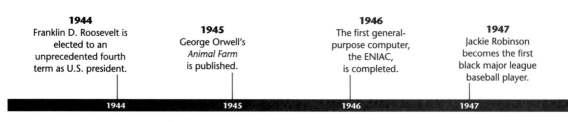

1944
Franklin D. Roosevelt is elected to an unprecedented fourth term as U.S. president.

1945
George Orwell's *Animal Farm* is published.

1946
The first general-purpose computer, the ENIAC, is completed.

1947
Jackie Robinson becomes the first black major league baseball player.

1944   1945   1946   1947

will assist any nation in the world being threatened by communist expansion.

June 5, 1947 U.S. secretary of state George C. Marshall announces the Marshall Plan, an ambitious economic aid program to rebuild Western Europe from World War II destruction.

July 26, 1947 Congress passes the National Security Act, creating the Central Intelligence Agency (CIA) and the National Security Council (NSC).

October 23, 1947 Actor Ronald Reagan testifies before the House Un-American Activities Committee (HUAC), a Congressional group established to investigate and root out any communist influences within the United States.

December 5, 1947 The Soviets establish the Communist Information Bureau (Cominform) to promote the expansion of communism in the world.

February 25, 1948 A communist coup in Czechoslovakia topples the last remaining democratic government in Eastern Europe.

March 14, 1948 Israel announces its independence as a new state in the Middle East.

June 24, 1948 The Soviets begin a blockade of Berlin, leading to a massive airlift of daily supplies by the Western powers for the next eleven months.

April 4, 1949 The North Atlantic Treaty Organization (NATO), a military alliance involving Western Europe and the United States, comes into existence.

May 5, 1949 The West Germans establish the Federal Republic of Germany government.

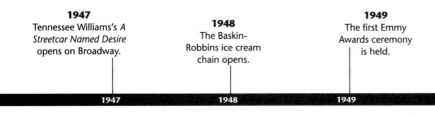

1947
Tennessee Williams's *A Streetcar Named Desire* opens on Broadway.

1948
The Baskin-Robbins ice cream chain opens.

1949
The first Emmy Awards ceremony is held.

1947   1948   1949

May 12, 1949 The Soviet blockade of access routes to West Berlin is lifted.

May 30, 1949 Soviet-controlled East Germany establishes the German Democratic Republic.

August 29, 1949 The Soviet Union conducts its first atomic bomb test.

October 1, 1949 Communist forces under Mao Zedong gain victory in the Chinese civil war, and the People's Republic of China (PRC) is established, with Zhou Enlai as its leader.

January 1950 Former State Department employee Alger Hiss is convicted of perjury but not of spy charges.

February 3, 1950 Klaus Fuchs is convicted of passing U.S. atomic secrets to the Soviets.

March 1, 1950 Chiang Kai-shek, former leader of nationalist China, which was defeated by communist forces, establishes the Republic of China (ROC) on the island of Taiwan.

April 7, 1950 U.S. security analyst Paul Nitze issues the secret National Security Council report 68 (NSC-68), calling for a dramatic buildup of U.S. military forces to combat the Soviet threat.

June 25, 1950 Forces of communist North Korea invade pro-U.S. South Korea, starting the Korean War.

October 24, 1950 U.S. forces push the North Korean army back to the border with China, sparking a Chinese invasion one week later and forcing the United States into a hasty retreat.

June 21, 1951 The Korean War reaches a military stalemate at the original boundary between North and South Korea.

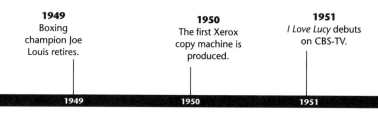

1949
Boxing champion Joe Louis retires.

1950
The first Xerox copy machine is produced.

1951
I Love Lucy debuts on CBS-TV.

1949　　　　　　　1950　　　　　　　1951

September 1, 1951 The United States, Australia, and New Zealand sign the ANZUS treaty, creating a military alliance to contain communism in the Southwest Pacific region.

October 3, 1952 Great Britain conducts its first atomic weapons test.

November 1, 1952 The United States tests the hydrogen bomb on the Marshall Islands in the Pacific Ocean.

March 5, 1953 After leading the Soviet Union for thirty years, Joseph Stalin dies of a stroke; Georgy Malenkov becomes the new Soviet leader.

June 27, 1953 An armistice is signed, bringing a cease-fire to the Korean War.

August 12, 1953 The Soviet Union announces its first hydrogen bomb test.

May 7, 1954 Vietminh communist forces defeat the French at Dien Bien Phu, leading to a U.S. commitment to containing communist expansion in Vietnam.

September 8, 1954 The Southeast Asia Treaty Organization (SEATO) is formed.

February 8, 1955 Nikolai Bulganin replaces Georgy Malenkov as Soviet premier.

May 14, 1955 The Warsaw Pact, a military alliance of Soviet-controlled Eastern European nations, is established; the countries include Albania, Bulgaria, Czechoslovakia, East Germany, Hungary, Poland, and Romania.

October 31, 1956 British, French, and Israeli forces attack Egypt to regain control of the Suez Canal.

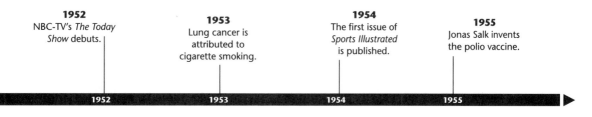

1952
NBC-TV's *The Today Show* debuts.

1953
Lung cancer is attributed to cigarette smoking.

1954
The first issue of *Sports Illustrated* is published.

1955
Jonas Salk invents the polio vaccine.

1952   1953   1954   1955

November 1, 1956 In Hungary, the Soviets crush an uprising against strict communist rule, killing many protestors.

March 7, 1957 The Eisenhower Doctrine, offering U.S. assistance to Middle East countries facing communist expansion threats, is approved by Congress.

October 5, 1957 Shocking the world with their new technology, the Soviets launch into space *Sputnik*, the first man-made satellite.

November 10, 1958 Soviet leader Nikita Khrushchev issues an ultimatum to the West to pull out of Berlin, but later backs down.

September 17, 1959 Soviet leader Nikita Khrushchev arrives in the United States to tour the country and meet with U.S. president Dwight D. Eisenhower.

May 1, 1960 The Soviets shoot down over Russia a U.S. spy plane piloted by Francis Gary Powers, leading to the cancellation of a planned summit meeting in Paris between Soviet leader Nikita Khrushchev and U.S. president Dwight D. Eisenhower.

April 15, 1961 A U.S.-supported army of Cuban exiles launches an ill-fated invasion of Cuba, leading to U.S. humiliation in the world.

June 3, 1961 U.S. president John F. Kennedy meets with Soviet leader Nikita Khrushchev at a Vienna summit meeting to discuss the arms race and Berlin; Kennedy comes away shaken by Khrushchev's belligerence.

August 15, 1961 Under orders from Soviet leader Nikita Khrushchev, the Berlin Wall is constructed stopping the flight of refugees from East Germany to West Berlin.

1957
West Side Story opens on Broadway.

1959
Alaska and Hawaii become the 49th and 50th U.S states.

1961
Soviet cosmonaut Yuri Gagarin becomes the first man to orbit Earth.

1962
Jim Beatty becomes the first person to run the mile in less than four minutes.

1956   1958   1960   1962

October 1962 The Cuban Missile Crisis occurs as the United States demands that the Soviets remove nuclear missiles from the island.

January 1, 1963 Chinese communist leaders denounce Soviet leader Nikita Khrushchev's policies of peaceful coexistence with the West; the Soviets respond by denouncing the Chinese Communist Party.

August 5, 1963 The first arms control agreement, the Limited Test Ban Treaty, banning above-ground nuclear testing, is reached between the United States, Soviet Union, and Great Britain.

August 7, 1964 U.S. Congress passes the Gulf of Tonkin Resolution, authorizing U.S. president Lyndon B. Johnson to conduct whatever military operations he thinks appropriate in Southeast Asia.

October 16, 1964 China conducts its first nuclear weapons test.

March 8, 1965 The first U.S. ground combat units arrive in South Vietnam.

June 23, 1967 U.S. president Lyndon B. Johnson and Soviet prime minister Aleksey Kosygin meet in Glassboro, New Jersey, to discuss a peace settlement to the Vietnam War.

January 30, 1968 The communist Vietcong forces launch the Tet Offensive, convincing the American public that the Vietnam War is not winnable.

July 15, 1968 Soviet leader Leonid Brezhnev announces the Brezhnev Doctrine, which authorizes the use of force where necessary to ensure maintenance of communist governments in Eastern European nations.

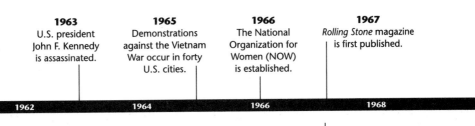

| **1963** U.S. president John F. Kennedy is assassinated. | **1965** Demonstrations against the Vietnam War occur in forty U.S. cities. | **1966** The National Organization for Women (NOW) is established. | **1967** *Rolling Stone* magazine is first published. |

1962   1964   1966   1968

August 20, 1968 The Warsaw Pact forces a crackdown on a Czechoslovakia reform movement known as the "Prague Spring."

August 27, 1968 Antiwar riots rage in Chicago's streets outside the Democratic National Convention.

March 18, 1969 The United States begins secret bombing of Cambodia to destroy North Vietnamese supply lines.

July 20, 1969 The United States lands the first men on the moon.

April 16, 1970 Strategic arms limitation talks, SALT, begin.

April 30, 1970 U.S. president Richard Nixon announces an invasion by U.S. forces of Cambodia to destroy North Vietnamese supply camps.

May 4, 1970 Four students are killed at Kent State University as Ohio National Guardsmen open fire on antiwar demonstrators.

October 25, 1971 The People's Republic of China (PRC) is admitted to the United Nations as the Republic of China (ROC) is expelled.

February 20, 1972 U.S. president Richard Nixon makes an historic trip to the People's Republic of China to discuss renewing relations between the two countries.

May 26, 1972 U.S. president Richard Nixon travels to Moscow to meet with Soviet leader Leonid Brezhnev to reach an agreement on the strategic arms limitation treaty, SALT I.

January 27, 1973 After intensive bombing of North Vietnamese cities the previous month, the United States and North Vietnam sign a peace treaty, ending U.S. involvement in Vietnam.

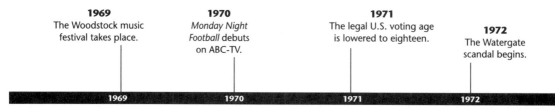

1969
The Woodstock music festival takes place.

1970
Monday Night Football debuts on ABC-TV.

1971
The legal U.S. voting age is lowered to eighteen.

1972
The Watergate scandal begins.

1969   1970   1971   1972

September 11, 1973 Chilean president Salvador Allende is ousted in a coup in Chile.

June 27, 1974 U.S. president Richard Nixon travels to Moscow for another summit conference with Soviet leader Leonid Brezhnev.

August 9, 1974 Under threats of impeachment due to a political scandal, Richard Nixon resigns as U.S. president and is replaced by Vice President Gerald R. Ford.

November 23, 1974 U.S. president Gerald R. Ford and Soviet leader Leonid Brezhnev meet in the Soviet city of Vladivostok.

April 30, 1975 In renewed fighting, North Vietnam captures South Vietnam and reunites the country.

August 1, 1975 Numerous nations sign the Helsinki Accords at the end of the Conference on Security and Cooperation in Europe.

December 25, 1977 Israeli prime minister Menachim Begin and Egyptian president Anwar Sadat begin peace negotiations in Egypt.

September 17, 1978 Israeli prime minister Menachim Begin and Egyptian president Anwar Sadat, meeting with U.S. president Jimmy Carter at Camp David, reach an historic peace settlement between Israel and Egypt.

January 1, 1979 The United States and the People's Republic of China (PRC) establish diplomatic relations.

January 16, 1979 The shah of Iran is overthrown as the leader of Iran and is replaced by Islamic leader Ayatollah Ruhollah Khomeini.

June 18, 1979 U.S. president Jimmy Carter and Soviet leader Leonid Brezhnev sign the SALT II strategic arms limitation agreement in Vienna, Austria.

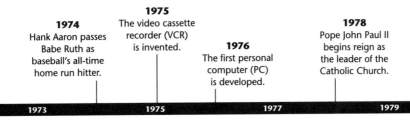

1974
Hank Aaron passes Babe Ruth as baseball's all-time home run hitter.

1975
The video cassette recorder (VCR) is invented.

1976
The first personal computer (PC) is developed.

1978
Pope John Paul II begins reign as the leader of the Catholic Church.

1973   1975   1977   1979

July 19, 1979 Sandinista rebels seize power in Nicaragua with Daniel Ortega becoming the new leader.

November 4, 1979 Islamic militants seize the U.S. embassy in Tehran, Iran, taking U.S. staff hostage.

December 26, 1979 Soviet forces invade Afghanistan to prop up an unpopular pro-Soviet government, leading to a decade of bloody fighting.

April 24, 1980 An attempted military rescue of American hostages in Iran ends with eight U.S. soldiers dead.

August 14, 1980 The Solidarity labor union protests the prices of goods in Poland.

January 20, 1981 Iran releases the U.S. hostages as Ronald Reagan is being sworn in as the new U.S. president.

November 12, 1982 Yuri Andropov becomes the new Soviet leader after the death of Leonid Brezhnev two days earlier.

March 23, 1983 U.S. president Ronald Reagan announces the Strategic Defense Initiative (SDI).

September 1, 1983 A Soviet fighter shoots down Korean Airlines Flight 007 as it strays off-course over Soviet restricted airspace.

October 25, 1983 U.S. forces invade Grenada to end fighting between two pro-communist factions.

February 13, 1984 Konstantin Chernenko becomes the new Soviet leader after the death of Yuri Andropov four days earlier.

February 1985 The United States issues the Reagan Doctrine, offering assistance to military dictatorships in defense against communist expansion.

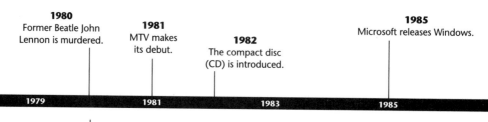

1980
Former Beatle John Lennon is murdered.

1981
MTV makes its debut.

1982
The compact disc (CD) is introduced.

1985
Microsoft releases Windows.

1979   1981   1983   1985

March 11, 1985 Mikhail Gorbachev becomes the new Soviet leader after the death of Konstantin Chernenko the previous day.

October 11–12, 1986 Soviet leader Mikhail Gorbachev and U.S. president Ronald Reagan meet in Reykjavik, Iceland, and agree to seek the elimination of nuclear weapons.

October 17, 1986 Congress approves aid to Contra rebels in Nicaragua.

November 3, 1986 The Iran-Contra affair is uncovered.

June 11, 1987 Margaret Thatcher wins an unprecedented third term as British prime minister.

December 8–10, 1987 U.S. president Ronald Reagan and Soviet leader Mikhail Gorbachev meet in Washington to sign the Intermediate Nuclear Forces Treaty (INF), removing thousands of missiles from Europe.

February 8, 1988 Soviet leader Mikhail Gorbachev announces his decision to withdraw Soviet forces from Afghanistan through the following year.

May 29, 1988 U.S. president Ronald Reagan journeys to Moscow for a summit meeting with Soviet leader Mikhail Gorbachev.

January 11, 1989 The Hungarian parliament adopts reforms granting greater personal freedoms to Hungarians, including allowing political parties and organizations.

January 18, 1989 The labor union Solidarity gains formal acceptance in Poland.

March 26, 1989 Open elections are held for the new Soviet Congress of People's Deputies, with the communists suffering major defeats; Boris Yeltsin wins the Moscow seat.

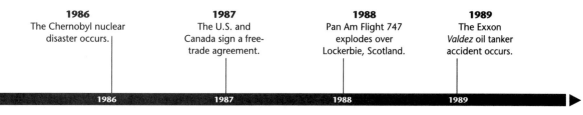

1986
The Chernobyl nuclear disaster occurs.

1987
The U.S. and Canada sign a free-trade agreement.

1988
Pan Am Flight 747 explodes over Lockerbie, Scotland.

1989
The Exxon *Valdez* oil tanker accident occurs.

1986   1987   1988   1989

May 11, 1989 Soviet leader Mikhail Gorbachev announces major reductions of nuclear forces in Eastern Europe.

June 3–4, 1989 Chinese communist leaders order a military crackdown on pro-democracy demonstrations in Tiananmen Square, leading to many deaths.

June 4, 1989 The first Polish free elections lead to major victory by Solidarity.

October 7, 1989 The Hungarian communist party disbands.

October 23, 1989 Massive demonstrations begin against the East German communist government, involving hundreds of thousands of protesters and leading to the resignation of the East German leadership in early November.

November 10, 1989 East Germany begins dismantling the Berlin Wall; Bulgarian communist leadership resigns.

November 24, 1989 Czechoslovakia communist leaders resign.

December 1, 1989 U.S. president George Bush and Soviet leader Mikhail Gorbachev begin a three-day meeting on a ship in a Malta harbor to discuss rapid changes in Eastern Europe and the Soviet Union.

December 20, 1989 Lithuania votes for independence from the Soviet Union.

December 22, 1989 Romanian communist leader Nicolae Ceausescu is toppled and executed three days later.

March 1990 Lithuania declares independence from Moscow.

March 14, 1990 Mikhail Gorbachev is elected president of the Soviet Union.

March 18, 1990 Open East German elections lead to a major defeat of Communist Party candidates.

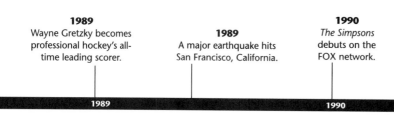

1989
Wayne Gretzky becomes professional hockey's all-time leading scorer.

1989
A major earthquake hits San Francisco, California.

1990
The Simpsons debuts on the FOX network.

1989

1990

May 29, 1990 Boris Yeltsin is elected president of the Russian republic.

June 1990 Russia declares independence as the Russian Federation.

October 15, 1990 Soviet leader Mikhail Gorbachev is awarded the Nobel Peace Prize for his reforms that ended the Cold War.

November 14, 1990 Various nations sign the Charter of Paris for a New Europe, ending the economic and military division of Europe created by the Cold War.

July 1, 1991 The Warsaw Pact disbands.

August 19, 1991 Soviet communist hardliners attempt an unsuccessful coup of Soviet leader Mikhail Gorbachev, leading to the banning of the Communist Party in Russia and other Soviet republics.

August 20–September 9, 1991 The various Soviet republics declare their independence from the Soviet Union, including Estonia, Latvia, Lithuania, Ukraine, Belorussia, Moldovia, Azerbaijan, Uzbekistan, Kirgizia, and Tadzhikistan.

October 3, 1991 West and East Germany reunite as one nation.

December 8, 1991 Russia, Ukraine, and Belorussia create the Commonwealth of Independent States organization as an alliance replacing the Soviet Union.

December 25, 1991 Soviet leader Mikhail Gorbachev resigns as the Soviet president, and the Soviet Union ceases to exist.

January 28, 1992 In his Annual State of the Union Address, U.S. president George Bush declares victory in the Cold War.

1990 The Hubble Space Telescope is deployed in space.

1991 The Persian Gulf War takes place.

1992 Hurricane Andrew causes $15 billion in damage in Florida.

1990   1991   1992

Research and Activity Ideas

The following research and activity ideas are intended to offer suggestions for complementing social studies and history curricula, to trigger additional ideas for enhancing learning, and to provide cross-disciplinary projects for library and classroom use.

- **Newspaper search:** Old issues of local newspapers are likely available at your public library, a nearby college or university library, or from the local newspaper office itself. Locate and review newspapers for the following events using the approximate dates given. Assess if reporters grasped the major points of the crisis. Choose interesting accounts to read to the class. The events are: Cuban Missile Crisis (October 23, 1962, through the end of October 1962); Berlin, Germany, Airlift (mid-July 1948 to mid-May 1949); Building the Berlin Wall (August 14, 1961, through the end of August 1961); and Tearing Down the Berlin Wall (November 10, 1989, through the end of November 1989).

- **The bomb scare:** At the height of the Cold War (1945–91), many individuals attempting to protect family members considered building bomb shelters in case of nuclear attack. At your local library, secure an old copy of the September 15, 1961, issue of *Life* magazine. Look for an article titled "Fallout Shelters." Also note the preceding letter to the American public from President John F. Kennedy.

- **Make an important decision:** Would you choose to build a shelter or rely on public bomb shelters being identified at that time by the Civil Defense? If you decide you would build, consider the same issues as those 1960s families did in the article. Where would you place your shelter, what kind would you build, could you afford to build it, and what and how many provisions would you stock it with? In the event of an attack warning, how long would it take to gather your family at the shelter?

- **Pretend you are a 1960s teenager:** Would a family shelter represent comfort and security, or a constant reminder of a possible doomsday event? Write what your thoughts might have been as the shelter was constructed.

- **Arms control treaties:** Create a timeline of nuclear weapons control treaties. Briefly describe the substance of each treaty and indicate which countries signed onto them. Begin with the 1963 Limited Test Ban Treaty. In addition to information found in books, check out information on the Internet at www.atomicarchive.com.

- **Strategic Triad:** To defend the United States from a nuclear attack, the U.S. government and military developed a system known as the Strategic Triad. Triad, meaning three, incorporated: (1) long-range bombers carrying nuclear weapons; (2) land-based intercontinental ballistic missiles; and (3) missile-carrying submarines. The reasoning behind the Triad was that an enemy could not hope to destroy all three systems in a first attack—at least one system would be left to retaliate. Hence, an enemy should be discouraged from launching an attack. Choose one of the three systems and report to the class. To learn more about the history of these systems, go to these Web sites on the Internet: U.S. Strategic Air Command, http://www.stratcom.af.mil; Titan Missile Museum, http://www.pimaair.org/titan_01. htm; Ballistic Missile Submarines (SSBNs), http://www. stratcom.af.mil/factsheetshtml/submarines.htm; and U.S. Navy Fact File, http://chinfo.navy.mil/navpalib/factfile/ships/ship-ssn.html.

- **At the movies:** Watch one of the following movies, each of which have Cold War overtones: *I Married a Communist* (1950); *My Son John* (1952); *Storm Center* (1956); *On the Beach* (1959); *The Manchurian Candidate* (1962); *Dr. Strangelove* (1963); *The Russians Are Coming, the Russians Are Coming* (1966); *The Deer Hunter* (1978); *Red Dawn* (1984); and *The Hunt for Red October* (1990). Applying your knowledge of the Cold War, how was the superpower rivalry portrayed in the movie? Whether the movie was dramatic and suspense-filled or a comedy spoof, what ideas about the Cold War did it relay to the audiences?

- **Map project:** Create the two following maps, then compare and contrast them. First, create a map of Europe and the Soviet Union as the countries existed in the late 1960s. Include the democratic Western European countries and the communist Eastern European countries and the Soviet Union. Second, create a map of the same geographical area in 2000 after the breakup of the Soviet Union during the 1990s.

- **U.S. Cold War military sites:** On a map of the western United States, locate the following sites involved in top secret Cold War military activities. Using a numbered key, on the map briefly describe the mission charged to each site. Using your favorite Internet search engine, enter these terms: Los Alamos, White Sands, Titan II Museum, Trinity Site, Nevada Test Site, Long Beach Navy Yard, Mare Island Naval Shipyard, North American Air Defense Command (NORAD) Headquarters, and Strategic Air Command (SAC) Headquarters.

- **Spying from above:** Research and report on aircraft and satellite spies. Include the U-2, Corona Satellite project, SR71 Blackbird (succeeded the U-2), and drone-type aircraft such as the U.S. Air Force Predator.

- **International Spy Museum, Washington, D.C.:** Go to the website of the International Spy Museum (http:// www.spymuseum.org) and find out about such fascinating topics as the tools of the trade of spying, lives of the spies of the Cold War, the Berlin Tunnel, or any other topic that catches your imagination at this exciting site.

- **VENONA Project:** Research the VENONA Project, which was the U.S. Army's Signal Intelligence Service's attempt, beginning in 1943, to decode the encrypted messages of the Soviet intelligence agencies, the KGB and GRU. The National Security Agency (NSA) ended a fifty-year silence on VENONA when it released documents in 1995 for the general public to study. The intelligence secrets uncovered by deciphering codes helped expose Soviet espionage activities carried out in the United States. For information, go to the National Security Agency's Web site, http://www.nsa.gov/docs/VENONA and the Public Broadcasting Service's *NOVA Online* Web site at http://www.pbs.org/wgbh/nova/venona.

- **CNN's "Cold War Experience":** Media giant CNN produced a documentary series on the Cold War for television broadcast in 1998. It won the prestigious George Foster Peabody Award for an excellent documentary series. To coincide with the programming, CNN developed an Internet interactive website, the *Cold War Experience,* that allows you to explore many facets of key situations and events of the Cold War. Go to this website at http://www.cnn.com/SPECIALS/cold.war/ for spellbinding information about the bomb, culture, technology, espionage, and more.

- **Development of nuclear weapons:** Divide the class into two groups, the Americans and the Soviets. Research and then write a class play on the development of the early nuclear technology. First act: The successful American development of an atomic bomb by 1945 with leading characters J. Robert Oppenheimer and Brigadier General Leslie R. Groves. Second act: The successful Soviet development of an atomic bomb by 1949 with leading characters Igor Kurchatov (physicist) and Lavrenti Beria (head of the KGB, the Soviet secret police). Third act: Follow Oppenheimer and Kurchatov until their deaths. What conclusions did they both independently come to concerning nuclear development, and how did they promote their views?

- **Coded or encrypted messages:** Divide the class into small groups for creating secret codes. Have each group make up an encrypted message using three letters for one letter, such as "abc" standing for "t." Make a tiny code deciphering book. Exchange code books and messages with another group. All students then become codebreakers employed by the National Security Agency and break the code. Remember, in real situations, code books changed from week to week and month to month, making deciphering very difficult.

- **Fission and fusion:** Explore the scientific basis of and difference between the nuclear reactions of fission and fusion. Explain the difference in destructive force between the atomic bomb based on fission and the hydrogen bomb based on fusion. Define what is meant by strategic and tactical nuclear weapons.

- **Terrorist thievery:** In the era of terrorists in the early twenty-first century, why do government officials fear that plutonium and uranium isotopes (two or more forms of an element that differ from each other according to their mass number) might be stolen. Which type of bomb, fission or fusion, might a terrorist produce with the stolen material? Would that bomb destroy a large part of the world or would it be, however devastating, limited in its destructive effects?

- **Interviews:** Make a list of persons who students know lived during much of the Cold War. Parents or grandparents born in the 1940s would be good candidates. Develop questions ahead of time. Tape record the interview if possible or take careful notes. Transcribe the recording or notes into a clear written retelling of the interview. This process is known as taking and recording an oral history. Share the oral history with the class.

- **Cartoon creation:** Cartoons are common features in newspapers and magazines. Used to illustrate the artist's viewpoint of an occurrence or common issue of the day, cartoons draw reactions from readers ranging from laughter to quiet agreement with the artist to howls of disgust. Use your imagination and artistic skills to create a cartoon about some aspect of the Cold War. Take either the side of the United States or of the Soviets. Suggestions for topics are Winston Churchill's phrase the "Iron Curtain," the Berlin Airlift, the Berlin Wall, the nuclear arms race, the space race, Senator Joseph R. McCarthy, the mutual assured destruction policy, détente, and President Ronald Reagan's "Star Wars" program. Be sure to convey an emotion such as humor, fear, or surprise. Write a caption for the cartoon that captures the essential message or spirit of the cartoon.

- **Debate #1:** Divide the class into two groups: (1) democratic, capitalists of Western Europe and the United States and (2) the communists of the Soviet Union. Debate thoroughly the differences in the two systems of government and economies. In reality, both sides believed their system was best. So staunchly defend what you think is right about your respective system. Were there any similarities or common ground in the two systems, or were they hopelessly incompatible?

- **Debate #2:** Divide the class into two groups: U.S. government officials and Soviet government officials. Set the debate in the time frame of 1945 to approximately 1949, post–World War II. Remember, the two groups were becoming more distrustful of each other with each passing day. Explore the reasons why, then debate over a "summit" table such issues as why the Soviets insisted on occupying Eastern European countries, why German reunification was such a stumbling block, and why Americans were suspicious of a communist conspiracy to take over the world and therefore began a policy of "containment."

- **Debate #3:** Divide the class into two groups: one in favor of a massive arms buildup to deter the Soviets and the other opposed to an arms buildup and instead vigorously pressing for arms control talks. Debate the advantages and problems with mutual assured destruction (MAD).

- **Debate #4:** Research and debate the ideas of the domino theory, particularly relating it to China, Korea, and Vietnam. How did it impact tensions of the Cold War?

- **Debate #5:** Study and debate President Ronald Reagan's "Star Wars" project. How did Reagan's insistence on the program affect the Soviets and did it prolong or hasten an end to the Cold War?

- **The image of Nikita Khrushchev:** At your public library, or a nearby college or university library, locate *Nikita Khrushchev and the Creation of a Superpower* (2000) by the late Soviet leader's son, Sergei Khrushchev. In the 1960s, most Americans thought of Nikita Khrushchev as an evil, stubborn Soviet leader determined to blow up the United States with nuclear weapons. From your reading of the book, construct your own personality and leadership profile of Nikita Khrushchev.

- **Mikhail Gorbachev:** Study in depth the life and ideologies of the Soviet Union's final president, Mikhail Gorbachev. Why was he chosen for the Nobel Peace Prize in 1990?

Cold War
Almanac

Origins of the Cold War

"There are two great peoples on the earth today who, starting from different points, seem to advance toward the same goal: these are the Russians and the Anglo-Americans. Both have grown larger in obscurity [relatively unnoticed by the rest of the world]; and while men's regards were occupied elsewhere, they have suddenly taken their place in the first rank of nations, and the world has learned of their birth and of their greatness almost at the same time." French traveler Alexis de Tocqueville (1805–1859) made this statement, quoted in his book *Democracy in America,* in the 1830s. Over a century later, the United States and the Union of Soviet Socialist Republics (also known as the Soviet Union or the U.S.S.R.; a country made up of fifteen republics, the largest of which was Russia, that in 1991 became independent states) had risen to the status of superpowers, extremely powerful nations that dominated world politics. Eventually, the two countries were involved in what became known as the Cold War.

The Cold War was a period of mutual fear and distrust, brought about by the differing ideologies, or set of beliefs, of these two nations. The Cold War did not begin on a

Words to Know

Allies: Alliances of countries in military opposition to another group of nations. In World War II, the Allied powers included Great Britain, the United States, and the Soviet Union.

Big Three: The trio of U.S. president Franklin D. Roosevelt, British prime minister Winston Churchill, and Soviet leader Joseph Stalin; also refers to the countries of the United States, Great Britain, and the Soviet Union.

Bolshevik: A member of the revolutionary political party of Russian workers and peasants that became the Communist Party after the Russian Revolution of 1917; the terms Bolshevik and Communist became interchangeable, with Communist eventually becoming more common.

Cold War: A prolonged conflict for world dominance from 1945 to 1991 between the two superpowers, the democratic, capitalist United States and the communist Soviet Union. The weapons of conflict were commonly words of propaganda and threats.

Communism: A system of government in which the nation's leaders are selected by a single political party that controls almost all aspects of society. Private ownership of property is eliminated and government directs all economic production. The goods produced and accumulated wealth are, in theory, shared relatively equally by all. All religious practices are banned.

Isolationism: A policy of avoiding official agreements with other nations in order to remain neutral.

Truman Doctrine: A Cold War–era program designed by President Harry S. Truman that sent aid to anticommunist forces in Turkey and Greece. The Soviet Union had naval stations in Turkey, and nearby Greece was fighting a civil war with communist-dominated rebels.

United Nations: An international organization, composed of most of the nations of the world, created to preserve world peace and security.

Yalta Conference: A 1944 meeting between Allied leaders Joseph Stalin, Winston Churchill, and Franklin D. Roosevelt in anticipation of an Allied victory in Europe over the Nazis. The leaders discussed how to manage lands conquered by Germany, and Roosevelt and Churchill urged Stalin to enter the Soviet Union in the war against Japan.

precise date, and it was not a shooting war, at least not directly between the two superpowers—the United States of America and the Soviet Union. As a result, the actual start of the Cold War is open to debate. The term "Cold War" comes from the title of a 1947 book by influential American journalist Walter Lippmann (1889–1974). He had heard presidential advisor Bernard Baruch (1870–1965) use the phrase "cold war" in a congressional debate that same year. Various political events between 1945 and 1947 were crucial to the Cold War's beginning. By the end of World War II (1939–45), the European powers—Great Britain, France, and Germany—had collapsed, while the U.S. and Soviet empires were thriving. U.S. and Soviet foreign policies, domestic priorities, economic decisions, and military strategies (including the development of nuclear weapons), all formulated in response to the war, created an atmosphere of hostility and fear that lasted almost half a century.

 People to Know

Clement Attlee (1883–1967): British prime minister, 1945–51.

James Byrnes (1879–1972): U.S. secretary of state, 1945–47.

Winston Churchill (1874–1965): British prime minister, 1940–45, 1951–55.

Adolf Hitler (1889–1945): Nazi party president, 1921–45; German leader, 1933–45.

Vladimir I. Lenin (1870–1924): Leader of Bolshevik Revolution, 1917; head of Soviet government, 1918–24; founder of the Communist Party in Russia, 1919.

Franklin D. Roosevelt (1882–1945): Thirty-second U.S. president, 1933–45.

Joseph Stalin (1879–1953): Dictatorial Russian/Soviet leader, 1924–53.

Harry S. Truman (1884–1972): Thirty-third U.S. president, 1945–53.

Distinct differences, distant enemies

Although the Cold War did not begin until the mid-1940s, many historians look back to 1917 for the first signs of U.S.-Soviet rivalry. In Russia, members of a rising political party, known as the Bolsheviks, gained control of the country in November 1917 through the Bolshevik Revolution. The Bolsheviks supported the communist ideologies of Vladimir I. Lenin (1870–1924), who established the Communist Party in Russia in 1919. Communism is a system of government in which a single party controls nearly all aspects of society; leaders are selected by top party members. Under the communist system, the government directs all economic production. Goods produced and accumulated wealth, are, in theory, shared relatively equally by all; there is no private ownership of property. Religious practices were not tolerated under communism.

On the other hand, the United States viewed the world differently than did Lenin and the Bolsheviks. The U.S.

Bolshevik leader Vladimir I. Lenin (left) and associate Leon Trotsky. *Reproduced by permission of Getty Images.*

system of government is democratic, which means that government leaders are elected by a vote of the general population; members of the government represent the people. Multiple political parties represent differing political views. The United States operates under a capitalist economic system. This means prices, production, and distribution of goods are determined by competition in a market relatively free of government interference. Property and businesses are privately owned. Religious freedom is absolute; it was a cornerstone in the founding of the United States in 1776. In response to the Bolshevik Revolution, the president of the United States, Woodrow Wilson (1856–1924; served 1913–21), condemned the Bolsheviks and sent troops to Russia in 1918 to restore the old government. However, this attempt was unsuccessful; the communist Bolsheviks prevailed and renamed Russia, calling it the Soviet Union. Still, the United States refused to officially recognize the new government as the official government of the Russian people. President Wilson did not think the communist rule would last long; he did not think the Russian people would tolerate the loss of private property and individual freedoms. As communist leaders worked to re-shape the Russian economy, the United States began a waiting game, hoping these leaders would fail. The unfriendly relations between the two countries would continue for the next twenty years, until an alliance during World War II brought them together.

During the 1920s and 1930s, neither the capitalist United States nor the communist Soviet Union was a world military power. Both countries isolated themselves from the political events in Europe and in other regions of the world. The United States wanted to avoid involvement in another European war after its bitter experience in World War I (1914–18), and the Atlantic Ocean seemed to offer a safe buffer against any foreign conflicts.

In contrast, Russia had no geographic buffer to protect it from land invasions. Historically, most military invasions of Russia had come from the west. Therefore, long before the communist takeover, Russian leaders had traditionally sought new western territories to protect their country from future threats. Joseph Stalin (1879–1953), a Bolshevik who became head of the Soviet communist state in 1924, wanted to avoid interaction with the capitalist governments in bordering Europe. Seeking security buffers and eager to spread the communist philosophy, Stalin pushed for expansion of Soviet influence in neighboring countries. However, denunciation of the Bolsheviks by various foreign leaders fed Soviet insecurities. The Bolsheviks feared external foreign invasion and an internal West-supported revolution to take back the government from the communists. During the 1920s, Soviet leaders were routinely excluded from international diplomacy such as European security pacts, because other countries viewed the Soviets' communist influence as a threat to international stability.

In November 1933, spurred by economic needs during the Great Depression (1929–41), the worst financial crisis in American history, U.S. president Franklin D. Roosevelt (1882–1945; served 1933–45) established formal diplomatic relations with the Soviet Union. Still, America remained quite hostile to the idea of communism, because Stalin's suppression of political, economic, and religious freedoms under the communist regime offended fundamental American ideals.

The Bolshevik Revolution

Shortly after 1900, members of the Russian Social Democratic Labor Party agreed that a revolution in Russia was needed. The tsars, Russia's monarchy, ruled harshly, decreasing local rule and appointing aristocrats to administer over the industrial workers and peasants. This led to poor working conditions, greater poverty and hunger, and growing discontent among the populace. But party members split into two major groups after they could not agree on how to conduct a revolution. Vladimir I. Lenin (1870–1924) was the leader of one side; his group believed in the overthrow of the tsars, or rulers, by a revolutionary army made up of peasants and workers. In a 1903 London meeting, Lenin's group gained control of the revolutionary movement and adopted the name Bolsheviks, derived from a Russian word meaning majority.

Major food shortages and other economic crises resulting from Russia's participation in World War I (1914–18) led to increasing public unrest and dissatisfaction with the oppressive ruling Russian monarchy. Strikes and demonstrations were becoming more common. With this momentum assisting him, Lenin led the Bolshevik Revolution in October 1917, and he and his communist followers took control of the Russian government.

Lenin strongly believed in the economic and social theories of German political philosopher Karl Marx (1818–1883). Marx stressed that free-enterprise capitalist economic systems, such as that seen in the United States, are unstable because they produce wide gaps in wealth between industry owners and workers; he argued that this system would inevitably lead to worker uprisings and revolution. Marx promoted a system in which workers would own industry and other means of production and share equally in the wealth. Through this

The Grand Alliance

In the 1930s, German dictator Adolf Hitler (1889–1945) began a military campaign to gain more territory for Germany. As conditions in Europe became increasingly troubling, President Roosevelt nudged the United States to give up its isolationist position, a policy of avoiding official agreements with other nations in order to remain neutral. He wanted the United States to help Great Britain and other countries resist Germany's expansion.

In contrast to the United States' new stance, Stalin sought a position of neutrality for the Soviet Union. He signed

Bolshevik leader Vladimir I. Lenin. *Reproduced by permission of the Corbis Corporation.*

Communist Party in March 1918. This party ran the Russian government and sought to establish a classless communist society in which all property was to be communally owned. All other political parties were banned, and Lenin ruled as a dictator, making use of force and terror to maintain control.

Lenin believed Communist revolutions would occur around the world as other nations followed Russia's lead. Therefore, he was dedicated to supporting communist movements in other countries. In December 1922, the Bolsheviks and their Communist Party government formed the Union of Soviet Socialist Republics (U.S.S.R., or Soviet Union), a union of four existing countries—Russia, the Ukraine, and two others. Other countries would be added to the Soviet Union through the years. Lenin remained the leader of the Soviet Union until he died in 1924.

system, he theorized, social classes would be eliminated.

After their victory in the revolution, Lenin's followers formed the All-Russian

the Nazi-Soviet Non-Aggression Pact with Germany in August 1939. The agreement gave the Soviet Union control of eastern Poland, Moldavia, and the Baltic States (Estonia, Latvia, and Lithuania). Stalin hoped this expansion would provide security from future attack while the capitalist countries fought among themselves. The extra land would also act as a screen, limiting Soviet contact with the West in general. Stunned by the Soviet-German agreement, the West claimed that this pact encouraged Germany's invasion of Poland the following month. With that invasion, in September 1939, World War II officially began. The Soviet buffer zone gave Russians less than two years of security: In June 1941, Germany violated its pact

with the Soviet Union and launched a massive offensive against the Russians. More than three million German troops pushed into Russia; by October, the German forces had reached the outskirts of Moscow, the capital city.

In the meantime, Japan was conducting a similar military campaign of expansion in the Far East. On December 7, 1941, Japan launched a surprise attack on the U.S. naval base at Pearl Harbor, Hawaii, in an effort to cripple the U.S. Pacific fleet and prevent U.S. intervention in Japan's expansion efforts. Germany declared war on the United States three days later. These events quickly brought the United States into the world war.

The joint struggle against Hitler's Germany led to the formation of the Grand Alliance—the United States, the Soviet Union, and Great Britain; the three powers referred to themselves as the Allies. However, this alliance was not a true, well-formed partnership. Instead, the three nations found themselves facing the same threat—the aggression of

Germany and Japan—and recognized that they needed to work together to defeat their common enemy. Yet even under these circumstances, the Americans and Soviets did not fully trust each other. For example, Roosevelt did not inform Stalin of the Manhattan Project, an American program (that began in 1942) to develop the atomic bomb. Stalin knew, nonetheless, thanks to well-placed spies, and secretly began his own atomic program.

Great Britain and the Soviet Union managed to repel the German onslaught on both the eastern and western fronts. On the eastern front, the Soviets defeated the invading German forces at Stalingrad in February 1943. In a counteroffensive, the Soviets pursued retreating German forces through eastern Europe. Meanwhile, Britain had survived the prolonged German bombing of England, including the capital city of London. On the western front, U.S. and British forces landed at Normandy on the French coast in June 1944 and pushed the Germans eastward. Caught between Allied forces approaching from the east and the west, Germany was defeated by the spring of 1945. The victory brought U.S. and Soviet forces face-to-face in central Europe. In several locations, young American and Russian soldiers eagerly shook hands with each other and celebrated together.

The Big Three

Roosevelt, Stalin, and British prime minister Winston Churchill (1874–1965) had begun meeting during the war to design a postwar world. The Big Three (a term that referred not only to the trio of Roosevelt, Stalin, and Churchill, but to the United States, the Soviet Union, and Great Britain as well) held friendly meetings, first in Tehran, Iran, in 1943, and then, in February 1945, in Yalta, a town on the Black Sea, in the Ukrainian region of the Soviet Union. During this time, President Roosevelt tried hard to overlook differences with Stalin. Furthermore, in early discussions Roosevelt had privately conceded to Stalin that the Soviets could control Eastern Europe under their communist government. Churchill was less willing to concede territory to the Soviet Union, particularly Poland. However, Stalin considered Poland crucial for protecting Moscow. He wanted to maintain the border es-

Soviet leader Joseph Stalin.
Reproduced by permission of the Corbis Corporation.

tablished in his 1939 nonaggression agreement with Germany. Churchill relented at the Tehran meetings, in exchange for British control over Greece.

In February 1945, the Big Three met in Yalta to discuss critical issues such as the Soviet entry into the war against Japan, the future of Eastern European governments, voting arrangements at the newly formed United Nations (UN; an international organization, composed of most of the nations of the world, created to preserve world peace and security), and a postwar government for Germany. The Allies were close to victory in Europe, but the outcome of the war with Japan in the western Pacific was still uncertain. The United States believed it needed help from the Soviets. Therefore, Roosevelt was willing to overlook the growing Soviet influences in Eastern Europe—at least temporarily—if the Soviets would promise to attack Japan. To formalize their plan for postwar Europe, the three leaders signed the Declaration on Liberated Europe. Under this agreement, the Soviet Union would retain control of the eastern region of Poland. Poland's western boundary was redrawn to include part of Germany; this change would displace the German population residing there. The agreement also stated that countries freed from German control would be allowed to hold free elections to establish their new governments. Nevertheless, many in the United States saw the Yalta agreements as a sellout; in other words, they felt that Roosevelt and Churchill had simply handed Eastern Europe to Stalin and his communist influence.

Relations decline

On April 12, 1945, Roosevelt died suddenly from a cerebral hemorrhage, a type of stroke where a blood artery in the brain bursts. He was replaced by Vice President Harry Truman (1884–1972; served 1945–53). Truman was more hostile to communism than Roosevelt and had little previous experience in foreign affairs; these two factors would play an important role in the buildup to the Cold War. During the spring of 1945, Stalin had established a communist government in a part of Poland that was beyond the accepted western boundary of Soviet influence. The United States charged that Stalin was violating the Yalta agreements by not allowing free elections in Poland and by suppressing the Polish people's freedom of speech, press, and religion. President Truman, newly in office, challenged the Soviets.

On April 16, four days after President Truman took office, he and Prime Minister Churchill sent a joint message to Stalin insisting the Soviets respect the agreements made in Yalta. On April 23, in a meeting in Washington, D.C., Truman made an unusually blunt comment to Soviet foreign minister Vyacheslav M. Molotov (1890–1986) about Soviet influences in Poland. As noted on the *Cold War International History Project* Web site, an irked Molotov said, "I have never been talked to like that in my life." Truman replied, "Carry out your agreements and you won't get talked to like that." Stalin responded the next day, saying that the United States was trying to dictate Soviet foreign policy. The German defeat had left Stalin an unprecedented opportunity to secure the buffer he was seeking in Eastern Europe. Stalin deemed Poland especially important as a first line of defense against future western invasions of the Soviet Union. Therefore, he would not budge, even under diplomatic pressure from Truman and Churchill; with Soviet troops occupying Poland since 1944, Stalin had the advantage.

The feuding spread to the United Nations organizational conference that was taking place in San Francisco, California. One part of the voting structure was to give the top world powers such as the United States and Great Britain veto power over key UN decisions. The Soviets insisted on having the veto power as well to overrule any proposed UN actions they found disagreeable. The dispute disrupted progress of the meetings.

Meanwhile on May 7, the defeated Germans officially surrendered. Four days later, on May 11, Truman abruptly ended shipments of wartime supplies to the Soviets, which

Postwar Economic and Political Order

By late 1944, President Franklin D. Roosevelt (1882–1945; served 1933–45) was focused on establishing international economic cooperation and a lasting peace for the postwar world. He did not want America to go back to the isolationism of the 1930s, when U.S. policy was to avoid official agreements with other nations in order to remain neutral, and be caught by surprise and be unprepared again as it had been when the Japanese attacked Pearl Harbor, Hawaii, on December 7, 1941. To help build the stable and prosperous world Roosevelt envisioned, he had supported the creation of international organizations such as the United Nations (UN), the International Monetary Fund (IMF), and the World Bank.

At Dumbarton Oaks, a private estate in the Washington, D.C., area, diplomats representing the United States, Great Britain, the Soviet Union, and China met between August 21 and October 7, 1944, to discuss and agree on the general purpose, structure, and operation of a new international organization that came to be known as the United Nations. At Yalta in February 1945, the Big Three—Roosevelt, Great Britain's Winston Churchill (1874–1965), and the Soviet Union's Joseph Stalin (1879–1953)—discussed how decisions would be made through a UN Security Council. Then, in a meeting in San Francisco that began on April 25, 1945—just thirteen days after Roosevelt's death—representatives from fifty nations developed the final charter of the United Nations. The charter was signed on June 26 and went into effect on October 24.

The UN is headquartered in New York City. Its main goals are to maintain

had begun in 1940. This put an end to all aid except what the Soviets needed to fight Japan. An infuriated Stalin viewed the sudden termination as concealed hostility fueled by disagreements over Poland and the UN.

To smooth over matters with the Soviets, Truman sent former Roosevelt advisor Harry Hopkins (1890–1946) to Moscow. Over a two-week period from May 25 to June 6, Hopkins was able to craft a compromise on various matters including composition of the Polish government. He also extracted from the Soviets a promise not to interfere in U.S. foreign relations in the Western Hemisphere. Furthermore, the Soviets promised to recognize U.S. dominance in Japan and China and to retreat from their UN veto demands. In return, the United States extended formal recognition to the com-

peace and security for its member nations, promote human rights, and address humanitarian needs. During the first forty-five years of the organization's existence, Cold War conflicts between the United States and the Soviet Union took top priority. The number of member nations continues to grow, from the original 50 in 1945 to 191 in 2003.

Two organizations related to the UN were designed to build a postwar international economic system. The World Bank and the IMF were both established at the Bretton Woods Conference in New Hampshire in July 1944. The IMF went into operation on December 27, 1945. It is focused on monitoring exchange rates to promote international trade and investments, which in turn stimulate economic growth around the world. The IMF can serve to stabilize a nation's economy by providing loans to ease the payment of debts. Often the loans are tied to an agreement that requires the receiving nation to make certain adjustments or reforms in its monetary system to avoid future problems. The World Bank was created to finance projects and promote economic development in UN member nations. It began operation in June 1946, and for the next half century the Bank would be the largest source of funds for developing nations. Loans are provided for hydroelectric dams, seaports, airports, water treatment plants, and improved roads. The World Bank also provides guidance to developing nations as they restructure their economic systems. The permanent headquarters of both the IMF and the World Bank are in Washington, D.C.

munist Polish government on July 5. With this agreement in place, delegates at the UN conference were able to complete work on the UN charter.

The Potsdam Conference

With the war in Europe over and relations between the West and the Soviets somewhat repaired, U.S., British, and Soviet leaders met again in Potsdam, Germany, near Berlin, in July 1945. Since the Big Three meeting in Yalta five months earlier, some changes had taken place: Roosevelt had died and Truman had taken over; and on July 16, just before the conference began, the United States had successfully conducted its first atomic bomb test—secretly, in a remote New

The Big Three shake hands at the beginning of the Potsdam Conference in July 1945. From left to right: British prime minister Winston Churchill, U.S. president Harry S. Truman, and Soviet leader Joseph Stalin. *Reproduced by permission of the Corbis Corporation.*

Mexico desert. Truman casually informed Stalin about the new weapon after a conference session. Stalin accepted the news so calmly that Truman believed Stalin did not fully understand what he had been told. However, Stalin's spies had already informed him of the U.S. effort to build an atomic bomb, so after hearing Truman's announcement, Stalin immediately sent orders to step up the Soviet atomic bomb effort at home.

One other notable event took place during the Potsdam Conference. A general election in Great Britain was being held as the meetings began. Conservative Party candidate Churchill and Labour Party candidate Clement Attlee (1883–1967) both traveled to Germany and awaited the results. The Labour Party was victorious, meaning Attlee became prime minister, replacing Churchill in the Big Three.

At the Potsdam Conference, tensions quickly surfaced over the future of Germany. Still taken aback over the German attack on their country during the war, the Soviets wanted a weak Germany. The United States wanted a strong, united Germany. The Western allies also wanted to rid Germany of Nazism (known primarily for its brutal policies of racism), break apart its military, control its industrial production, and set up a democratic government. In addition, they wanted to put the surviving Nazi leaders on trial for war crimes, or crimes against humanity. At the time, Germany was under military rule and divided into four geographic zones based on the location of the various occupational forces at war's end. The Russians held the east zone, which was mainly an agricultural area; Britain had the industrial region in the northwest; the Americans controlled the south; and France had parts of the southwest. Berlin, the German capital, was located well within the Russian zone, but it, too, was divided into four sectors. Berlin became headquarters of the new Four-Power Allied Control Council created to rule Germany. This arrangement was to stay in place until a more permanent arrangement could be worked out.

To further punish Germany, Stalin insisted on large reparations, payments that Germany would have to make to compensate the Soviet Union for the massive wartime destruction caused by German forces. Stalin particularly wanted Germany's industrial equipment and raw materials. Earlier at the Yalta Conference, Foreign Minister Molotov of the Soviet Union proposed that Germany provide $20 billion to the wartime allies, including the United States, with half of that amount going to the Soviet Union and half going to the Western countries. Some U.S. leaders felt such demands would greatly hinder Germany's economic recovery, so Roosevelt offered a compromise: He stated that the United States did not want reparations; however, he supported the Soviet request for $10 billion as a justified demand.

U.S. president Harry S.
Truman, Soviet leader Joseph
Stalin, British prime minister
Clement Attlee, and other
government officials meet at
the Potsdam Conference in
July 1945. *Reproduced by
permission of Getty Images.*

At Potsdam, U.S. secretary of state James Byrnes
(1879–1972) drew up a plan largely restricting the Soviet
Union to receiving reparations from its own occupation
zone. Though Stalin was displeased, Byrnes's plan inciden-
tally served to more formally partition Germany, giving the
Soviet Union a relatively free hand in its zone. As time
passed, the United States would become increasingly concerned that the Soviets were keeping east Germany econom-

ically repressed, in preparation for long-term control of the territory.

War's aftermath

Shortly after the Potsdam meeting, a rapid sequence of major events unfolded in Japan. Truman issued the Potsdam Declaration on July 26, which called for Japan's unconditional surrender from the war. The Japanese government rebuffed that request. With military officials believing that a war against Japan could result in the loss of five hundred thousand lives, the United States decided to force a quick surrender by dropping atomic bombs on two Japanese cities—Hiroshima on August 6 and Nagasaki on August 9. Approximately 150,000 people were killed outright. On August 8, the Soviets had declared war on Japan and invaded Japanese-held Manchuria several days later. On August 14, Japan surrendered; formal surrender documents were signed on the USS *Missouri* on September 2. With both Germany and Japan defeated, the Grand Alliance no longer had any reason to stay together.

Great war losses left Britain and the Soviet Union considerably weakened. Britain was heavily in debt and no longer had the resources to be a world leader. Britain still had substantial military forces and colonies around the world, but its superpower status would soon fade. Similarly the Soviet Union was economically crippled near the war's end. Over twenty million Soviets had died, and the country's agricultural and industrial economies were in ruin; Stalin's immediate goal following the war was to avoid further military conflict. In contrast to Britain and the Soviet Union, the United States emerged from the war as a world power in a league of its own. Its gross national product, or total market value of the country's goods and services, had increased from $90 billion in 1939 to $211 billion in 1945. The U.S. population had also increased during the war, from 131 million to 140 million. The United States was the world's economic leader and major source of financial credit. Its military was vast, and it was the only country with atomic weapons.

A meeting of the Council of Foreign Ministers, held in London in September 1945 to determine terms of peace treaties and other end-of-the-war matters, ended in disarray.

The United States and the Soviet Union strongly disagreed over draft treaties concerning Romania and Bulgaria and the Soviet role in postwar Japan. Some diplomats left the meeting feeling that the two nations were clearly on an unavoidable collision course. Many of them had begun to understand that the United States and other Western nations held basic economic and political values that were loathsome to the Soviets. Likewise, Western governments were inherently opposed to Soviet values.

In order to resolve differences, Truman sent Secretary of State Byrnes to Moscow, the Soviet capital. Byrnes was able to reach substantial compromises with the Soviets, including recognition of general spheres of influence for both nations; the Soviets were given control over Romania and Bulgaria. U.S. and Soviet diplomats agreed to meet in May 1946 in Paris to develop a series of peace treaties for other European nations. They also created the UN Atomic Energy Commission. Byrnes faced intense criticism when he returned to the United States; some Americans felt he was too soft in his negotiations with the communists. Because of this perception, his influence over foreign policy would substantially decline.

A mushroom cloud hovers over Nagasaki, Japan, after the United States dropped an atomic bomb on that city on August 9, 1945.
Reproduced by permission of the Corbis Corporation.

A fateful year

In 1946, a continuous sequence of events clearly established the emerging rivalry between the West and the Soviet Union. In January, at a UN meeting in London, British foreign minister Ernest Bevin (1881–1951) spoke out strongly against growing Soviet intimidation in Turkey and Iran, and

he called for united opposition from the West. This set the tone for the following month, which would mark a major turning point in U.S. foreign policy. On February 3, the American public was stunned when U.S. newspapers reported that a Soviet spy ring had been sending U.S. atomic bomb secrets to Moscow. Public support for negotiations with the Soviets over nuclear arms control plummeted. Then on February 9, Stalin gave his "Two Camps" speech, in which he announced a five-year postwar economic plan. Some considered the speech more like a declaration of war on capitalist nations, because Stalin contended that capitalism and communism were incompatible.

On February 22, less than two weeks after Stalin's speech, George Kennan (1904–), an American diplomat in Moscow, sent what became known as the "Long Telegram." The eight-thousand-word telegram warned that the Soviet leaders could not be trusted and recommended that the United States give up its isolationist attitudes and take on more of a leadership role with regard to international politics. The transmission, confirming the anti-Soviet beliefs already held by many Washington officials, would change the course of U.S. foreign policy. The United States, according to Kennan, would have to deal with the Soviets from a position of power.

The first direct confrontation between the two superpowers began the same day the Long Telegram was sent. Since 1941, both British and Soviet forces had occupied Iran, a country in the Middle East. Following the war, both sides agreed to withdraw by March 1946. However, the Soviet government, with an eye on Iran's oil, kept troops in Azerbaijan, a northern province of Iran (now divided into East and West Azerbaijan, and not the same Azerbaijan that was once part of the Soviet Union and is now an independent country). The Soviets looked to aid separatists, who were fighting against the Iranian government. In the United States, concerns rose over maintaining access to the vast oil reserves located in Iran and elsewhere in the Middle East, due to the Soviets' presence in Azerbaijan. On February 22, Secretary of State Byrnes went before the UN Security Council to condemn Soviet actions in Azerbaijan. In response, Soviet representative Andrey Gromyko (1909–1989) staged a dramatic walkout of the session. Days later, Byrnes sent the USS *Missouri,* the world's most powerful warship at that time, to neighboring Turkey as a warning to the Soviets. On February 28, Byrnes confirmed the new confrontational approach in U.S. foreign policy in a speech considered by many as a declaration of the Cold War. On March 5, Byrnes sent a note to Moscow demanding Soviet withdrawal from Iran.

At the same time, European leaders were feeling particularly threatened by the growing Soviet presence in Eastern Europe. On March 5, Winston Churchill, Britain's former prime minister, delivered a speech at Westminster College in Fulton, Missouri, with President Truman near his side. Churchill warned Americans of a descending Soviet "Iron Curtain" extending from Stettin, a key Polish port city on the Baltic Sea, to Bulgaria on the Black Sea. Behind the "Iron Curtain," communist governments ruled over closed societies, in which the ruling communist party in each country, such as Poland and Bulgaria, dictated the production levels of industry and determined what could and could not be printed; the population was shielded from outside social and political in-

fluence. Churchill urged the United States to take a more assertive role in European affairs to stop any further expansion of Soviet influence. In Moscow, Stalin expressed alarm over the aggressive tone of Churchill's speech.

By April 14, the Soviets responded to Byrnes's note, promising to remove their forces from Iran by May 1946. In exchange, with the support of the United States, Iran promised the Soviets access to Iranian oil, a promise never

The USS *Missouri* was sent to Turkey as a warning to the Soviets after they began their presence in the nearby Iranian province of Azerbaijan. *Courtesy of the National Archives and Records Administration.*

fulfilled by Iran or the United States. Iran was the first test of strength between the United States and the Soviet Union. The encounter demonstrated to the United States the benefit of being tough.

During the spring and summer of 1946, the Soviet Union had begun significantly pulling back from interaction with the West. Stalin stopped efforts to obtain a $1 billion loan from the United States and declined Soviet membership in the World Bank and the International Monetary Fund. He purged the Kremlin, or Soviet government, of any remaining Western sympathizers in influential positions. Meanwhile, on June 14, Bernard Baruch (1870–1965), U.S. representative on the UN Atomic Energy Commission, presented a plan for international control of atomic energy. The Soviets rejected the proposed plan because it required international inspection of scientific, industrial, and military facilities in the Soviet Union and would potentially end Soviet atomic energy development. The Soviets offered a counterproposal on June 19, but the UN adopted the U.S. plan. However, that plan would have little meaning without Soviet acceptance. The lack of agreement between the superpowers on this issue laid the foundation for a nuclear arms race.

That summer, White House aides Clark Clifford (1906–1998) and George Elsey (1918–) wrote a report to President Truman emphasizing that the Soviets would consider any U.S. compromise or concession as a weakness. They urged a continued show of strength—that is, not giving in to Soviet demands—because they believed that Stalin's ultimate goal was world domination. The report further supported Truman's evolving anti-Soviet stance.

Through 1946, Truman's anti-Soviet position solidified. As noted on the Truman Presidential Museum & Library Web site, the president stated that he was "tired of babying the Soviets." In defining the U.S. position, Truman seemed most influenced by the strongest anti-Soviet advisors in his administration, including Navy secretary James V. Forrestal (1892–1949), ambassador to Moscow William Averell Harriman (1891–1986), and World Bank president John J. McCloy (1895–1989). Alarmed by this trend, Nikolai Novikov, Soviet ambassador to the United States, exclaimed that it was the United States, not the Soviets, seeking world supremacy. In addition some U.S. officials questioned Truman's tough stance. Even a member of Truman's cabinet, Secretary of Commerce Henry A. Wallace (1888–1965), began speaking out in public in opposition. Wallace, who preceded Truman as vice president, was fired by Truman on September 20.

The Truman Doctrine

A clear announcement of the new U.S. policy toward the Soviets came in early 1947, triggered by events in the eastern Mediterranean. A civil war was raging in Greece, and the Soviets were pressing the Turkish government to gain control of the straits, or passageway, between the Black Sea and the Mediterranean Sea. Many believed communists were behind the rebel forces fighting the Greek government. The Soviets wanted to control the Turkish straits to guarantee freedom of passage for their warships operating in the region. Greece and Turkey had been under British influence following the war. On February 21, 1947, however, the British announced they could no longer afford to provide those two countries with substantial military and economic aid.

On February 27, U.S. administration officials Dean Acheson (1893–1971) and George Marshall (1880–1959) met with key congressional leaders to determine what the United States might do about the situation in Greece and Turkey. They decided Truman needed to address the nation, strongly emphasizing the perceived communist threat in the Mediterranean region. On March 12, 1947, Truman addressed Congress, stressing the growing Cold War tensions and the political differences between East and West. Truman asked Congress and the American public for support in providing $400 million of aid to the Mediterranean region, an area in which the United States had traditionally shown little interest. The ideas he expressed in this speech became known as the Truman Doctrine. The actions of the United States prompted the Soviets to pull back from both Greece and Turkey.

In the Truman Doctrine speech, the president proposed to provide aid to any nation in the world where free peoples were threatened by the spread of communism, especially in areas where poverty was threatening to undermine capitalist institutions. Truman's speech set U.S. foreign policy for the next twenty-five years. As a result, the United States would become increasingly involved in the internal politics of other nations.

Overview of Cold War origins

To Europeans, steeped in a long history of territorial shifts, the Cold War was yet another struggle for power and land in Europe. To Americans, however, the Soviet takeover of such areas as east Germany and Poland, along with Soviet activity in Iran, Greece, and Turkey, had the appearance of a communist conspiracy that might spread worldwide. In an effort to stop further communist expansion, the United States adopted a policy of intervention in the affairs of other countries. President Truman's speech of March 1947, in which he announced this new policy—called the Truman Doctrine—has traditionally been considered the beginning point of the Cold War.

The Cold War pitted the Western Bloc countries, composed of the United States and its allies in Western Europe, Latin America, Asia, and Africa, against the Eastern Bloc, composed of the Soviet Union and its allies and satellite governments in Eastern Europe, the Caribbean, Asia, and Africa. (Bloc refers to a group of nations.) The international rivalry fully evolved in the 1945-to-1947 time period and posed many significant global impacts. While producing a dramatic nuclear arms race, the Cold War would ironically provide prolonged international stability and a lack of war between the two great superpowers through the use of fear of nuclear annihilation (total destruction) as a deterrence to hostilities. Secret intelligence agencies became integrated with diplomatic and military affairs. The struggle for dominance would affect the daily lives of millions of people for over forty years. Developing countries became the location of armed conflicts leading to great loss of life.

The exact causes of the Cold War continue to be the subject of energetic debate in the twenty-first century. Many historians believe that Soviet expansionism provoked a strong U.S. reaction and a firm foreign policy, thereby initiating the Cold War. Others claim that massive foreign economic aid programs offered by the United States raised Soviet fears of worldwide capitalist expansion. With long-held fears of foreign invasion, the Soviets believed the United States was involved in a conspiracy to encircle the Soviet Union with hostile capitalist states.

Other historians point to the personalities of Truman and Stalin as the keys to the Cold War. Truman was free-speaking; Stalin could be testy and ruthless. Whereas Roosevelt had seemed to be trying to develop a friendly relationship with Stalin, the more blunt Truman was harsher and more hostile in his dealings with the Soviet leader; Truman was, to the Soviets, a threatening figure. He was also much less experienced in foreign affairs than Roosevelt and relied heavily on his strongly anticommunist advisors, such as Ambassador Harriman and Chief of Staff William Leahy (1875–1959). As a result, misunderstanding and misinterpretation of actions played a significant role in U.S.-Soviet relations.

Basic differences in political and economic goals lay beneath the specific events and misunderstandings that triggered the Cold War. The United States desired a world order based on democracy and capitalism; U.S. leaders wanted American businesses to be able to compete and profit on a global scale. The Soviets wanted a different economic and governmental system, one based on the theory of communism. Because they believed this system could not coexist with Western capitalism, the Soviets sought a geographic buffer against increasing American influence in European economic affairs. With these conflicting goals, the United States and the Soviet Union became adversaries on an international stage.

For More Information

Books

Gaddis, John L. *The United States and the Origins of the Cold War, 1941–1947*. New York: Columbia University Press, 1972. Reprint, 2000.

Harbutt, Fraser. *The Iron Curtain: Churchill, America, and the Origins of the Cold War*. New York: Oxford University Press, 1986.

Larson, Deborah W. *Anatomy of Mistrust: U.S.-Soviet Relations during the Cold War*. Ithaca, NY: Cornell University Press, 1997.

Leffler, Melvyn P. *The Specter of Communism: The United States and the Origins of the Cold War, 1917–1953*. New York: Hill and Wang, 1994.

Lippmann, Walter. *The Cold War: A Study in U.S. Foreign Policy.* New York: Harper and Brothers, 1947. Reprint, 1972.

McCauley, Martin. *The Origins of the Cold War, 1941–1949.* 2nd ed. New York: Longman, 1995.

Mee, Charles L. *Meeting at Potsdam.* New York: Evans, 1975.

Messer, Robert L. *The End of an Alliance: James Byrnes, Roosevelt, Truman, and the Origins of the Cold War.* Chapel Hill: University of North Carolina, 1982.

Paterson, Thomas G. *On Every Front: The Making of the Cold War.* New York: Norton, 1979.

Reynolds, David, ed. *The Origins of the Cold War in Europe.* New Haven, CT: Yale University Press, 1994.

Rose, Lisle A. *After Yalta: America and the Origins of the Cold War.* New York: Scribner, 1973.

Sircusa, Joseph M. *Into the Dark House: American Diplomacy and the Ideological Origins of the Cold War.* Claremont, CA: Regina Books, 1998.

Tocqueville, Alexis de. *Democracy in America.* London: Saunders and Otley, 1835–1840. Multiple reprints.

Web Sites

"Origins of the Cold War." *Truman Presidential Museum & Library.* http://www.trumanlibrary.org/hst/g.htm (accessed on June 16, 2003).

"Understanding Documents: Molotov and Truman Meet April 23, 1945." *Truman Presidential Museum & Library.* http://www.arthes.com/truman/molotov.html (accessed on June 13, 2003).

Woodrow Wilson International Center for Scholars. *The Cold War International History Project.* http://wwics.si.edu/index.cfm?fuseaction=topics.home&topic_id=1409 (accessed on June 13, 2003).

Conflict Builds   2

The United States and the Soviet Union had emerged from World War II (1939–45) as superpowers. The two countries had different political and economic philosophies, and each believed its own governmental system was superior to the other. The United States, with its multiparty democratic form of government, valued an open, free society: American citizens elected their government leaders and were guaranteed freedom of speech, freedom of the press, and freedom of religion. The U.S. capitalist economic system allowed private ownership of property and businesses. Prices, production, and distribution of goods were determined by competitive markets, with minimal government involvement. U.S. leaders believed that all countries would benefit from following democratic, capitalist principles.

The Soviet Union had a completely different form of government than did the United States. A single political party, the Communist Party, controlled most aspects of Soviet society. Top members of the party selected government leaders from among their own ranks. The government directed all economic production; private ownership of property

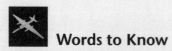

Words to Know

Capitalism: An economic system in which property and businesses are privately owned. Prices, production, and distribution of goods are determined by competition in a market relatively free of government intervention.

Cold War: A prolonged conflict for world dominance from 1945 to 1991 between the two superpowers, the democratic, capitalist United States and the communist Soviet Union. The weapons of conflict were commonly words of propaganda and threats.

Communism: A system of government in which the nation's leaders are selected by a single political party that controls almost all aspects of society. Private ownership of property is eliminated and government directs all economic production. The goods produced and accumulated wealth are, in theory, shared relatively equally by all. All religious practices are banned.

Containment: A key U.S. Cold War policy to restrict the territorial growth of communist rule.

Isolationism: A policy of avoiding official agreements with other nations in order to remain neutral.

Korean War (1950–53): A conflict that began when North Korean communist troops crossed the thirty-eighth parallel into South Korea.

Marshall Plan: A massive U.S. plan to promote Europe's economic recovery from the war; officially known as the European Recovery Program for Western Europe, it was made available to all nations, though the communist regime rejected it.

Molotov Plan: A Soviet series of trade agreements—made after the rejection of the Marshall Plan—designed to provide economic assistance to eastern European countries.

National Security Act: An act that created the National Security Council, which advised the president on national security policy.

National Security Council Document 68, or NSC-68: A plan for keeping Soviet influence contained within its existing areas; the strategy required dramatic increases in U.S. military spending.

North Atlantic Treaty Organization (NATO): A peacetime alliance of the United States and eleven other nations, and a key factor in the attempt to contain communism; the pact meant that the United States became the undisputed global military leader.

and businesses was not allowed. In theory, all the goods produced and any accumulated wealth were to be shared equally by all citizens. Whereas the United States was protected from invasion by two oceans, the Soviet Union had been plagued by land invasions from the west, including the German invasion in World War II. The Soviet Union sought to expand its sphere of influence into neighboring countries to create a security buffer against western invasion and to protect its communist system of government from such capitalist nations as the United States.

After World War II, the basic differences between the two superpowers began to cause conflict. The United States and the Soviet Union quickly became locked in a power struggle known as the Cold War. The Cold War was generally not fought with armies and guns (though that would later change during the Korean War), but it was like other wars in one major respect: It was based on mutual fear and failure to communicate.

In 1945, the two countries had been allies, or alliances of countries in military opposition to another group of nations. At that time, their common goal was to stop German and Japanese aggression. By 1947, however, they were adversaries, or opponents. Case in point: At the February 1945 Yalta meeting of the Big Three—U.S. president Franklin D. Roosevelt (1882–1945; served 1933–45), British prime minister Winston Churchill (1874–1965), and Soviet leader Joseph Stalin (1879–1953)— Roosevelt projected that all American troops would be withdrawn from Europe within two years. However, in March

 People to Know

Chiang Kai-shek (1887–1975): Ruler of China's Nationalist (Kuomintang) party, 1943–49.

George Kennan (1904–): Long-time U.S. Cold War advisor.

Douglas MacArthur (1880–1964): Supreme commander of occupational forces in Japan, 1945–51, and of the UN forces in Korea, 1950–51.

Mao Zedong (1893–1976): Chairman of the People's Republic of China and its Communist Party, 1949–76.

George C. Marshall (1880–1959): U.S. secretary of state, 1947–49; secretary of defense, 1950–51.

Joseph R. McCarthy (1908–1957): U.S. senator from Wisconsin, 1947–57; adopted an anticommunism campaign and became a national figure in Cold War politics.

Joseph Stalin (1879–1953): Dictatorial Russian/Soviet leader, 1924–53.

Harry S. Truman (1884–1972): Thirty-third U.S. president, 1945–53.

1947, President Harry S. Truman (1884–1972; served 1945–53) announced that the United States planned to take an active role in combating the spread of communism in Europe and worldwide; in other words, the U.S. military was not going to withdraw after all.

Germany: Focal point of the Cold War

At the close of World War II the Allies had divided defeated Germany into four zones. Military troops from the United States, Great Britain, France, and the Soviet Union each occupied one zone. The three Western powers soon allowed their zones to act as one economic and political unit; these three zones became known as West Germany. The Soviets placed their zone under a communist political system, and that zone became known as East Germany. Officials in West Germany and those in East Germany did little to cooperate with each other, and attempts to negotiate a peace treaty acceptable to all four powers failed. As a result, Germany would remain divided for almost half a century. West Germany and East Germany would become the focal point of the power struggle between the United States and the Soviet Union.

The Marshall Plan

In January 1947, George C. Marshall (1880–1959) replaced James Byrnes (1879–1972) as U.S. secretary of state. Marshall announced that the U.S. military would stay in Europe to ensure that the economic reconstruction of West Germany was successful. U.S. officials hoped that a revitalized democratic and capitalist West Germany would prevent Soviet expansion toward Western Europe.

As Soviet influence expanded into Eastern Europe, communist parties were also gaining popularity in France and Italy. Postwar economic conditions were poor in these countries. During the war years, factories had been destroyed, agricultural lands ravaged, and millions of families displaced. Some poverty-stricken people looked to the communists to improve their living conditions, and with its economies in danger of collapsing, Western Europe was ripe for communist intervention. During a visit to Europe in April 1947, Secretary of State Marshall was struck by the dire conditions he saw. Europe was facing critical food and fuel shortages and increasing monetary inflation (increasing consumer prices). He was convinced the United States had to act to save Western Europe from economic and political collapse.

On June 5 in a speech at Harvard University, Marshall announced a massive new U.S. plan to promote Europe's economic recovery from the war. The plan was to be made available to all nations, even those under communist control. Later in June, leaders of the United States, Great Britain, and the Soviet Union met to examine the proposed plan. After reading the details of the plan and listening to discussions, the Soviets became alarmed; they felt that the plan put too much emphasis on capitalist values. They abruptly withdrew from further discussions on July 2 and pressured Eastern European countries under their influence to refuse the plan as well. The Soviets charged that the plan would undermine their national independence and that it was primarily a means to spread capitalism. (Indeed, U.S. business and corporate interests were a prominent consideration in shaping the Marshall Plan; one of the goals of the plan was to establish foreign markets for U.S. goods and ensure access to needed raw materials found in Europe.) Other European nations met in Paris, France, later in July to consider the Marshall Plan, and by early fall the plan was adopted. Though more formally named the European Recovery Program for Western Europe, it was still referred to as the Marshall Plan.

Before the Marshall Plan could go into action, the American public and Congress had to support the expensive financial aid package. In December 1947, President Truman requested $17 billion from Congress for the program. Congressional debate over the proposal carried on for weeks. Then in February 1948, a communist takeover in Czechoslovakia caused great alarm. Czechoslovakia had been the last democracy in Eastern Europe; its collapse heightened fears about the political stability of Europe. A new presidential advisory group called the National Security Council (NSC) issued a report, NSC-20, concluding that the goal of the Soviet Union was world domination. The report stated that the United States and its allies needed to stop or at least reduce Soviet influence. Another report, NSC-30, advocated the use of nuclear weapons as a deterrent to further communist expansion. This was a bold new strategy for the United States—an aggressive foreign policy that used the threat of force to influence other nations.

After the fall of the democratic Czech government and the release of the NSC reports, Congress passed the Marshall Plan. Passage of the plan essentially divided Europe economically: The Eastern half kept its communist economic principles, and the Western half accepted capitalist support from the United States. The Marshall Plan would provide over $12 billion by 1952 to help maintain political stability in western Europe, and the United States continued to support a large foreign aid program through the second half of the twentieth century.

The Molotov Plan

In reaction to the Marshall Plan, the Soviets held a meeting with Eastern European nations in September 1947

and formed the Communist Information Bureau (Cominform) to create a tighter bond between the Soviet Union and its Eastern European satellite states (countries politically and economically controlled by the Soviets). Cominform's primary mission was to combat the spread of American capitalism and imperialism, the process of expanding the authority of one government over other nations and groups of people. On October 5, the Soviets announced their own economic assistance plan for Eastern Europe, called the Molotov Plan. The plan was named after Soviet foreign minister Vyacheslav M. Molotov (1890–1986). It consisted of a series of trade agreements between the Soviet Union and the eastern European countries.

In January 1949, the Soviets enhanced the agreements of the Molotov Plan by creating the Council of Mutual Economic Assistance (Comecon), which more closely tied Eastern European economies to the Soviet economy. Each country was to specialize in the production of particular kinds of products or crops. The council included the Soviet

The Communist Coup in Czechoslovakia

Edvard Beneš (1884–1948) was president of Czechoslovakia from 1935 to 1938. In 1938, Germany annexed Czechoslovakia, and Beneš left the country. He then taught briefly in the United States and spent time in France before moving to London. At the same time, Klement Gottwald (1896–1953), a prominent member of the Czech Communist Party, also fled German rule, going to Moscow. In London, Beneš formed the Czech National Committee. The Western allies recognized this committee as the official provisional (temporary) government of Czechoslovakia while Germany occupied that country. In 1943, Beneš gained Soviet support by signing with them a pact that would help deal with a postwar Czechoslovakia.

When the war in Europe ended in May 1945, resulting in the defeat of the German Nazi government, Beneš returned to the Czech capital of Prague and resumed his role as president of the Czech government. The communist Gottwald also returned. Facing pressure from the Soviet communists, Beneš first named Gottwald deputy premier in the newly reestablished government; Gottwald became premier in 1946. Gottwald also assumed leadership of the Czech Communist Party. Beneš mistakenly believed he had the support of Soviet leader Joseph Stalin to participate in the Marshall Plan, the U.S. program of financial assistance for war-torn European nations. However, Beneš came under intense criticism for his attempts to participate in the plan, and by

Union, Poland, Czechoslovakia, Hungary, Romania, Bulgaria, Yugoslavia, and the Communist parties of France and Italy.

National Security Act

When the Soviets rejected the proposed Marshall Plan in the summer of 1947, U.S. concerns over Soviet intentions escalated. These concerns led Congress to pass the National Security Act, which President Truman signed into law on July 26, 1947. The act, which had been intensely debated for two years, brought major changes to the federal government. It created the National Security Council within the executive branch to advise the president on national security policy. It also created the Central Intelligence Agency (CIA) to gather and interpret the meaning of information on foreign activities. The CIA was also designed to carry out secret foreign operations.

Edvard Beneš in 1919. *Reproduced by permission of the Corbis Corporation.*

late 1947 Gottwald began planning a coup to overthrow Beneš. In February 1948, Gottwald launched his coup, first gaining control of the Czech militia, police, and other agencies. By June 7, Beneš retired from public life, and Gottwald became the new president. Gottwald formed a close alliance with Stalin and instituted a harsh communist rule that led to the arrest and execution of many leading Czech officials.

Czechoslovakia was Western Europe's next-door neighbor; it had been the last democracy in Eastern Europe. Therefore, when it fell to communism, Western European and American fears intensified: The threat of communist world domination seemed one step closer to becoming a reality.

A 1949 amendment to the act created the Department of Defense, which united all the U.S. armed services. The new department was headquartered in the Pentagon building, across the Potomac River from Washington, D.C. Some consider the National Security Act one of the most important pieces of U.S. legislation of the Cold War period.

Containment

In July 1947, Truman administration policy analyst George Kennan (1904–), using the pseudonym "X," published a highly influential article, entitled "The Sources of Soviet Conduct," in the journal *Foreign Affairs*. In the article, Kennan outlined a foreign policy strategy to block further communist expansion: The United States was to contain Soviet expansion through economic, military, and political means. Economic aid would be offered to countries that might be vulnerable to communist influence because of poverty and lack of jobs. The U.S. military would respond in areas where noncommunist forces might be threatening to undermine a communist government. Political containment included efforts to cause friction between the Soviet Union and other communist countries, such as China. The idea of containment continued to take shape over the next few years, and until 1953 containment was America's primary foreign policy strategy. The goal was to limit the Soviet Union's activity outside its existing sphere of influence and counter other communist threats of expansion around the world.

Rio Pact—OAS

The United States turned its attention to Latin America at this time as well. The United States had long desired to keep foreign influence and intervention out of Latin America. In 1823, the Monroe Doctrine was established, declaring that the United States would not tolerate interference from European nations in North and South America. The fear of global communist expansion in the late 1940s renewed this desire to guard against what were considered outside influences. In September 1947, in Rio de Janeiro, Brazil, U.S. diplomats met with representatives from nineteen Latin American countries and signed an agreement called the Inter-American Treaty of Reciprocal Assistance. More commonly known as the Rio Pact, this agreement established a security zone around North and South America. The alliance guarded against the potential growth and expansion of communism. The U.S. Senate approved the treaty on December 8, but some Latin Americans were dismayed that the agreement did not include economic assistance as the Marshall Plan had for western Europe.

The Western Hemisphere nations met again in April 1948, this time in Bogotá, Colombia. Building on the Rio Pact, representatives established the Organization of American States (OAS), which sought to maintain political stability in the region by providing a means to resolve disputes. The OAS went into effect in December 1951.

North Atlantic Treaty Organization (NATO)

Western Europe did not have a postwar military agreement with the United States. The Marshall Plan primarily addressed political and economic issues. Financially weakened by World War II, Western Europe felt highly vulnerable to future attack; the Soviet Union had the strongest military in the region. Western Europeans wanted the United States, with its atomic bomb capabilities, to ensure their security. However, the United States had a history of isolationism, that is, not entering into formal agreements or alliances that might require U.S. military support in foreign wars. After World War II, the American public was in a mood for peace and retreat from European affairs. Initially Great Britain, France, Belgium, the Netherlands, and Luxembourg formed the Western European Union (WEU), or Brussels Pact, for mutual military assistance. However, the WEU alone could not act as a serious deterrent to a potential Soviet attack; the alliance remained weak without the United States. Seeing this, President Truman began to lobby Congress for support of U.S. entry into a European alliance.

A couple of key events in 1948 helped Truman get the support he needed for joining Western Europe in a military alliance. Early in the year, the communist coup d'état, a sudden change in government leadership by violent force, in Czechoslovakia convinced the American public and Congress that the Soviets were a real threat. Then, that summer, Berlin became the stage for further conflict. Like the whole of Germany, Berlin had been divided into sectors after World War II. West Berlin included three sectors; the United States, Great Britain, and France each occupied one sector. The East Berlin sector was occupied by the Soviet Union. The divided city was located deep within East Germany, the Soviet-controlled portion of the country. Hoping to force the Western powers out of Berlin, the Soviets blocked transportation routes running through East Germany so that the western sectors of the city could not receive supplies. The blockade lasted until May 1949. It took a massive airlift of supplies, which went on for almost a year, to break the blockade. Forced to confront the Soviet threat in this situation, Americans realized they could not remain uninvolved in European affairs. Truman soon received congressional go-ahead to negotiate an alliance with western Europe.

On April 4, 1949, Truman and other Western leaders signed the North Atlantic Treaty. The new alliance, called the North Atlantic Treaty Organization (NATO), included twelve nations—the United States, the five WEU nations, Iceland, Norway, Denmark, Canada, Portugal, and Italy. The Senate approved the treaty in July. Article 5 of the treaty stated that an attack on any one of the member nations would be considered an attack on all members; U.S. military assistance in Europe was thus ensured. The treaty was the first peacetime alliance for the United States since its treaty with France in the late eighteenth century. The United States was now the global military leader, and NATO would be key in the attempt to contain communism.

While forming NATO, the allies also decided to make the occupied west German area into a new nation; the Federal Republic of Germany came into being on September 21, 1949. On October 7, the Soviets responded by creating the German Democratic Republic from their east German occupation zone. (The countries were still more commonly known as West Germany and East Germany.) The division of Germany between East and West was complete. The official boundary was the line where the communist East and democratic West stood face-to-face amid Cold War tensions, neither backing down. With the formation of NATO, the West had a military defense alliance in place and an organization that clearly increased Soviet fears of an attack by the West.

Communist expansion in the Far East

For centuries, a vast Chinese empire existed in the Far East. However, China's influence began to decline through the eighteenth and nineteenth centuries with the expansion of European influence. By 1911, a revolution had brought an end to the empire and replaced it with economic and political instability. However, by 1928 the United States had officially recognized the new Chinese government. In the early 1930s, civil war broke out in China. The Nationalists (Kuomintang) were led by Chiang Kai-shek (1887–1975), who had ruled China since the 1920s. Nationalism refers to the strong loyalty of a person or group to its own country. The Chinese Nationalists wanted to once again raise the world prominence of China. Challenging the Nationalists were commu-

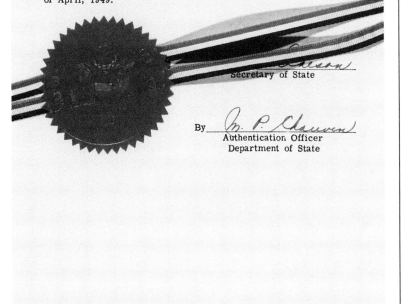

I CERTIFY THAT the foregoing is a true copy of the North Atlantic Treaty signed at Washington on April 4, 1949 in the English and French languages, the signed original of which is deposited in the archives of the Government of the United States of America.

IN TESTIMONY WHEREOF, I, DEAN ACHESON, Secretary of State of the United States of America, have hereunto caused the seal of the Department of State to be affixed and my name subscribed by the Authentication Officer of the said Department, at the city of Washington, in the District of Columbia, this fourth day of April, 1949.

Secretary of State

By _____
Authentication Officer
Department of State

A signed document by U.S. secretary of state Dean Acheson attesting to the authenticity of the North Atlantic Treaty document. *Reproduced by permission of the Corbis Corporation.*

nist forces led by Mao Zedong (1893–1976). The communist forces were largely composed of peasants in agricultural areas; their strength was in northeastern China.

When Japan invaded China in 1937, the two Chinese leaders called a truce and together turned their attention to halting Japanese aggression. But when Japan surrendered to the Allies in August 1945, ending World War II, China's civil war resumed. In the United States, Chinese Nationalist sup-

Top Chinese officials in 1943, from left to right, finance minister H. H. Kung, President Lin Sen, Nationalist Party leader Chiang Kai-shek, and minister of military operations Chang Chu-Chung. *Reproduced by permission of the Corbis Corporation.*

porters known as the China Lobby tried to gain active U.S. support for Chiang, and they wielded a good deal of influence. Yet President Truman was hesitant to provide much help, in part because of the poor support the Nationalists received within China. He also knew that Chiang had a reputation for corruption and oppression. On the other hand, Truman knew Mao represented a threat: Despite major philosophical differences between Mao and Soviet leader Stalin, U.S. officials considered Mao a puppet (a leader who is controlled or influenced by outside forces) of the Soviet communists. Taking all of this into consideration, Truman agreed to send some U.S. troops and limited economic aid to help Chiang and the Nationalists. Perhaps in reaction to this U.S. aid, Stalin began providing support to Mao's communist forces.

In November 1945, Truman decided to send former U.S. Army chief of staff George Marshall to China to work out a settlement between the Nationalist and communist factions. Meanwhile, the Soviets withdrew their military forces

China leader Mao Zedong applauds his troops.
Reproduced by permission of the Corbis Corporation.

in May 1946. In July, the Nationalists began an ill-fated military offensive against Mao's forces in northern China. Marshall worked to resolve the conflict but with little success. By the end of 1946, he concluded that no prospect for a peaceful settlement existed. The Nationalist military offensive soon lost strength, and the Communist forces began what would be a victorious counteroffensive.

Mao's communist forces swept southward through China in 1948. In January 1949, Chiang pleaded for military assistance from both the United States and the Soviet Union. The Soviets asked Mao to stop his offensive and seek a settlement, but Mao's forces pushed on. In the fall of 1949, the Nationalists fled Mainland China and went to the island of Formosa. They renamed the island Taiwan and established the Republic of China (ROC). Mao proclaimed communist rule over Mainland China on October 1 and established the People's Republic of China (PRC). The Soviets recognized the PRC government the following day, while the United States, under continued pressure from the China Lobby, recognized the ROC as the official government of China. However, in January 1950, Truman announced that the United States would not take action to challenge communist control of Mainland China. Feeling nonetheless spurned by the lack of U.S. recognition, Mao adopted a strong anti-American foreign policy and seized U.S. diplomatic property. On February 14, 1950, PRC and Soviet leaders signed the Sino-Soviet Treaty (the term Sino means Chinese), and Stalin promised communist China their full support as well as $300 million in loans.

Japan and Indochina

During the late 1940s, after Japan's surrender in World War II, General Douglas MacArthur (1880–1964), commander of the U.S. Army, guided a political, economic, and social revolution in Japan. A new Japanese constitution was partly written by Americans. The United States was helping rebuild Japan's industrial base, which had been destroyed during the war. After the communist victory in China in 1949, Japan became an important base for American military operations in the West Pacific.

Also in the late 1940s a communist liberation movement in Vietnam was escalating. Vietnam is part of Indochina, a region of Southeast Asia extending south from the southern border of China. Indochina also includes Cambodia, Laos, Myanmar, Thailand, and West Malaysia. France had established colonies throughout Indochina, which is rich in resources such as rubber and rice. Japanese forces overran the area during World War II, but the French returned after the war to reassert their rule. Led by Ho Chi Minh (1890–1969), the communist Vietminh army battled against French control. Ho Chi Minh had received military training in the Soviet Union in 1946. He quickly moved into Vietnam after the Japanese departure and proclaimed establishment of the Democratic Republic of Vietnam. War between the Vietminh and French forces broke out in November 1946. In January 1950, China and the Soviet Union extended diplomatic recognition to Ho Chi Minh's government. In opposition to this communist challenge, the United States affirmed its support of French colonial rule.

The Red Scare

The world events of 1948 and 1949 caused great alarm in America. With the communist coup in Czechoslovakia, the Soviet blockade of West Berlin, the communist victory in China, and communist advances in Indochina, it appeared that a massive wave of communism was engulfing the world and would soon encircle the United States. The so-called Red Scare was occurring in the United States. (Red is a synonym for communist.)

On August 29, 1949, the Soviets successfully tested an atomic bomb for the first time, further heightening American fears. The world was stunned by the Soviets' rapid atomic development. American experts immediately suspected theft of U.S. nuclear secrets, and in fact, nuclear secrets were being transmitted to Soviet agents by spies at the U.S. atomic bomb laboratory in New Mexico. As a result, the United States no longer had a monopoly on atomic weapons, which meant it no longer had a deterrent to potential Soviet aggression. In the months following the Soviet test, American scientists and politicians debated the development of a hydrogen bomb (H-bomb) based on nuclear fusion; this type of bomb would be even more powerful than the atomic bomb. By late January 1950, Truman decided to build the hydrogen bomb in addition to smaller-scale, tactical atomic weapons. The Soviets had already chosen to develop an H-bomb as well. The race to produce more powerful nuclear weapons in greater numbers led to the most dramatic example of the Cold War deadlock: The Soviet Union and the United States faced the threat of mutual nuclear annihilation if either country dared to defy the other.

With fear of the Soviets running high in the United States, Senator Joseph R. McCarthy (1908–1957) of Wisconsin dramatically pronounced in February 1950 that hundreds of communists were employed in the U.S. State Department. Since he took office in 1947, McCarthy's senatorial career had largely been uneventful and ineffective; his often rude behavior branded him a troublemaker. When he adopted the anticommunism campaign, however, McCarthy instantly became a national figure in Cold War politics. He steadily became more outrageous in his charges, often claiming to have lists of communist sympathizers but then failing to show proof. Even so, he was feared by many, because in this atmosphere of anti-Soviet hysteria, the mere suggestion of having communist ties could seriously damage a person's reputation. Hundreds of college professors, actors, filmmakers, and teachers who were suspected to be communist sympathizers appeared in congressional hearings in front of the House Un-American Activities Committee. Many lost their jobs. McCarthy even questioned the allegiance of Secretary of Defense George Marshall in June 1951 before the Senate. McCarthy's activities gained him a place in the dictionary: The term "McCarthyism" refers to the suspicion, hostility, and often groundless accusations that were directed at U.S. citizens who held nonmainstream political beliefs in the mid-twentieth century.

Other politicians besides McCarthy, who won reelection in 1952, benefited from the charged political climate. Future U.S. vice president and president Richard M. Nixon (1913–1994) won his first political election in 1946, becoming a congressman for California, by naming his opponent, Jerry Voorhis (1901–1984), as a communist sympathizer. Nixon then became nationally known after successfully seeking the conviction of Alger Hiss (1904–1996) for passing secret documents to the Soviets. Hiss, a former official of the U.S. State Department, denied the charge. However, he was never able to clear his name, because the American public, spurred on by news stories and Senator McCarthy's example, had become obsessed with the possibility of communist subversion within the United States.

A plan for security: NSC-68

In January 1950, with the Red Scare running high, Paul H. Nitze (1907–), head of the Policy Planning Staff in the State Department, assembled a team of administration officials to write a top-secret report that would offer a new strategy for U.S. foreign policy. Completed in April and known as National Security Council Document 68, or NSC-68, it outlined a plan for keeping Soviet influence contained within its existing areas. The strategy would require dramatic increases in military spending, unprecedented for the United States in peacetime. NSC-68 proposed to increase the military budget from less than $14 billion a year to $50 billion a year. Nitze contended that the United States needed to be prepared to respond to a surprise attack from the Soviets at any point in the world at any time and be ready to address communist efforts in Southeast Asia. However, Truman and the Republican-controlled Congress were not prepared to launch into such substantial deficit spending. (Deficit spending is when the government spends more money than it receives into the treasury, which causes the country to go into debt.) The secret report was shelved, but only briefly.

Korean War (1950–53)

The proposals in NSC-68 were adopted only weeks after Congress originally rejected them. An invasion of South Korea carried out by Soviet-supported North Korean troops meant that the United States would have to substantially increase its military spending to contain this new communist threat. Prior to World War II, Korea was a province of Japan, though the Soviets and the Chinese both tried to gain the territory for themselves. The United States had little interest in the region. After Japan's World War II defeat in August 1945, the Soviet Union and the United States divided Korea into two parts at the thirty-eighth parallel. The North, under Soviet influence, operated under a communist system of politics and economics. The South came under the influence of the democratic United States. The North had been well armed during Soviet occupation; the United States had done little to bolster forces in the South. National elections and UN actions failed to reunify the country, so the divisions were formalized: The Democratic People's Republic of Korea (DPRK) was established in the North and led by communist Kim Il Sung (1912–1994); the Republic of Korea (ROK) was established in the South and led by Syngman Rhee (1875–1965), who had lived in the United States for over thirty years. When Soviet and U.S. forces pulled out of the region in June 1949, Kim and Rhee both claimed leadership over the whole of Korea, and limited military skirmishes grew more frequent.

Early in 1950, Secretary of State Dean Acheson (1893–1971) commented that Korea lay outside the U.S. perimeter of defense. This remark, coupled with the fact that the United States had not attempted to reinstate former Chinese Nationalist president Chiang Kai-shek in Mainland China, convinced the Soviets and North Korea that the United States would not give South Korea military support in the event of a war. Thus, North Korean communist leader Kim Il Sung, possibly with Soviet approval, boldly launched a surprise military assault on South Korea on June 25, 1950. Invoking the strategies offered in NSC-68, Truman quickly determined it was in America's best interest to respond to the assault. Korea became a symbolic test of the U.S. policy to confront communist expansion worldwide, rather than in Europe or with the Soviet Union directly. Korea was also the first hot spot in the Cold War.

The United States did not have any treaty or alliance with South Korea that would justify a military response to the North Korean attack. Therefore, Truman went to the UN on the day of the attack to recommend a Security Council resolution condemning North Korean aggression. The council passed the resolution that day and two days later voted to assist South Korea in fighting off the attack. Ironically, the Soviet Union was caught off guard. The Soviets had been boycotting the UN in protest over the UN rejection of membership for the People's Republic of China. Therefore, no Soviet representatives were present to veto the resolution. Eventually sixteen nations provided troops to fight the communist North, but the United States was by far the major contributor, providing key air and naval support.

On June 27, Truman authorized the use of U.S. naval and air forces on behalf of the UN and on June 30 the use of U.S. ground forces. American troops were sent to participate in a "police action," the term used to describe this undeclared war. Truman thought an official congressional declaration of war could potentially escalate the conflict. The North Korean troops had quickly pushed south, trapping South Korean forces. However, on September 15, 1950, UN forces under the command of General MacArthur of the U.S. Army made a spectacular counterattack by an amphibious (water) landing on the west coast of South Korea at Inchon. UN forces landed behind enemy lines, cutting North Korean forces in half and sending North Korean troops on a hasty retreat, back across the thirty-eighth parallel.

The U.S. strategy soon changed from defending South Korea to defeating the North Korean Communist government. MacArthur led the UN forces into North Korea and pushed all the way to the Yalu River, along the border of China. The Chinese considered this action a direct threat to China's security, but MacArthur did not take warnings from China seriously. So with a force of more than two hundred thousand troops, China attacked, driving into North Korea on November 25 and pushing MacArthur back south, below the thirty-eighth parallel. MacArthur, who had earlier advised Truman that China would not become involved, insisted that the United States needed to retaliate and attack China, perhaps with nuclear weapons. But Truman resisted the idea and ended up firing MacArthur on April 11, 1951. It was a highly unpopular move, demonstrated by MacArthur's return from Korea a hero, which included a parade in New York City and a speech in front of Congress. MacArthur continued to be an outspoken critic of U.S. foreign policy during the final two years of Truman's administration.

U.S. paratroopers herd together a large group of prisoners on Koje Island in Korea. *Reproduced by permission of the Corbis Corporation.*

UN forces launched another counterattack, slowly pushing the Chinese troops back north, and reached the thirty-eighth parallel once again by early spring 1951. Truman entered peace negotiations with China on July 10, 1951. However, fighting would go on for another two years as the peace talks continued. By the fall of 1952, the American public was tired of the war and wanted a change in national leadership: The Democrats had been in control in the United States since 1933. Republicans who favored a policy of isolationism nominated U.S. senator Robert A. Taft (1889–1953) of Ohio to be the party's presidential candidate, but internationalist Republicans, or those who favored a policy of cooperation among nations, drafted retired U.S. general Dwight Eisenhower (1890–1969) to run. Eisenhower, also known as "Ike," was a popular figure who had served as supreme commander of Allied forces in Europe during World War II, leading the Allies to victory over Germany's leader, Adolf Hitler (1889–1945). Eisenhower won the Republican nomination and defeated the Democratic candidate, Illinois governor Adlai Stevenson (1900–1965), in the presidential election. When Eisenhower moved into the White House in January 1953, he mentioned using nuclear weapons as a possibility to ending the Korean War. An armistice agreement, or truce, was finally signed in June 1953, leaving the boundary between North Korea and South Korea the same as before the war. Over 54,000 Americans and 3.6 million Koreans had been killed, yet little had been gained. One million Chinese also were killed or wounded, including Mao's son. Some forty thousand U.S. troops stayed in South Korea following the armistice, and the U.S. military would remain there for the rest of the twentieth century.

Implications of the Korean War era

In response to the North Korean invasion of South Korea and other events between 1948 and 1950, U.S. defense spending dramatically increased. The North Korean invasion had confirmed the need to adopt the strategies of NSC-68. The United States began a massive military buildup to be ready to counter any possible communist aggression. The number of U.S. military personnel rose from less than 1.5 million in 1950 to over 3.5 million by 1954; the number of

General Douglas MacArthur.
Painting by Rodolphe Kiss.
Reproduced by permission of
the National Portrait Gallery,
Smithsonian Institution.

personnel stationed in foreign countries rose from 280,000 to almost a million.

Congress adopted a plan to provide technical assistance to less developed regions, including Taiwan and Southeast Asia. Called the Point Four Program, the plan was designed to fight the spread of communism in impoverished Third World, or underdeveloped, countries. The United States set aside almost $35 million for this program in 1950,

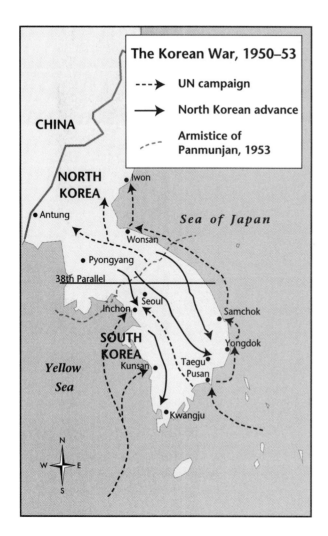

The Korean War, 1950–53

- - -> UN campaign

——> North Korean advance

- - - Armistice of Panmunjan, 1953

CHINA

NORTH KOREA

Antung

Iwon

Sea of Japan

Wonsan

Pyongyang

38th Parallel

Seoul

Inchon

Samchok

SOUTH KOREA

Yongdok

Yellow Sea

Kunsan

Taegu

Pusan

Kwangju

N W E S

A map of the Korean War.
Map by Eastword Publications Development. Reproduced by permission of the Gale Group.

and the amount would rise to over $155 million by 1953. The program provided assistance for health care, farming, irrigation, and transportation in locations such as India, Paraguay, Iran, and Liberia.

Intent on building a line of defense against communist expansion in the Far East, the United States increased aid in the region. Truman extended aid to the island of Taiwan, the adopted home of Chinese Nationalists. Taiwan would become part of a defense chain of islands in the western Pacific. Truman sent the powerful Seventh Fleet to patrol the Taiwan Strait and protect against any possible attacks by the People's Republic of China. Truman also approved military aid to France for their fight against communists in Indochina (this approval came on June 27, 1950, two days after the initial North Korean attack on South Korea). In June 1952, Truman secretly adopted a policy that the United States would hit key targets in Mainland China if the Chinese communists invaded Indochina. In addition, the United States signed a peace treaty and security pact with Japan in September 1951, restoring Japan's national sovereignty, meaning it could once again make decisions without the oversight of the United States and other occupational forces established at the end of World War II, and guaranteeing U.S. defense of Japan. (U.S. occupation of Japan ended on April 28, 1952.) The United States also established an alliance with Australia and New Zealand, known as the ANZUS Pact, and a defense agreement with the Philippines. The United States thus formed a defensive chain of allies running from north to south in the western Pacific.

The invasion of South Korea by communist forces led to U.S. fears that similar attacks could happen in Europe. The

Yugoslavia: Communist but Independent

As World War II came to a close, the Communist Party gained control of many parts of Eastern Europe, including Yugoslavia. However, unlike the other countries coming under Soviet influence, Yugoslavia maintained some independence, much to the disfavor of the Soviets. This unusual development—an independent communist nation—can be largely attributed to the strong personality of Josip Broz Tito (1892–1980). Tito, a Communist Party leader, had exceptional leadership qualities and directed Yugoslavia without Soviet assistance. It was no small accomplishment bringing together such ethnically diverse provinces as Montenegro, Serbia, Slovenia, Macedonia, and Bosnia and Herzegovina, but Tito succeeded in doing just that.

Tito became an internationally known figure, and this status enhanced his independence from the Soviets. At first, Soviet leader Joseph Stalin respected Tito's achievements and did not pressure Yugoslavia into strict obedience of Soviet rule as he did with other Eastern European countries. But by early 1948, tension built between Moscow and Belgrade, the capital of Yugoslavia. Stalin had grown tired of Yugoslavia's independence. On June 28, four days after beginning the West Berlin blockade, the Soviet Union evicted Yu-

Yugoslav president Josip Broz Tito.

goslavia from the community of communist states and demanded that other Soviet satellites break their ties with Yugoslavia as well. The Soviets essentially established an economic blockade against Yugoslavia, just as they had against West Berlin. By the fall of 1949, economic conditions inside Yugoslavia were deteriorating. Somewhat reluctantly, Yugoslavia negotiated a trade agreement with the United States. While remaining an independent communist state, Yugoslavia would ultimately receive $150 million of aid from the United States. It maintained its unique standing in Europe throughout the Cold War.

United States decided to rearm West Germany (disarmament had been part of the World War II peace treaty) and send more American troops there to provide a stronger defense against any likely Soviet aggression. The United States increased economic aid to Western Europe from $5.3 billion in 1950 to over $8 billion in 1951, and in January 1951 Congress approved an expansion of NATO. (Greece joined NATO in 1951; Turkey, in 1952; West Germany, in 1955.) The United States also extended diplomatic relations to Spain and Yugoslavia.

As NATO membership grew and the United States built alliances in the Far East, Stalin increased the size of his army from 2.8 million in 1948 to 5 million in 1953. The overwhelming strength of the Soviet army ensured the allegiance of the Soviet satellite nations, which extended from the Baltic States (Estonia, Latvia, and Lithuania) to the Balkan States (countries along the Balkan Peninsula of southeast Europe). The Soviets closely controlled the politics and economies of most Eastern European nations. The Soviet Union also increased economic and military aid to the People's Republic of China, its communist partner in the Far East.

Some historians consider the Truman-Stalin era of 1945 to 1953 the most intense period of global rivalry. But a new direction was taking shape. When Eisenhower was inaugurated in January 1953, he became the first Republican president in America in twenty years. The Soviet Union experienced an even more dramatic change in leadership: On March 5, Joseph Stalin died; a two-year power struggle between Nikita Khrushchev (1894–1971) and Georgy Malenkov (1902–1988) followed, with Khrushchev ultimately winning out. With new leadership in both the United States and the Soviet Union, a new era of the Cold War would begin.

For More Information

Books

Cook, Don. *Forging the Alliance: NATO, 1945–1950.* London: Secker and Warburg, 1989.

Feis, Herbert. *From Trust to Terror: The Onset of the Cold War, 1945–1950.* New York: Norton, 1970.

Gimbel, John. *The Origins of the Marshall Plan.* Stanford, CA: Stanford University Press, 1976.

Goncharov, Serge N., John W. Lewis, and Xue Litai. *Uncertain Partners: Stalin, Mao, and the Korean War.* Stanford, CA: Stanford University Press, 1993.

Grasso, June M. *Harry Truman's Two-China Policy, 1948–1950.* Armonk, NY: M. E. Sharpe, 1987.

Hogan, Michael J. *The Marshall Plan: America, Britain, and the Reconstruction of Western Europe, 1947–1952.* Cambridge, MA: Cambridge University Press, 1987.

Kaplan, Lawrence S. *The United States and NATO: The Formative Years.* Lexington: University Press of Kentucky, 1984.

Kaufman, Burton I. *The Korean War: Challenges in Crisis, Credibility, and Command.* New York: Knopf, 1986.

McCullough, David G. *Truman.* New York: Simon and Schuster, 1992.

Miscamble, Wilson D. *George F. Kennan and the Making of American Foreign Policy, 1947–1950.* Princeton, NJ: Princeton University Press, 1992.

Stueck, William W., Jr. *Rethinking the Korean War: A New Diplomatic and Strategic History.* Princeton, NJ: Princeton University Press, 2002.

Talbott, Strobe. *The Master of the Game: Paul Nitze and the Nuclear Peace.* New York: Vintage Books, 1989.

Web Sites

"The Cold War International History Project." *Woodrow Wilson International Center for Scholars.* http://wwics.si.edu/index.cfm?fuseaction=topics.home&topic_id=1409 (accessed on July 8, 2003).

United States of America Korean War Commemoration. http://korea50.army.mil (accessed on July 8, 2003).

Germany and Berlin

3

On May 7, 1945, Germany surrendered to the Allies in Reims, France, bringing an end to World War II (1939–45) in Europe. The "Big Four" allies were the United States, Great Britain, France, and the Soviet Union. Allies are alliances of countries in military opposition to another group of nations. Immediately upon Germany's surrender, an Allied plan that divided Germany into four zones became effective. Each zone was occupied by troops from one of the Big Four countries; each country appointed a military governor to oversee its zone. Within a few years, the democratic U.S., British, and French zones were collectively referred to as West Germany. The communist Soviet zone became known as East Germany.

Although Germany's capital, Berlin, was located well within the Soviet zone, the four Allies divided the capital city into four sectors, in the same way as they had divided the whole of Germany. The same four Allied powers each occupied a sector of Berlin. The U.S., British, and French sectors soon became known as West Berlin. The Soviet-occupied sector was called East Berlin. Road, rail, water, and air routes running from West Germany through and over East Ger-

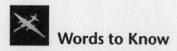

Allied Control Council: An organization of military governors from each of the four zones of Germany.

Berlin airlift: Massive shipments of food and goods, airlifted into the Western sector of Berlin, organized by the Western powers, after the Soviets halted all shipments of supplies and food from the eastern zone into West Berlin. The Americans nicknamed the airlift Operation Vittles, while the British dubbed the effort Operation Plain Fare.

Berlin blockade: A ten-and-a-half-month stoppage by the Soviets of shipments of supplies and food through East Germany into West Berlin. The Soviets also cut all coal-generated electricity supplied from East Germany to Berlin's western sectors, and land and water routes from West Germany into Berlin were closed.

Berlin Wall: A wall dividing the Soviet-controlled sector of Berlin from the three Western-controlled zones, built in

an attempt to stem the tide of refugees seeking asylum in the West.

Capitalism: An economic system in which property and businesses are privately owned. Prices, production, and distribution of goods are determined by competition in a market relatively free of government intervention.

Cold War: A prolonged conflict for world dominance from 1945 to 1991 between the two superpowers, the democratic, capitalist United States and the communist Soviet Union. The weapons of conflict were commonly words of propaganda and threats.

Communism: A system of government in which the nation's leaders are selected by a single political party that controls all aspects of society. Private ownership of property is eliminated and government directs all economic production. The goods produced and accumulated wealth are, in theory, shared relatively equally by all. All religious practices are banned.

many to Berlin made trade possible. The three Western powers identified specific trade and supply routes from West Germany into Berlin and expected the Soviets to grant free access to Berlin through these corridors.

Different points of view

At the end of the war, the cities of Germany lay in ruin. The British Royal Air Force and the U.S. military had relentlessly released bombs on German targets. Particularly in the last year of the war, bombs rained down on Germany day and night, and Berlin was not spared. Many of Berlin's stately buildings were reduced to shells and rubble. One-third of Berlin's population, approximately 1.5 million people, had fled or had been killed. The urgent task of governing a shattered Germany fell to the four Allied powers. Yet each of the four powers had differing points of view on how to deal with postwar Germany. From the start, neither negotiations nor cooperative efforts among the four proceeded smoothly.

 People to Know

Dwight D. Eisenhower (1890–1969): Thirty-fourth U.S. president, 1953–61.

John F. Kennedy (1917–1963): Thirty-fifth U.S. president, 1961–63.

Nikita S. Khrushchev (1894–1971): Soviet premier, 1958–64.

Walter Ulbricht (1893–1973): Head of the East German government, 1949–71.

The Soviet Union had suffered greatly at the hands of the invading Germans. The Soviets strongly opposed rebuilding Germany's economic base. They did not want to fear another German invasion in the future, as they had experienced on several occasions in the past. Throughout 1946 and 1947, the Soviets demanded billions of dollars in reparations from Germany—repayment for the heavy damage German troops had inflicted on their country. Within the Soviet zone of Germany, they disassembled entire factories that had not been damaged by the war and shipped the equipment to Russia for reassembly.

The Soviet Union operated under a communist government. Communism is a system of government in which a single party controls almost all aspects of society. In theory, a communist economy eliminates private ownership of property so that goods produced and accumulated wealth are shared relatively equally by all. At the war's end, the Soviet Union immediately began expanding its influence into the Eastern European countries it occupied by establishing communist governments. Included was Poland, which lay between the Soviet Union's western boundary and Germany. The Soviets also established communist governments in their zone of Germany (East Germany) and in the Soviet sector of Berlin (East Berlin). In these regions of Germany, the entire economic base—factories, banks, and farms—was seized and organized under the communist system. The Soviets appointed German communists to leadership positions in local government offices.

A Soviet soldier raises his country's flag in Berlin on May 2, 1945, just days before the Germans surrendered to the Allies.
Photograph by Yevgeny Khaldei. Reproduced by permission of the Corbis Corporation.

The United States believed that controlling Germany and deliberately keeping the German people in an impoverished state (as a result of reparations) would only breed defiance among the strong-willed Germans and lead to more struggles in the future. In conflict with Soviet wishes, the United States wanted to end reparations and rebuild a strong democratic Germany with a capitalist economy. A democratic system of government consists of several political parties whose members are elected to various government offices by a vote of the people. In a capitalist economy, property can be privately owned. Prices, production, and distribution of goods are determined by competition in a market relatively free of government intervention. The United States was becoming increasingly concerned about the Soviets' rapidly expanding communist influence in Europe. American leaders believed a strong democratic Germany could stop the westward spread of communism.

Badly damaged during the war and still resentful of Germany's wartime aggression, Great Britain somewhat re-

luctantly agreed that a democratic Germany with a revitalized economic base could be essential for a strong democratic and capitalist Western Europe. Britain held the key to Germany's revitalization because the Ruhr River region was part of the British-occupied zone. This region was home to large coal mining operations and the great iron and steel factories where cars and machinery were manufactured. Britain and the United States soon agreed on rebuilding Germany; both countries also favored dissolving the four zones to make one united Germany.

France did not want to rebuild Germany any more than the Soviets did. France had been invaded by the Germans three times in the twentieth century alone. The French people dreaded the prospect of a strong, reunited Germany. Nevertheless, given the choice of aligning with the communist Soviet Union or the Western democratic nations of the United States and Britain, France moved to the democratic side, reluctantly dropping its opposition to rebuilding Germany.

People of German descent who lived in eastern countries at war with Germany await transportation out of Germany, upon the end of the war in 1945. They had been forced out of their home countries to live in Berlin during the war. *Reproduced by permission of the Corbis Corporation.*

A map of Germany showing the 1939 and 1945 boundaries, the latter including the four power zones. *Map by XNR Productions, Inc. Reproduced by permission of the Gale Group.*

Focal point of the Cold War

The Cold War was usually not fought on battlefields with large armies; it was a conflict between the ideologies, or political orientations, of the communist Soviet Union and the democratic, capitalist Western nations. Because of its geographic position between Western Europe and the Soviet Union, Germany became a focal point of the Cold War.

By early 1948, the three Western powers were making plans to unite their occupied zones of Germany, both economically and politically. They also planned to unite their sections of Berlin. In February, leaders from the United States, Britain, and France, along with representatives of Belgium, the Netherlands, and Luxembourg, met in London to discuss a new West German state. Having well-placed spies, the Soviet Union knew of the meeting. The Soviets believed that the proposed West German state would pose a military and political threat to the Soviet zone of Germany and the Soviet Union itself. When the Allied Control Council, an organization of military

YOU ARE LEAVING
THE AMERICAN SECTOR
ВЫ ВЫЕЗЖАЕТЕ ИЗ
АМЕРИКАНСКОЙ ЗОНЫ
VOUS SORTEZ
DU SECTEUR AMERICAIN

governors from each of the four zones, met in March, the Soviet delegation accused the Western-sector governors of conspiring against the Soviet Union and walked out of the meeting. This action brought an end to the Allied Control Council, the only organized body of all four occupying powers.

East Berliners buy Western sector newspapers.
Reproduced by permission of Getty Images.

Harassment

Within weeks of the Allied Control Council meeting, the Soviets began harassing train, automobile, and water traffic coming from the West German zones into Berlin. Soviet officials began randomly searching passengers and inspecting cargo on trains destined for Berlin. Restrictions popped up on automobile routes and river traffic routes. Soviet fighter planes called Yak-3s harassed planes on scheduled flights from West German air bases to Berlin. On April 5 a Yak-3 collided with a British European Airways transport plane, killing eleven people. Tensions escalated rapidly.

Berlin blockade

On June 18, 1948, a quarrel over German currency increased tensions even further. Unable to reach agreement with the Soviets on ways to stop German inflation (a rapid increase in consumer prices), the Western powers issued new currency in the western zones of Germany. For the moment, the new currency, called the deutsche mark (D-mark), was not issued in Berlin. Replacing the worthless reichsmark, the new currency had been secretly printed in the United States by the U.S. Mint. Soviet officials immediately rejected the new currency and moved that day to close off all automobile, rail, and water traffic into Berlin from the western zones. On June 23, the Soviets introduced into the Soviet zone—and into all of Berlin—the ostmark. Soviet authorities insisted that all of Berlin use the ostmark, because all sectors of Berlin were within the Soviet zone of Germany. However, the Western powers rejected the ostmark and introduced the deutsche mark in West Berlin. In response, at dawn on June 24, the Soviets halted all shipments of supplies and food through East Germany into West Berlin. They cut all coal-generated electricity supplied from East Germany to Berlin's western sectors, and land and water routes from West Germany into Berlin were closed. The 2.3 million Berliners living in the western sectors of the city, as well as the military personnel stationed there, were marooned within Soviet-controlled territory. A total blockade was in place.

Berlin airlift

The Soviets hoped the blockade would force the Western powers to leave Berlin. Above all else, the Soviets wanted to prevent West Berlin from becoming part of the newly proposed West German state, because they feared that the Western powers might place U.S. atomic weapons in West Berlin, right next door to Soviet-controlled territory. The Soviets also hoped that the blockade would weaken the spirit of West Berliners, so that they would agree to communist rule. These hopes were dashed by a massive airlift organized by the Western powers. Rather than abandoning the city, they sent the British Royal Air Force (RAF) and the U.S. Air Force in Europe (USAFE) to fly the necessities of life into West Berlin.

Berlin Airlift Statistics

Between June 26, 1948, and September 30, 1949, approximately 586,901 flying hours were required to keep West Berlin supplied with the necessities of life. U.S. aircraft consisted of C-47s (which could carry a payload of 3 short tons), C-54s (carrying a payload of 10 tons), five C-82s (capable of carrying large machinery), one C-74, and one C-97. British aircraft consisted of Dakotas (similar to C-47s), Yorks, and Hastings. Thirty-one Americans died as a result of the airlifts, thirty-nine Brits, and nine or twelve Germans (unclear records). The following statistics are provided by the U.S. Air Force in Europe.

| | Flights | Cargo (short tons)[a] | | | | Passengers | |
		Food	Coal	Other[b]	Total	In	Out
USA	189,963	296,319	1,421,119	66,135	1,783,573	25,263	37,486
UK	87,841	240,386	164,911	136,640	541,937	34,815	130,091
France	424	unknown	unknown	unknown	896	10,000 (in and out)	
Total				278,228	2,326,406		

a: Short tons equal 2,000 lbs; long tons equal 2,240 lbs.

b: Included diverse items such as toothpaste, medical supplies, newspapers, steamrollers (for construction), and equipment for generating electrical power.

Source: "Berlin Airlift Quick Facts." U.S. Forces in Europe Berlin Airlift Web Site. http://www.usafe.af.mil/berlin/quickfax.htm (accessed on July 15, 2003).

Although both organizations had experience flying air supply missions, the scale of the operation seemed overwhelming. Military authorities calculated that approximately 4,500 tons (4,082 metric tons) of food, coal, and other supplies would be needed daily to keep West Berliners alive if the blockade carried on into the winter. All but the most optimistic believed an undertaking so large was doomed. Nevertheless, Ernst Reuter (1889–1953), a German anticommunist who had been elected mayor of West Berlin in 1948, announced that West Berliners would "tighten their belts" and make do with whatever supplies they received. The airlift began on June 26, when American C-47s flew 80 (73 metric tons) tons of food into West Berlin. The tonnage was a tiny percentage of what would be needed daily, but the operation was under way. On June 28, the U.S. Air Force ordered larger and faster planes—C-54s—

West Berlin children cheer as U.S. aircraft deliver supplies during the Berlin airlift.
Reproduced by permission of the Corbis Corporation.

from Alaska, Hawaii, and the Caribbean to aid in the airlift. The RAF flew Dakotas, similar to C-47s, for their part of the airlift. The RAF also pressed private commercial air carriers into service. Aircrews came from Australia, New Zealand, and South Africa to fly the supply missions.

The United States nicknamed the airlift Operation Vittles, and the British dubbed the effort Operation Plain Fare. At first, two airfields in Berlin were used, Tempelhof in the U.S. sector and Gatow in the British sector of the city. Volunteer German workers—men and women—labored to build a third airport, Fegel, in the French sector. (Fegel would receive its first supply missions on November 5.) By mid-July, the airlift was delivering nearly 2,000 tons (1,814 metric tons) of supplies a day, including the first shipments of coal.

Also in July, with much publicity, the United States sent three B-29 bomber squadrons (sixty aircraft) to England to stress how determined the Western allies were to resist Soviet pressure. The B-29s were capable of carrying atomic bombs and were

Coal and the Humble Duffel Bag

Coal was a critical necessity for marooned West Berliners; it was used for heat. Coal, which is very heavy, made up most of the tonnage airlifted into Berlin in 1948 and 1949. Coal is also very dirty, and coal dust crept everywhere in the airplanes, corroding the planes and irritating the crews' noses. Finally, the humble army surplus duffel bag proved to be the solution. Stuffed into the bags, the coal was contained. Half a million bags from World War II were located and pressed back into ser-

Germans stand near coal, a critical necessity used for heat. *Reproduced by permission of the Corbis Corporation.*

within easy reach of the Soviet Union. The bombers carried no atomic weapons, but the Soviet government was kept guessing.

In early September, three hundred thousand West Berliners gathered to demonstrate for continuance of the airlift. Seven thousand tons of cargo arrived on September 18. In mid-October, U.S. and British aircrews joined forces under a unified command, the Combined Airlift Task Force, headquartered in Wiesbaden in the U.S. zone of Germany. Flights landed every ninety seconds at Tempelhof and Gatow, often in bad weather conditions. Pilots flew exacting patterns at specified speed and altitude. They were locked into patterns so tight that if an aircraft failed to land on the first attempt, it had to return to West Germany rather than make a second attempt.

By spring 1949, the Soviets had lost hope that the airlift would fail. West Berliners neither starved nor froze but instead adjusted to supplies arriving by airlift. The West Berlin economy actually began to grow. By spring, 8,000 tons (7,256 metric tons) per day was the average delivery. Stockpiles grew. April 16

Twenty-Three Tons of Candy

Though carried out by military aircraft, the massive Berlin airlift was a humanitarian effort. Serving as a symbol of this effort were thousands of tiny parachutes that were dropped from the planes to deliver candy to delighted Berlin children. The effort came into being from one man's bright idea: Impressed by the friendliness of the Berlin children gathered to watch the planes land at the Tempelhof airport, U.S. Air Force pilot Lieutenant Gail S. Halvorsen of Garland, Utah, began dropping candy to the children. As word spread, donations of candy, handkerchiefs, and cloth reached Halvorsen. After crafting

the material into parachutes, Halvorsen would attach the candy; then, as he approached Tempelhof, he would wiggle his C-54's wings—and out came the treats.

Soon, other pilots picked up on Halvorsen's idea and began dropping the special cargo all over Berlin where they saw children playing. Halvorsen had several nicknames, including the Candy Bomber, Uncle Wiggly Wings, and the Chocolate Flier. Lieutenant Halvorsen received the Cheney Award in 1948 for his "sweet" idea and humanitarian action. He became one of the Berlin airlift's most famous figures.

was the record day for deliveries: Known as the "Easter Parade," 1,398 flights brought 12,940 short tons (11,700 metric tons) of cargo. (A short ton is 2,000 pounds; a long ton is 2,240 pounds.) The successful airlift was a huge propaganda victory for the Western powers. Propaganda is facts and ideas deliberately circulated to promote one's own cause or to damage the opposing side's cause.

At midnight on May 12, 1949, the Soviets stopped the blockade and reopened highway, train, and water routes into West Berlin. (The airlifts, however, would continue through September 30, 1949.) The city's residents began to celebrate; they—and many others around the world—hoped that the Cold War had come to an end.

Further separation of West and East Germany

The Western allies allowed West German officials to craft their own constitution, approved on September 21, 1949,

which combined the three West German zones into the Federal Republic of Germany. The new West German parliament selected Bonn as West Germany's capital. The West German people elected Konrad Adenauer (1876–1967), the chairman of the country's Christian Democratic party, as their first chancellor. Aided by the Marshall Plan, U.S. funding assistance for economic recovery and development, the West German economy was revitalized and began to thrive. In 1955, West Germany became a completely independent nation. That year it also joined the North Atlantic Treaty Organization (NATO), a Western military alliance for mutual protection.

In the Soviet-controlled zone of Germany, a communist-crafted constitution was approved on October 7, 1949. Under the new constitution, East Germany became the German Democratic Republic (GDR); its capital was East Berlin. Communist Walter Ulbricht (1893–1973) headed the East German government. Although it remained under strong Soviet influence, East Germany officially became independent of the Soviet Union in 1955. The Western powers consistently refused to recognize East Germany as an independent country.

Meanwhile, Berlin remained divided into the four sectors originally established after World War II. However, the three sectors occupied by the Western allies operated as one, both politically and economically. The Soviet sector remained under communist control.

Brain and labor drain

Although the East German economy began to recover, it lagged far behind West Germany's. Protests, even riots, broke out among workers and had to be quieted by the Soviet military. Through the 1950s, roughly three million East Germans left home for the freedom and better economic climate of West Germany.

The communists made travel between East and West Germany difficult. Ulbricht had closed the entire 900-mile border between East and West Germany. Barbed wire fences patrolled by armed guards made casual travel across the border impossible. West Germans had to have permission to enter East Germany. East Germans and East Berliners could rarely get permission to go into West Germany. However, East Germans could freely travel to East Berlin, and within Berlin, people could travel freely between all sectors of the city.

For example, using public transportation systems—the underground U-Bahn train or the elevated S-Bahn trains—thousands of East Berliners crossed into West Berlin daily for jobs and shopping and returned home at night. Berlin therefore became the place to escape permanently to

West Germany if a person wished to do so (making the person a refugee). First, an East German individual or family would come into East Berlin. Over a period of days, weeks, or months they could inconspicuously take a few belongings at a time into West Berlin. When ready, the fleeing East Germans simply registered at a refugee assembly camp in the western sector of the city. Most refugees resettled in West Germany, where jobs were plentiful in the rapidly growing economy. A smaller number stayed in West Berlin.

Three-quarters of the refugees were under forty-five years of age, and more than half were under twenty-five years of age. The refugees were farmers, skilled industrial craftspeople, scientists, and professionals such as engineers, doctors, lawyers, and teachers. These were precisely the people East Germany needed to build a strong economy. They had been educated in East Germany; then they left for the West. Their loss was devastating to East Germany.

Renewed Berlin crisis

On November 10, 1958, Soviet premier Nikita S. Khrushchev (1894–1971) announced that the Soviet Union intended to turn over its administrative control responsibilities in East Berlin to East Germany. This statement was a threat to the West since the United States and other Western countries did not formally recognize East Germany. They would be forced to establish relations and further formalize a divided Germany. The situation turned even more threatening when, on November 27, Khrushchev sent a letter to the Western powers giving them a six-month ultimatum to withdraw their military forces from West Berlin. He demanded that they enter into serious negotiations for an overall German peace treaty acceptable to the Soviet Union. It angered Khrushchev that thirteen years after the end of World War II no formal German peace treaty had yet been signed. Khrushchev still feared that Germany might reunite, side with the Western powers, and provide an attack base against the Soviet Union.

Khrushchev also demanded negotiations on the problem of West Berlin. He proposed a city with no further military occupation, which meant Western troops would have to withdraw from Berlin. Khrushchev stated that if substantial progress was not made on these issues by May 27, 1959, he would sign a separate peace treaty with East Germany and turn over to East Germany control of the transportation routes into Berlin. Khrushchev reasoned that if the East Germans controlled the routes into Berlin, the Western powers would be forced to talk directly to East Germany, not the Soviets, about transportation concerns. This, in effect, would force the West to recognize East Germany as a nation. Forcing this recognition was Khrushchev's primary reason for renewing Berlin tensions. He knew that keeping Germany divided would prevent an alliance between Germany and the Western powers—and thereby protect the Soviet Union against potential united attacks from the west.

Khrushchev made political points in the Soviet Union by taking a tough stance on the issue of Germany. He believed the West would never risk a war over Berlin, because the Soviet Union possessed atomic weapons that could destroy West Germany, England, and France in a matter of minutes; it also had missiles that could hit the United States directly. This put U.S. president Dwight D. Eisenhower (1890–1969; served 1953–61) in a difficult position.

Western allies hold firm

The United States and its Western allies rejected Khrushchev's demands. They had drawn the line in Berlin during the blockade. They vowed to maintain their presence in West Berlin while at the same time pushing for a united Germany. President Eisenhower opted not to use force to defend West Berlin. He favored diplomatic negotiations with the Soviets but did not rule out a nuclear conflict; he considered the latter a last resort and vowed that the United States would never fire the first shot. Khrushchev backed down from his six-month deadline, and May 27, 1959, passed quietly.

Negotiations between the United States and the Soviet Union continued. John F. Kennedy (1917–1963; served 1961–63) was elected U.S. president in 1960 and met with Khrushchev in June 1961. In classic Cold War language, both stated they wanted peace, but they both refused to budge on their positions regarding Germany and Berlin. Khrushchev's style was to yell, growl, and generally create an uproarious clamor. The young American president was taken aback but never wavered in his determination to hold the line in Berlin.

Berlin Wall

Even as negotiations went on, a flood of East Germans departed daily for the West through West Berlin. From January through July 1961, approximately two hundred thousand East Germans abandoned most of their belongings and headed to the western sectors of Berlin. The East German economy could not afford the population drain. Walter Ulbricht continually demanded economic assistance from the Soviet Union as East Germany's economic woes continued. By 1961, Soviet officials were grumbling about Ulbricht and the undue strain his demands put on the Soviet economy. It was clear something had to be done to end the exodus from East Germany to the West. Ulbricht had been requesting for years that the Soviet Union do something about West Berlin. Ulbricht favored a Soviet takeover of West Berlin, which could then be made part of East Germany; alternatively, he urged that a separate peace treaty be made between the Soviet Union and East Germany, one that would give the East Germans total control of access routes to West Berlin. Ulbricht believed this second option would allow him to eventually take over West Berlin. Khrushchev believed such action was too aggressive and likely to provoke war with the West. Not willing to risk a war, Khrushchev rejected Ulbricht's ideas. Nevertheless, he knew the tide of refugees must be stopped, so he decided to put another plan, an old plan developed years before, into place: Khrushchev ordered that a wall be constructed between East and West Berlin, to seal off the western sectors of the city from the eastern sector.

In the early-morning hours of Sunday, August 13, 1961, East German crews began to erect a fence of barbed wire connected to concrete posts—a barrier that ran through the heart of Berlin. Constructed street by street, it followed the boundary between the Soviet-controlled East Berlin sector and the sectors controlled by the Western allies. Soviet tanks sat poised a few blocks back. However, neither the Soviets nor the East Germans made any attempt to invade West Berlin. By

dawn, crowds of West Berliners came in amazement to view what was happening to their city. East Berliners set off for their jobs in West Berlin, but their trains did not proceed past the boundary. The border between East and West was closed. Families whose members lived in various sectors of the city suddenly found themselves permanently split apart.

The three western-sector military governors quickly huddled but could not act until they had orders from their respective governments. Construction of the wall had caught American intelligence completely off guard. President Kennedy was informed at mid-morning on Sunday as he set out with his family to picnic and sail off Hyannis Port, Massachusetts. Many years later, according to *Time* magazine's special Web site commemorating the ten years following the fall of the Berlin Wall, when Kennedy returned to the Oval Office, he told Brigadier General Chester Clifton, his military aide, that the wall would stay until the Soviets tired of it. Kennedy later stated, "We could have sent tanks over and knocked the

Wall down. What then? They build another one back a hundred yards? We knock that down, then we go to war?"

Khrushchev had guessed right. As long as West Berlin was left unharmed and its access routes were open to West Germany, the United States would not risk war. However, the wall was actually a huge defeat for communism: It was an ugly physical reminder that the communist system would not work unless people were denied any other options. Nevertheless, Khrushchev had succeeded in stopping the refugee flood to the West. Many thought Khrushchev had yet another reason for the wall. In sealing off East Berlin from West Berlin, he had also effectively sealed off Ulbricht, thwarting any effort Ulbricht might make to take matters into his own hands and provoke a war with the West. Khrushchev told Ulbricht that the population drain had been halted and demanded that Ulbricht get on with building the East German economy.

It took the entire Sunday to wire off West Berlin's 103-mile (166-kilometer) perimeter. A few days later, at least within

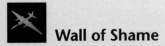

Wall of Shame

Construction of the Berlin Wall began August 13, 1961. It was originally a fence made of barbed wire, twisting through the heart of Berlin, but the fence was immediately replaced by a concrete block wall. Because a few daring individuals still managed to escape over the wall, the barrier grew more complex, and the area around the concrete structure became a sinister no-man's-land. The wall was meant to keep East Berliners in East Berlin and East Germans out of West Berlin. This objective was accomplished. Another wall was constructed around the outskirts of West Berlin restricting travel to East Germany. Known as the "country wall," it was not as elaborate as the wall that ran through the middle of the city dividing East and West Berlin. However, it was equally effective in isolating West Berlin.

The completed wall complex consisted of the following elements, which except for the memorials, are all on the east side:

- **Two steel-reinforced concrete walls:** These walls were 12 to 15 feet (3.7 to 4.6 meters) high, topped with large round concrete piping that could not be gripped in an effort to hoist oneself over.

- **Tank traps:** Large objects resembling in appearance giant jacks from a child's game of ball and jacks were lined up in a row on the East Berlin side of the concrete wall. They could disable any vehicle attempting to drive through them.

- **"Death strip":** The strip was a no-man's-land between the tank traps and the barbed wire fence. Within the strip were ditches, land mines, and a concrete pathway for East German soldiers on patrol, both on foot and in vehicles. Vicious dogs also patrolled. A strip of sand and gravel ran by the concrete pathway. Routinely raked smooth, it exposed footprints of would-be escapees.

the city, crews began construction of a steel-reinforced concrete wall topped with barbed wire. As the construction continued, a few East Germans made desperate, last-minute attempts to escape. Some tried to jump from windows of apartments that were right on the boundary. Those windows were quickly bricked over. Others tried to drive cars through the wire fence. Soon East German guards began to shoot would-be escapees. In 1962, eighteen-year-old Peter Fechter, a bricklayer from East Berlin, tried to climb over the wall; he was shot by machine-gun-carrying East German guards and bled to death in plain sight of Western police and reporters. The wall that actually ran

Two guards face each other on opposite sides of the Berlin Wall. *Reproduced by permission of Getty Images.*

along and high above the wall. Guards with orders to shoot to kill were always present. Pillboxes were concrete-reinforced boxlike guardhouses with slit openings from which guards could fire.

- **Automatic guns:** These unmanned guns were activated by wires an escapee could stumble into. The guns not only fired bullets but triggered shrapnel explosions within the "death strip."
- **Lights:** Floodlights covered most areas.
- **Memorials:** Standing in tribute to those who died trying to escape to the West, over two hundred memorials lined the walls on their west sides. The west sides of the walls gradually were filled by graffiti artists. In contrast, the east sides were painted white to expose anyone trying to flee East Germany.

- **Barbed wire:** A barbed wire barrier ran the entire length of the "death strip" (no-man's-land).

- **Watchtowers and pillboxes:** Several hundred watchtowers were placed

When the Berlin Wall was built, no one imagined how long it would remain. The wall did not come down until November 1989.

through the city was 28.5 miles (45.9 kilometers) long. Within a few years, the wall was topped with round piping that made escape over the wall impossible. Over time, the area around the concrete wall became a deadly no-man's-land of guard towers, barbed wire, land mines, and a patrol track.

West Berliners were allowed very limited access into East Berlin. They could cross only at specific crossing points. Other Westerners, including U.S. citizens, could cross into East Berlin only at the Friedrichstrasse Crossing, known as Checkpoint Charlie. It was here, in a sixteen-hour standoff

"Checkpoint Charlie," the only crossing point for non-West Berliners along the Berlin Wall. *Reproduced by permission of the Corbis Corporation.*

beginning October 27, 1961, that Soviet tanks faced directly at U.S. tanks. The standoff was a result of a dispute over passport procedures. Fortunately, diplomatic efforts resolved the problem before the tanks fired a shot. Some historians believe this confrontation came as close as any in the Cold War to igniting a hot war, an actual armed conflict.

Global significance

In West Berlin, the Berlin Wall was called the "Wall of Shame"; to the rest of the world, the barbed-wire-and-concrete structure was simply the Wall. It stood as a testimony to the divisions brought about during the Cold War. Many thought of Checkpoint Charlie as the place where the communist East came face-to-face with the democratic West. When President Kennedy went to West Berlin in June 1963, he stopped at Checkpoint Charlie. After climbing to a viewing stand and surveying the no-man's-land below, he spotted three women in a window in an East Berlin apartment waving handkerchiefs toward him. He stood for a moment in tribute to them. Back at West Berlin's city hall, he addressed 250,000 Berliners. Having thrown out a speech prepared for him, he spoke from the heart. If anyone in the world does not understand the issues between a free world and a communist one, Kennedy thundered repeatedly, "Let them come to Berlin." He concluded by showing support for a united, democratic Berlin by saying, "Ich bin ein Berliner [I am a Berliner]." The crowd cheered wildly. Despite the significance of Kennedy's Berlin visit, the Berlin Wall stood for twenty-eight years. As President Kennedy once noted, no one wanted the wall, but perhaps a wall was better than war. (Amid fireworks and celebration, the border between East and West Berlin opened on November 9, 1989, and the wall was torn down; see Chapter 15, End of the Cold War.)

For More Information

Books

Ayer, Eleanor H. *Germany.* San Diego: Lucent Books, 1999.

Gelb, Norman. *The Berlin Wall: Kennedy, Khrushchev, and a Showdown in the Heart of Europe.* New York: Times Books (Random House), 1986.

Grant, R. G. *The Berlin Wall.* Austin, TX: Raintree Steck-Vaughn, 1999.

Isaacs, Jeremy, and Taylor Downing. *Cold War: An Illustrated History, 1945–1991.* Boston: Little, Brown, 1998.

Parrish, Thomas. *Berlin in the Balance, 1945–1949: The Blockade, the Airlift, the First Major Battle of the Cold War.* Reading, MA: Perseus Publishing, 1998.

Shlaim, Avi. *The United States and the Berlin Blockade: A Study in Crisis Decision-Making.* Berkeley: University of California Press, 1983.

Tusa, Ann. *The Last Division: A History of Berlin, 1945–1989.* Reading, MA: Addison-Wesley, 1997.

Tusa, Ann, and John Tusa. *The Berlin Airlift.* New York: Atheneum, 1988.

Tusa, Ann, and John Tusa. *The Berlin Blockade.* London: Hodder and Stoughton, 1988.

Wyden, Peter. *Wall: The Inside Story of Divided Berlin.* New York: Simon and Schuster, 1989.

Web Sites

"The Berlin Wall: Ten Years Later." *Time.com.* http://www.time.com/time/daily/special/berlin/index.html (accessed on July 14, 2003).

"Cold War History: 1949–1989." *U.S. Air Force Museum.* http://www. wpafb.af.mil/museum/history/coldwar/cw.htm (accessed on July 14, 2003).

"A Concrete Curtain: The Life and Death of the Berlin Wall." *Deutsches Historisches Museum, Berlin.* http://www.wall-berlin.org/gb/berlin. htm (accessed on July 14, 2003).

U.S. Air Forces in Europe Berlin Airlift Web Site. http://www.usafe.af.mil/ berlin/berlin.htm (accessed on July 14, 2003).

Dawning of the Nuclear Age

4

On Monday, July 16, 1945, at exactly 5:29:45 A.M. Mountain War Time, the world's first successful detonation, or explosion, of an atomic bomb occurred. Referred to by scientists as "the gadget" or "the thing," it exploded with the force of 21,000 tons (19,047 metric tons) of TNT (a commonly used high explosive). A flash of light brighter than people had ever witnessed before illuminated the landscape of the test site near Alamogordo, New Mexico, in an area called *Jornada del Muerto* (commonly translated as Journey of the Dead). The code name for the test was "Trinity."

As noted on the Los Alamos National Laboratory Web site, General Leslie R. Groves (1896–1970), the U.S. Army officer in charge, later recalled, "As we approached the final minute the quiet grew more intense. As I lay there in the final seconds, I thought only what I would do if the countdown got to zero and nothing happened." Later, General Thomas Farrell, deputy to Groves, wrote that the "whole country was lighted by a searing light with the intensity many times that of the midday sun. It was golden, purple, violet, gray and blue. It lighted every peak, crevasse and ridge

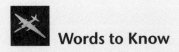

Words to Know

Atomic bomb: An explosive device that releases nuclear energy (energy that comes from an atom's core). All previous explosive devices were powered by rapid burning or decomposition of a chemical compound; they only released energy from the outermost electrons of an atom. Nuclear explosives are energized by splitting an atom, a process called fission.

Atomic Energy Commission (AEC): A unit established by Congress in July 1946 that managed the nuclear research facilities in Oak Ridge, Tennessee, Hanford, Washington, and Los Alamos, New Mexico.

Cold War: A prolonged conflict for world dominance from 1945 to 1991 between the two superpowers, the democratic, capitalist United States and the communist Soviet Union. The weapons of conflict were commonly words of propaganda and threats.

Communism: A system of government in which the nation's leaders are selected by a single political party that controls all aspects of society. Private ownership of property is eliminated and government directs all economic production. The goods produced and accumulated wealth are, in theory, shared relatively equally by all. All religious practices are banned.

Manhattan Project: A project begun in 1942—during World War II (1939–45)—with the goal of building an atomic weapon before scientists in Germany or Japan did.

Strategic Air Command (SAC): A unit established by the U.S. military with the goal of identifying targets in the Soviet Union and being ready to deliver nuclear weapons to those targets.

of the nearby mountain range with a clarity and beauty that cannot be described but must be seen to be imagined. Seconds after the explosion came first the air blast pressing hard against the people, to be followed almost immediately by the strong sustained awesome roar that warned of doomsday and made us feel we puny things were blasphemous [showing a lack of reverence] to dare tamper with the forces heretofore [previously] reserved for the Almighty." The world's first successful detonation of an atomic bomb was the climax of a secret effort known as the Manhattan Project.

The Manhattan Project began during 1942 in the middle of World War II (1939–45). The goal of the project was to build an atomic weapon before scientists in Germany or

Japan did. The United States was at war with these two nations. During the 1930s, scientists in both the United States and Germany greatly expanded knowledge in the field of nuclear physics, the study of the structure and reactions of an atom. Late in 1938, nuclear physicists in Germany discovered nuclear fission. Fission is the splitting of the nucleus of an atom; when the nucleus is split, a substantial amount of energy is released. Aware of this discovery, German physicists who had left Germany to live and work in the United States, due to Adolf Hitler (1889–1945) and his politics of Nazism (which stressed racism), feared the Germans could and would build powerful atomic bombs.

Albert Einstein's letter

Three Hungarian scientists who lived in Germany and then moved to the United States—Leo Szilard (1898–1964), Edward Teller (1908–2003), and Eugene Wigner (1902–1995)—asked the German-born Albert Einstein (1879–1955), America's most famous physicist, to write a letter to U.S. president Franklin D. Roosevelt (1882–1945; served 1933–45) expressing their fears and stressing the urgency of the atomic bomb situation. As noted on the Manhattan Project Heritage Preservation Association Web site, Einstein penned his letter on August 2, 1939, stating that recent breakthroughs in nuclear research led him to believe "the element uranium may be turned into a new and important source of energy in the immediate future" and that "extremely powerful bombs [could be] constructed." Einstein requested increased funding for American nuclear physicists working throughout the country in university laboratories and urged better communication among them. Realizing

 People to Know

Lavrenty Beria (1899–1953): Leader of the Soviet secret police and manager of the Soviet bomb project.

Leslie R. Groves (1896–1970): The U.S. Army officer in charge of the Manhattan Project.

Adolf Hitler (1889–1945): Nazi party president, 1921–45; German leader, 1933–45.

Igor Kurchatov (1903–1960): The Soviet Union's premier nuclear physicist, who led the building of the Soviets' atomic bomb in 1948.

J. Robert Oppenheimer (1904–1967): A theoretical physicist who led the building of the United States' atomic bomb during World War II.

Franklin D. Roosevelt (1882–1945): Thirty-second U.S. president, 1933–45.

Harry S. Truman (1884–1972): Thirty-third U.S. president, 1945–53.

The mushroom cloud from the United States' "Trinity" test on July 16, 1945, thirty seconds after detonation. *Photograph by Berlyn Brixner. Reproduced by permission of the Corbis Corporation.*

30 SEC.
N

100 METERS

that Germany's Hitler could develop these powerful new weapons and use them to hold the world hostage, Roosevelt established the Uranium Committee in October 1939. This was the first step toward organized development of an atomic bomb (A-bomb) in the United States.

Long-distance difficulties

Across the country, many institutes of advanced learning (including the University of California's Radiation Laboratory and the physics departments at Columbia, Stanford, and Cornell Universities; the California Institute of Technology; and the Universities of Wisconsin and Illinois) stepped up research into preparing nuclear materials such as uranium-235 and plutonium. Uranium-235 and plutonium are fissionable elements and the bases of atomic bombs. The National Academy of Sciences announced that its number one priority was to build atomic weapons before anyone else in the world did so. Scientists met at conferences to share their knowledge, but coordinating the scattered research projects proved problematic. Long-distance communication between scientists was all but impossible because government security regulations required that uranium and plutonium research be kept top-secret; scientists could not discuss their research over the phone or in writing. By the fall of 1942, a research facility in one location, where key scientists could speak in person and work together, was desperately needed.

The Manhattan Project

Vannevar Bush (1890–1974) was head of the Office of Scientific Research and Development (OSRD), the wartime civilian scientific mobilization group. He asked President Roosevelt to assign to the military the construction of a lab and production plants. Roosevelt assigned the army to work with OSRD. In September 1942, Leslie R. Groves of the Army Corps of Engineers was appointed to take charge of the weapons program. Groves was immediately promoted to brigadier general so that he would have sufficient rank to impress the senior civilian scientists in the project. Groves and the Manhattan Engineer District, headquartered in New York City, took charge. Groves named the weapons program the Manhattan Project after his home base. With directness and determined efficiency, Groves established two large production plants, the Clinton Engineer Works in Oak Ridge, Tennessee, and the Hanford Engineer Works in eastern Washington State. Oak Ridge would produce uranium-235; Hanford would produce plutonium. Construction of a third facility, the Manhattan Engineer District Laboratory, began in March 1943 in a remote desert area near Los Alamos, New Mexico. The first atomic bomb would be assembled at the Los Alamos site, dubbed Project Y, about a hundred miles north of Albuquerque.

In October 1942, Groves named J. Robert Oppenheimer (1904–1967), a theoretical physicist from the University of California at Berkeley, to lead the laboratory's scientists. In March 1943, before construction of the facility was anywhere near complete, the most renowned scientists in the country and their families began arriving at Los Alamos. Navigating primitive roads and dealing with inadequate cooking and sleeping accommodations, they began their work. No one knew how close the Germans were to completing a bomb, but if Germany won the bomb race, America would lose the war. Every month, week, and day counted.

A secret project, a secret town

Everything about the Manhattan Project was top-secret. When Robert Serber (1909–1997) of the University of Illinois, Oppenheimer's chief theoretical assistant, rose to give one of the first lectures to the gathered Los Alamos scientists, he announced that the project objective was to build a practical military weapon, a bomb based on nuclear fission. Upon hearing the word bomb, Oppenheimer sent a note up to the podium saying Serber should use the term "gadget," not bomb, because many carpenters and other workers were still present and might overhear. From then on, the bomb was always referred to as "the gadget."

Physicist J. Robert Oppenheimer, head of the Manhattan Project. *Courtesy of the National Archives and Records Administration.*

Within the year, thousands of personnel from all over the country had arrived, and Los Alamos became a small town. Everyone there had passed rigorous background checks. The name Los Alamos could not appear on any letters or parcels, incoming or outgoing. Instead the address was Box 1663, Santa Fe, New Mexico. The address on the birth certificates of babies born at the Los Alamos Engineers Hospital between 1942 and 1945 was simply "Box 1663."

Ultimately about 140,000 military and civilian individuals—physicists, chemists, engineers, teachers, carpenters, janitors, etc.—worked on the Manhattan Project at Los Alamos and in various secret locations throughout the United States. However, only a tiny percentage ever knew the ultimate goal was to build an atomic bomb.

Mission completed

On July 16, 1945, the "gadget" tested successfully. At that point, the United States had the only workable atomic bomb in the world. Los Alamos engineers did not realize that the German attempt to develop a bomb had been derailed years earlier. Lack of organization, then the devastation of World War II, had prevented any concerted effort by the scientists in Germany.

Los Alamos produced two bombs, code-named "Little Boy" and "Fat Man." Confident that Little Boy would work, scientists assembled the uranium-235-based bomb and readied it for shipment in early July 1945. Fat Man, which had a plutonium base, needed to be tested to confirm that it would detonate. The "Trinity" test near Alamogordo, New Mexico, was therefore a test of a plutonium-based bomb like Fat Man. When that bomb detonated, American scientists knew they had opened the age of nuclear weaponry; they also knew that this weapon would end World War II.

An aerial view of Los Alamos National Laboratory during the 1940s.
Reproduced by permission of the Corbis Corporation.

World War II ends

The results of the Trinity test were immediately conveyed to U.S. president Harry S. Truman (1884–1972; served 1945–53), who had taken office after President Roosevelt's death in April 1945. Truman was attending a conference in Potsdam, near Berlin, Germany. He casually informed Soviet premier Joseph Stalin (1879–1953), also in attendance, that the United States had a new weapon of great destructive power. On July 26, 1945, Truman and Clement Attlee (1883–1967), who had replaced Winston Churchill (1874–1965) as Great Britain's prime minister, issued an ultimatum to Japan: Surrender or face total destruction. Japan rejected the ultimatum.

In the early-morning hours of August 6, Little Boy rode in the belly of a U.S. B-29 bomber, the *Enola Gay*, that was part of the 509th Composite Air Group, stationed in the Mariana Islands in the western Pacific Ocean. At precisely

"Little Boy" and "Fat Man"

Between 1942 and 1945, Los Alamos scientists produced two types of bombs—or "gadgets," as they were called during development. The bombs were detonated in different ways. One bomb, code-named "Little Boy," used uranium-235 (U-235) and was detonated by a process called fission. Fission involves splitting the atomic nucleus of a heavy element to create two lighter elements. Natural uranium contains two forms of the element mixed together: U-235 and U-238. U-235 is fissionable (split-table); U-238 is not. Therefore, to gather material for bomb making, scientists have to separate U-235 from U-238.

The nuclear research plant in Oak Ridge, Tennessee, took charge of the task to produce the U-235 needed for Little Boy. To detonate Little Boy, a slug of U-235 would be fired like a bullet down a gun barrel into the center of another chunk of U-235. Adding its own fissionable material to the mix, the slug would split the nucleus of the U-235 chunk, causing it to release a tremendous amount of energy in the form of an explosion. Little Boy was 10 feet (3 meters) long and 28 inches (71 centimeters) in diameter; it weighed 9,000 pounds (4,086 kilograms). Scientists were certain that this type of bomb would work and did not actually test Little Boy.

The second type of bomb, code-named Fat Man, used implosion (an extreme inward collapse) to detonate plutonium. A University of California at Berkeley scientist, Glenn T. Seaborg (1912–1999), discovered that a new fissionable element could be made by bombarding uranium-238 with neutrons, one of two kinds of particles found inside the nucleus (central part) of an atom. He named the new element plutonium. The nuclear research plant in Hanford, Washington, was in charge of producing plutonium. Fat Man consisted of high explosives surrounding a plutonium ball. When detonated, the explosives would compress, or squeeze, the plutonium, causing a massive energy release, or explosion. Los Alamos scientists were not sure the plutonium bomb would work, so they conducted the Trinity test of Fat Man on July 16, 1945. The spectacular results confirmed that it indeed worked.

Both types of bombs release energy (explode) as a result of a change in the composition of the atomic nucleus; that is why they are called atomic or nuclear weapons.

8:16:02 A.M. Japanese time, Little Boy was dropped on the center of Hiroshima, Japan, instantly killing at least 80,000 people and seriously injuring at least 100,000 more. Many of the injured would die of burns and radiation exposure. Japan did not surrender. On August 9, at 11:02 A.M. Japanese time,

A-Bombs and H-Bombs

All the bombs mentioned in this chapter were created by altering the nucleus of the atom of an element, so all of them may be referred to as nuclear bombs or atomic bombs. However, technically, only bombs that are detonated by controlled fission, or the splitting of an atom's nucleus, are true atomic bombs, or A-bombs.

Bombs that are created by the fusion, or joining together, of atomic nuclei of the element hydrogen are called hydrogen bombs, or H-bombs. H-bombs are also called thermonuclear bombs, because of the incredible heat their reaction generates. H-bombs explode with a much greater force than A-bombs.

Although highly destructive, A-bombs are limited in power compared to the boundless destructive force of H-bombs. One kiloton equals the explosive force of (or the energy released by) 1,000 tons (907 metric tons) of TNT, a conventional (nonnuclear) explosive. One megaton equals the explosive force of 1,000,000 tons (907,000 metric tons) of TNT.

In August 1945, the United States dropped A-bombs on Japan over the cities of Hiroshima and Nagasaki. The Hiroshima bomb, using the code name "Little Boy," had a force of 13,000 tons (11,791 metric tons), or 13 kilotons, of TNT. Its element base was uranium-235. The Nagasaki bomb, using the code name "Fat Man," had a force of 22,000 tons (19,954 metric tons), or 22 kilotons, of TNT. Its element base was plutonium.

Two tests showed the tremendous force of H-bombs. One test, at Enewetak Atoll, on November 1, 1952, had a force of 10,400,000 tons (9,432,800 metric tons), or 10,400 kilotons, or 10.4 megatons, of TNT. Its element base was hydrogen. Another test (given the test code name of Bravo), at Bikini Atoll, on March 1, 1954, had a force of 15,000,000 tons (13,605,000 metric tons), or 15,000 kilotons, or 15 megatons, of TNT. Its element base was hydrogen.

Fat Man was dropped on Nagasaki, Japan, killing nearly 74,000 and injuring 75,000 of Nagasaki's 286,000 residents. Japan agreed to surrender on August 14, 1945.

Arms race begins

When President Truman mentioned to Stalin at Potsdam that the United States had a powerful new weapon, he did not realize that Stalin was already aware of the Manhattan Project; Soviet spies had been reporting to Stalin regular-ly. American officials no doubt hoped that U.S. possession of an atomic bomb would give them an advantage in postwar negotiations and make Stalin and the Soviets more manageable. Instead, Stalin accelerated the Soviet A-bomb effort. The Soviets vowed to produce their own atomic weapons and to break the U.S. monopoly as soon as possible. The Soviet Union and the United States were now locked in an arms race, with each side trying to equal or outdo the military strength of the other. This further promoted the "cold war" between the two countries: Neither could use its weapons without risking annihilation, but both continued the battle by building more powerful bombs.

"Joe-1"

Only a few weeks after the bombing of Hiroshima and Nagasaki, Stalin ordered forty-two-year-old Igor Kurchatov (1903–1960), the Soviet Union's premier nuclear physicist, to build an atomic bomb by 1948. The focus of the Soviet nuclear program was to detonate a nuclear bomb as soon as possible, no matter the cost. Stalin also selected Lavrenty Beria (1899–1953), leader of the dreaded Soviet secret police, to organize and manage the Soviet bomb project. Kurchatov had the same role in the Soviet program as Oppenheimer had had in the Manhattan Project. Beria was the Soviet counterpart to General Groves—with one major distinction: Apparently Beria had permission to shoot Kurchatov and his staff if they failed at their task. Beria was fond of announcing to Kurchatov, "You will become camp dust." Perhaps partly out of fear but overwhelmingly out of a sense of patriotic duty to his country that had been so injured by the Germans during World War II, Kurchatov set about his task immediately. Like most Soviets, he believed the United States intended to use its atomic power to gain influence around the world, perhaps to push its economic and political views onto the Soviet Union and its allies.

Both Kurchatov and Beria were talented organizers. They mobilized people and resources. Uranium was mined; a nuclear reactor (a device in which nuclear reactions took place) was built; and the super-secret atomic weapons laboratory, Arzamas-16, took shape. It was nicknamed "Los Arzamas," a play on words with the U.S. atomic weapons laboratory site of Los Alamos. Arzamas-16 was much like Los Alamos: It was developed at the site of a small town, Sarov. About 250 miles (400 kilometers) east of Moscow, Sarov soon disappeared from maps. All the great Soviet scientists would live and work at this top-secret location, and after several years, they created a plutonium bomb, code-named "Joe-1."

In early 1946, a two-story house called the "Forester's Cabin" was built at Los Arzamas for Kurchatov and his wife, Marina. It was within walking distance of Kurchatov's lab. Kurchatov was likable and capable—he even coped well with Beria—and he brought about intense loyalty from his fellow scientists. He often sat at a table with his staff, surrounded by the extensive flower and vegetable garden he had planted at his house, and invited them to discuss problems and working plans. At the end of the discussion, Kurchatov would assign a month's worth of work and send them back to the lab. Then, only hours later, he would head down his path through the woods to the lab to see how much progress had been made.

After a series of technical delays, Kurchatov delivered on August 29, 1949. The Soviets' first atomic test, code-named "First Lightning," was successful. A plutonium bomb named Joe-1, which closely resembled the U.S. "gadget" Fat Man, detonated at the Semipalatinsk Test Site in northeastern Kazakhstan. A few days later, the United States became aware of the test. A U.S. Air Force B-29 on a weather mission over the North Pacific encountered a very high radioactivity count. Analyzing the data, U.S. scientists realized the Soviets had detonated a plutonium atomic bomb.

"Enormous"

U.S. intelligence had figured that the earliest possible Soviet completion of a nuclear weapon would be about 1953. It seemed reasonable that Kurchatov and his scientists would need that much time to design and build their own atomic bomb. However, the Soviet project had been speeded up by information from "atomic spies" within the Manhattan Project. "Enormous" was the code word the atomic spies used to refer to the Manhattan Project. Between 1943 and 1945, Klaus Fuchs (1911–1988), Theodore Alvin Hall (1925–1999),

David Greenglass (1922–), Ruth Greenglass (1925–), Julius Rosenberg (1918–1953), Ethel Rosenberg (1915–1953), and Harry Gold (c. 1911–1972) helped deliver technical information from the Manhattan Project to Beria and Kurchatov and their colleagues at Los Arzamas. Fuchs, a Los Alamos scientist; Hall, a Los Alamos physicist; and David Greenglass, a Los Alamos machinist, passed detailed information to the Rosenbergs and Gold. In turn, the information was passed on to the Soviets. In retrospect, historians believe the information that the spies passed on speeded up Soviet atomic bomb development by one to two years.

On September 23, 1949, a shocked United States listened as President Truman revealed information about the Soviet atomic blast. Americans absorbed the news with dread rather than panic. Clearly the Soviets had caught up. Americans now questioned their own safety. Fuchs had sent detailed data about the American plutonium bomb, "Fat Man"; that explained Joe-1's resemblance. Hall was the only atomic spy U.S. officials knew about who was not caught.

Ground zero in Kazakhstan, the site of the first Soviet atomic explosion on August 29, 1949. This photograph, taken in November 1992, shows the desolation forty-three years later. *Photograph by Shepard Sherbell. Reproduced by permission of the Corbis Corporation.*

The Strategic Air Command and the Atomic Energy Commission

After the initial race to create an atomic bomb, two key groups came into being in the United States in 1946: the Strategic Air Command and the Atomic Energy Commission. The U.S. military established the Strategic Air Command (SAC), and by the late 1940s SAC's goal was to identify targets in the Soviet Union and be ready to deliver nuclear weapons to those targets. It was hoped that this would deter any Soviet aggression. The United States saw atomic weapons as a way to match the strength of the Soviet land armies in Eastern Europe.

The Atomic Energy Commission (AEC), established by Congress in July 1946, took over management of the nuclear research facilities at Oak Ridge, Hanford, and Los Alamos. Universities contracted with the AEC for research and development of weapons. The University of California contracted with the AEC to manage Los Alamos. Although World War II had ended, the United States and the Soviet Union were becoming entangled in a war over political and economic ideas—the Cold War. Increasingly, Americans believed that the United States needed to maintain superiority in weaponry to deter Soviet aggression. Subscribing to this view, the AEC favored development of weapons rather than pursuing ways to peacefully take advantage of nuclear energy.

Hydrogen bomb

President Truman shocked the United States and the world with his announcement that the Soviet Union had successfully detonated an atomic weapon. The United States had to reassess its position in the world: U.S. leaders were already worried about the strong and growing Soviet communist influence in Eastern Europe. Additionally the communists controlled China. Many Americans believed that only being on constant alert and having a strong military armed with nuclear weapons could keep the Soviets in check. Indeed, some feared a communist takeover of the United States if the United States let down its guard, even momentarily.

In the fall of 1949, after the Soviet atomic bomb test, a secret and heated debate raged among American government

The Strategic Air Command

In 1948, General Curtis E. LeMay (1906–1990), a decorated World War II pilot, assumed command of the U.S. Air Force Strategic Air Command (SAC), which was formed in 1946. Based in Nebraska at Offutt Air Base, the SAC bomber force became the cornerstone for the U.S. national air defensive and offensive strategy. Commanding the nerve center of an eventually worldwide bomber-missile force, LeMay started building his bomber teams into an elite, well-seasoned corps. Deciding that the best defense was indeed an overwhelming offense, LeMay pushed for a buildup of nuclear weapons and for bombers to carry them. As soon as the Soviets demonstrated nuclear capability, LeMay emphasized that SAC needed to have at its disposal enough weapons, and the planes to carry them, to hit thousands of targets in the Soviet Union. By 1952 he had identified up to six thousand Soviet targets. He reasoned that SAC's strength would deter Soviet aggression.

According to Isaacs and Downing in *Cold War: An Illustrated History, 1945–*

U.S. general Curtis E. LeMay. *Reproduced by permission of the Corbis Corporation.*

1991, the U.S. military had 298 atomic bombs in 1950, 2,422 nuclear weapons in 1955, and 27,100 by 1962. In 1951, SAC had 668 B-50 and B-29 bombers. By 1959 it had 500 long-range B-52 bombers and more than 2,500 B-47 bombers that could refuel in midair.

officials, scientists, and the U.S. military. Reevaluating U.S. strength in light of the Soviet atomic test, Truman turned first to the AEC. After completing the Manhattan Project, U.S. scientists had considered the development of a hydrogen bomb (H-bomb), which would be far more destructive than the bombs dropped in Japan. They knew that H-bombs could be created through fusion, or joining together, of the atomic nuclei of the element hydrogen. However, AEC director David Lilienthal (1899–1981) did not support further testing in peace-

David Lilienthal, director of the Atomic Energy Commission. *Courtesy of the Library of Congress.*

time. Because the Soviets had just developed their own A-bomb, others on the AEC wanted the United States to do immediate and concentrated research to develop the H-bomb. Lilienthal, fully aware of the H-bomb's boundless destructive power, still resisted. He then asked for direction from the AEC's General Advisory Committee (GAC), a group made up of scientists including Manhattan Project leader J. Robert Oppenheimer. The GAC supported Lilienthal, recommending a buildup of A-bombs but rejecting development of the H-bomb.

However, yet another group of scientists (including Edward Teller, who in 1939 had urged Einstein to write to then-President Roosevelt about development of the A-bomb) argued in favor of the H-bomb. Concurring, the U.S. military strongly urged development, emphasizing the need to produce such a weapon before the Soviets could produce one. President Truman managed to keep all the debate secret; he hoped the press and the American public would not hear about the H-bomb before he had decided what to do. He next appointed a three-man committee—Lilienthal, Secretary of State Dean Acheson (1893–1971), and Secretary of Defense Louis Johnson (1891–1966)—to debate the issue and advise him. Lilienthal remained opposed, but Acheson and Johnson supported development of the H-bomb. Truman believed that negotiating a mutual agreement with the Soviets not to pursue the H-bomb was hopeless, so in late January 1950 he announced to the American public that development would proceed on all types of nuclear weapons, including the H-bomb. Scientists at Los Alamos immediately began work on the H-bomb.

By the late 1940s, Soviet scientists knew that U.S. scientists were researching the H-bomb, so they began research, too. The Soviet investigation team was headed by physicist Yakov Zel'dovich (1914–1987) and included fellow physicists Andrey Sakharov (1921–1989), Vitali Ginzburg (1916–), and Viktor Davidenko. Sakharov would become known as the father of the Soviet hydrogen bomb.

Thermonuclear race

On November 1, 1952, from the tiny atoll, or coral island, of Enewetak, part of the western Pacific's Marshall Islands, a fireball arose. America's first hydrogen bomb had been detonated. The fireball's mushroom shape grew to 100 miles (160 kilometers) in diameter and rained down radioactive material. The H-bomb was 800 times more powerful than the A-bomb dropped on Hiroshima, exploding with a force of 10.4 megatons (9,432,800 metric tons) of TNT. The bomb could not be transported by aircraft; it was too heavy and had to be cooled by refrigeration until detonated.

On August 12, 1953, the Soviets successfully tested Joe-4 at Semipalatinsk Test Site. Although much smaller than the U.S. test bomb and not a true hydrogen bomb, Joe-4 brought the Soviets into the race. On March 1, 1954, the United States detonated a physically smaller, lithium-based hydrogen bomb that could be carried by a B-47 jet bomber. The test, known as "Bravo," occurred at the Bikini Atoll, 200 miles (321 kilometers) from Enewetak. The bomb yielded 15 megatons (13,605,000 metric tons) of destructive force.

The Soviets kept pace with U.S. progress. On November 22, 1955, again at Semipalatinsk, the Soviets' first true hydrogen

The view of the first hydrogen bomb, following its detonation near Enewetak, in the Pacific's Marshall Islands, November 1, 1952. *Reproduced by permission of the Corbis Corporation.*

bomb detonated. At 1.6 megatons (1,451,200 metric tons and a little over 100 times the force of the Hiroshima bomb), it was the world's first air-dropped hydrogen bomb. The Cold War and the thermonuclear race, referring to nuclear weapons that release atomic energy by joining hydrogen nuclei at high temperatures, had spiraled out of control. Although both the United States and the Soviet Union claimed they did not want to use the H-bombs, the world could only hold its breath and wait.

For More Information

Books

Badash, Lawrence. *Scientists and the Development of Nuclear Weapons: From Fission to the Limited Test Ban Treaty, 1939–1963.* Amherst, NY: Humanity Books, 1998.

Bethe, Hans A. *The Road from Los Alamos.* New York: Simon and Schuster, 1991.

Groves, Leslie R. *Now It Can Be Told: The Story of the Manhattan Project.* New York: Da Capo Press, 1983.

Holloway, David. *Stalin and the Bomb: The Soviet Union and Atomic Energy, 1939–1956.* New Haven, CT: Yale University Press, 1994.

Isaacs, Jeremy, and Taylor Downing. *Cold War: An Illustrated History, 1945–1991.* Boston: Little, Brown, 1998.

Kunetka, James W. *City of Fire: Los Alamos and the Birth of the Atomic Age, 1943–1945.* Englewood Cliffs, NJ: Prentice-Hall, 1978.

Maier, Pauline, Merritt R. Smith, Alexander Keyssar, and Daniel J. Kevles. *Inventing America: A History of the United States.* New York: W. W. Norton, 2003.

Rhodes, Richard. *Dark Sun: The Making of the Hydrogen Bomb.* New York: Simon and Schuster, 1995.

Seaborg, Glenn T. *Adventures in the Atomic Age.* Berkeley, CA: Farrar, Straus, and Giroux, 2001.

Shroyer, Jo Ann. *Secret Mesa: Inside Los Alamos National Laboratory.* New York: John Wiley and Sons, 1998.

Szasz, Ferenc M. *The Day the Sun Rose Twice: The Story of the Trinity Site Nuclear Explosion.* Albuquerque: University of New Mexico Press, 1984.

Web Sites

The Atomic Archive. http://www.atomicarchive.com (accessed on July 18, 2003).

Los Alamos National Laboratory. http://www.lanl.gov/worldview/ (accessed on July 18, 2003).

The Manhattan Project Heritage Preservation Association, Inc. http://www.childrenofthemanhattanproject.org (accessed on July 18, 2003).

National Atomic Museum. http://www.atomicmuseum.com (accessed on July 18, 2003).

Russian Research Centre, Kurchatov Institute. http://www.kiae.ru (accessed on July 18, 2003).

"Secrets, Lies, and Atomic Spies." *Nova Online.* http://www.pbs.org/wgbh/nova/venona (accessed on July 18, 2003).

United States Strategic Command. http://www.stratcom.af.mil (accessed on July 18, 2003).

Homeland Insecurities

5

"Are you now, or have you ever been, a member of the Communist Party?" This was the question members of the House Un-American Activities Committee (HUAC) asked each American who was brought before them. The HUAC, reaching its peak of power between 1947 and 1953, was at the center of the Red Scare, a period in U.S. history when Americans felt highly threatened by communism. Communism is a system of government in which a single political party controls almost all aspects of society. A communist system eliminates private ownership of property and business. Goods produced and accumulated wealth are in theory shared relatively equally by all. Under communism, people are not guaranteed individual liberties. In communist countries religious practices are not allowed.

Americans feared communists would gain strength in their country and might eventually take over. "Reds under the beds" and "better dead than Red" were common catchphrases. (The term "Red" was used to refer to communists and communist sympathizers.) Americans became obsessed with the fear of communism and looked with suspicion on subver-

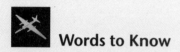

Words to Know

Cold War: A prolonged conflict for world dominance from 1945 to 1991 between the two superpowers, the democratic, capitalist United States and the communist Soviet Union. The weapons of conflict were commonly words of propaganda and threats.

Communism: A system of government in which the nation's leaders are selected by a single political party that controls almost all aspects of society. Private ownership of property is eliminated and government directs all economic production. The goods produced and accumulated wealth are, in theory, shared relatively equally by all. All religious practices are banned.

Hollywood Ten: Ten producers, directors, and screenwriters from Hollywood who were called before the House Un-American Activities Committee (HUAC) to explain their politics and reveal what organizations they were part of. Eight of the ten had communist affiliations.

House Un-American Activities Committee (HUAC): A congressional group established to investigate and root out any communist influences within the United States.

Red Scare: A great fear among U.S. citizens in the late 1940s and early 1950s that communist influences were infiltrating U.S. society and government and could eventually lead to the overthrow of the American democratic system.

sive, or revolutionary, groups within the United States. The HUAC was established to investigate and root out any communist influences within the country. In this atmosphere of suspicion and fear, "McCarthyism"—unfounded accusations of disloyalty to the U.S. government—was strong and continued to grow stronger. Even the U.S. Federal Bureau of Investigation (FBI) joined in the fight against the "Red Menace."

Communism and democracy

During the Red Scare, investigations and restrictions on liberties protected by the U.S. Constitution shook Americans. But Soviet and Eastern European citizens experienced far worse conditions under Communist Party leader Joseph Stalin (1879–1953). Many years earlier, in November 1917, members of a rising political party in Russia, the Bolsheviks, had gained

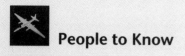

People to Know

Whittaker Chambers (1901–1961): A journalist who admitted at the House Un-American Activities Committee (HUAC) hearings that he had once been a communist but had later denounced communism; he named Alger Hiss as a communist.

Martin Dies (1900–1972): U.S. representative from Texas, 1931–44, 1953–58; chairman of the House Un-American Activities Committee (HUAC), often called the Dies Committee.

Dwight D. Eisenhower (1890–1969): Thirty-fourth U.S. president, 1953–61.

Alger Hiss (1904–1996): U.S. State Department official who was accused of being a communist; he served three years and eight months in prison after being convicted of perjury.

Joseph R. McCarthy (1908–1957): U.S. senator from Wisconsin, 1947–58; for four years, he sought to expose American communists by manipulating the public's fear of communism and by making false accusations and claims that a massive communist conspiracy threatened to take over the country.

Richard M. Nixon (1913–1994): Republican congressman from California, 1947–50; member of the House Un-American Activities Committee (HUAC), and closely involved with the investigation of accused communist Alger Hiss; was later a U.S. senator, vice president, and president.

Franklin D. Roosevelt (1882–1945): Thirty-second U.S. president, 1933–45.

Joseph Stalin (1879–1953): Dictatorial Russian/Soviet leader, 1924–53.

Harry S. Truman (1884–1972): Thirty-third U.S. president, 1945–53.

control of the Russian government. The Bolsheviks, later called the Communists, believed in the ideology of Vladimir I. Lenin (1870–1924), who established the Communist Party in Russia.

The American public soon realized the communist system of government was uncompromisingly different from U.S. democracy. In the United States, property and businesses are privately owned, and the Bill of Rights protects individual liberties. Americans are free to worship as they wish.

The first Red Scare

Near the end of the 1910s, many Americans began to fear that communism might spread and take over the Ameri-

Vladimir I. Lenin, founder of the Russian Communist Party. *Reproduced by permission of Getty Images.*

can way of life. Late in 1918, anarchists, people intent on overthrowing the government by violence, bombed the homes of a Philadelphia, Pennsylvania, businessman, a police official, and a state judge. Then, in June 1919, a bomb exploded outside the home of U.S. attorney general A. Mitchell Palmer (1872–1936), who was trying to make a name for himself by launching a major campaign against political radicals, or those advocating extreme change. Palmer and other politicians visiting his home at the time escaped injury, but the bomber was killed. Most Americans attributed the bombings to communists and immigrant anarchists because of Palmer's warnings to the public that the Bolsheviks were trying to overthrow the U.S. government. The first Red Scare swept across the country.

Attorney General Palmer announced to Congress that communists were intent on overthrowing the government as quickly as possible. Congress reacted by establishing the Anti-Radical Division within the Department of Justice. The name was soon changed to the General Intelligence Division (GID). Appointed to head the new division was twenty-four-year-old J. Edgar Hoover (1895–1972). Hoover would later head the FBI from 1924 until his death in 1972. Palmer and Hoover planned and carried out a series of raids known as the Palmer Raids in late 1919 and early 1920. During the raids, thousands of U.S. citizens, many of Russian ancestry, and aliens, or foreign-born people who live in the United States but are not citizens, were arrested across the country without warrants. Although most were released in a few days, hundreds of Russian immigrants, not yet citizens, were deported, or shipped back, to Russia. Many of them had no connection to any communist group and had not acted against the U.S. government in any way.

Later in 1920, the Red Scare subsided, but a pattern that would repeat many times in the future had been set. Fear of communism would rise and fall through the twentieth century. It would come to its most dangerous peak in the late 1940s and 1950s.

A. Mitchell Palmer, attorney general during the final two years of Woodrow Wilson's administration. *Reproduced by permission of the Corbis Corporation.*

1930s

During the 1930s, Americans suffered through the longest and worst economic crisis in U.S. history, the Great Depression. By 1932, roughly 25 percent of the American workforce were unemployed. Among those who kept their jobs, incomes dropped an average of 40 percent between 1929 and 1932. Many Americans went hungry; in cities, people stood in long lines at food kitchens. The inauguration of Franklin D. Roosevelt (1882–1945; served 1933–45) as president of the United States in March 1933 brought renewed hope that the economic problems could be solved. Roosevelt devised a variety of social and economic programs, known as the New Deal, to bring relief to the American people and encourage economic recovery. Nevertheless, the Depression lingered on through the 1930s.

Because of the serious economic problems, many Americans, especially intellectuals and youths, rethought what they had been taught about the American political system, which was that the system offered the American dream in which anyone could reach financial security through hard work and resourcefulness. They attended meetings to learn about other systems of government and economics. At meetings led by communists, speakers called for more rights for workers and for spreading America's wealth more evenly. Americans interested in communism hoped it might provide some answers for Depression-era America; they had no doubt that they could freely express such ideas. However, many of those who showed an interest in communism in the 1930s would eventually be labeled as subversives and have to answer to government questioning. (A subversive is a person who attempts to overthrow or undermine an established political system.)

In 1938, Congress passed the Hatch Act (named after its author, U.S. senator Carl A. Hatch [1889–1963] of New Mexico), which prohibited Americans who joined the Communist Party from holding federal jobs. In May 1938, U.S. representative Martin Dies (1900–1972) of Texas managed to get congressional funding for his favorite special committee, the House Un-American Activities Committee (HUAC), often called the Dies Committee. The HUAC was asked to investigate subversive activities by organizations that might try to overthrow the U.S. government.

The Dies Committee claimed to find communists in labor unions and government agencies and among African American groups. Many of those who were accused of communist sympathies were fired from their jobs. Several members of Congress argued that HUAC was going too far and violating the civil rights of those accused. Nevertheless, in 1940 Congress passed the Alien Registration Act, better known as the Smith Act, which made it illegal to be a member of any organization that supported a violent overthrow of the U.S. government. The Communist Party was the principal organization lawmakers had in mind.

By 1939, World War II (1939–45) was raging in Europe, and in 1941 Japan bombed Pearl Harbor, a U.S. naval station in Hawaii, thus bringing the United States into the war. Although America's attention turned to the war, Dies doggedly kept HUAC alive until 1944, when ill health and criticism of his often groundless accusations against fellow Americans finally caused him to step down. The HUAC ceased to function, and the hunt for subversives slowed.

War ends and the second Red Scare begins

During World War II, the United States found itself in the strange position of being an ally of the communist Soviet Union. These uneasy allies joined with Great Britain and France to halt the advance of the German troops of Nazi leader Adolf Hitler (1889–1945). The Allied forces were successful in defeating Hitler, and as the war wound down in Europe, U.S. president Franklin D. Roosevelt, Soviet leader Joseph Stalin, and British prime minister Winston Churchill (1874–1965) met in Yalta (a resort town in the Soviet republic of the Ukraine) in February 1945 to discuss postwar plans. All agreed that the European nations liberated from Germany's grasp would eventually have free elections, where citizens are free to vote for the candidate of their choice.

World War II officially ended on September 2, 1945, and shortly thereafter Stalin began ignoring postwar agreements. He established communist governments in the Eastern European nations of Poland, Albania, Bulgaria, Hungary, and finally Czechoslovakia. These Eastern European nations, along with Yugoslavia, became known as the Eastern Bloc. (Bloc refers to a group of nations.) Free elections were not held. Instead, Soviet leaders in Moscow controlled the communist governments that had been put in place. The United States became the leader of the Western European democratic nations.

Relations between the East and West were tense. A cold war replaced the hot war, an actual armed conflict. The Cold War was fought over ideologies—communism versus democracy. It was a war caused by mutual fear and distrust. To most Americans, describing someone as "communist" was the same as saying the person was un-American.

EUROPE
During the Cold War

North
Sea

NORWAY SWEDEN
Oslo
Stockholm

Tallinn

SOVIET UNION

Moscow

Riga

DENMARK
København
(Copenhagen)

Vilnius

Minsk

Belfast UNITED
KINGDOM

Dublin

IRELAND Irish
Sea

NETHERLANDS
Amsterdam
London

Berlin

POLAND

Kiev

WEST
Brussels GERMANY EAST

Warsaw

BELGIUM Bonn
GERMANY

LUXEMBOURG
Prague

ATLANTIC
English Channel
Guernsey (UK)
Jersey (UK)

CZECHOSLOVAKIA

OCEAN
Paris

Bratislava

LIECHTENSTEIN Vienna

Bay
of
Biscay

FRANCE

AUSTRIA
Budapest

Bern
SWITZERLAND
HUNGARY ROMANIA

Ljubljana
Zagreb

MONACO
SAN
MARINO

Belgrade
Bucharest

Black
Sea

YUGOSLAVIA

BULGARIA

SPAIN

ITALY

Sarajevo
Sofia

PORTUGAL
ANDORRA

Corsica

Rome
Podgorica

Skopje

VATICAN
CITY

ALBANIA

Sardinia

Tirana

Balearic Islands

Tyrrhenian
Sea

Corfu

GREECE
Aegean
Sea

Mediterranean Sea

Ionian
Sea

Athens

Rhodes

Crete

MALTA

☐ Eastern Europe
▨ Western Europe

0   300 mi
0   300 km

A map showing Eastern and
Western European nations
during the Cold War.
*Reproduced by permission of
the Gale Group.*

In the 1946 congressional elections, a number of
politicians engaged in "Red-baiting"; that is, they attacked
their opponents by accusing them of having communist
leanings. Republicans charged that President Harry S. Truman (1884–1972; served 1945–53) and other Democrats were
"soft" on, or indifferent to, communism. Robert McCormick
(1880–1955), the longtime owner and editor of the *Chicago
Tribune* and a leading Republican in Illinois, claimed that the
Democratic Party was not firm against feared communist influences. Republican Joseph R. McCarthy (1908–1957) of
Wisconsin, who would play a major role in the second Red
Scare, was elected to the U.S. Senate. Organizations such as
the American Legion and Daughters of the American Revolution, along with conservative newspaper chains such as
Hearst and Scripps-Howard, contributed to the anticommu-
nist hysteria again sweeping the nation.

Loyalty program

President Truman listened to the remarks that Democrats were soft on communism. He also had intelligence reports that there were Soviet spies within the U.S. government. In March 1947, he responded with Executive Order 9835. The order established a program to check on the loyalty of the 2.5 million federal employees and root out any subversives. Subversive activity included past or present membership in various organizations with communist-like ideologies. Attorney General Tom Campbell Clark (1899–1977) was ordered to draw up a list of subversive organizations; however, there were no set standards for judging organizations, and the groups named as subversive could not challenge the listing. The FBI, under J. Edgar Hoover, checked out millions of federal workers over the next four years. (See box.) Most loyalty boards denied the accused people their right to know who accused them. Some people were even asked about books and artwork they owned, which was an infringement of their personal liberties. Privately, Truman was beginning to become quite uncomfortable with the FBI's methods.

Truman announced the Truman Doctrine the same month as he announced the loyalty investigation program. The Truman Doctrine promised that the United States would help any nation threatened by an attempted communist takeover. Truman also revived the Smith Act of 1940, which had been somewhat forgotten during the war. The 1948 presidential election was looming, and Truman's efforts were directed at disproving the charge that Democrats were soft on communists. Truman also hoped his loyalty program would help protect innocent federal workers from the invasive HUAC, which had again come to life.

A reinstated HUAC

Although HUAC had stopped operating after Martin Dies's departure in 1944, the committee was reestablished and made permanent in 1945 at the insistence of Democratic congressman John E. Rankin (1882–1960) from Mississippi. (Rankin led the proposal to reinstate the committee, and the House voted in favor of his idea.) HUAC received funding

Protecting America from Communism, J. Edgar Hoover Style

In the mid-1930s, President Franklin D. Roosevelt asked J. Edgar Hoover, head of the U.S. Federal Bureau of Investigation (FBI), to monitor the activities of communists and any other subversives in the United States. Hoover undertook this mission with great enthusiasm. By the end of World War II, he had compiled an amazing amount of information, including files on the daily habits and group memberships of many people who he thought might turn into enemies of democracy.

The campaign against communism dominated Hoover's life and the activities of the FBI. In 1947, the FBI investigated the loyalty of two to three million federal employees at the request of President Harry S. Truman. Of those, six thousand were thoroughly investigated. About twelve hundred were dismissed from their jobs, but only 212 people were fired for loyalty issues. Hoover also uncovered alcoholics, homosexuals, and employees in great debt. Heavy debtors were considered a risk because they might sell U.S. government information to the Soviets. In all, about twelve hundred federal employees were let go. Hoover also eagerly supplied the House Un-American Activities Committee (HUAC) with incriminating information on organizations such as labor unions. Hoover's FBI was in charge of the investigation and arrests of the "atomic spies," including Julius Rosenberg (1918–1953), Ethel Rosenberg (1915–1953), Harry Gold (c. 1911–1972), and David Greenglass (1922–), who had passed top-secret technical information about the atomic bomb to the Soviets.

To educate the public about the threat of communism within the United States, Hoover authored *Masters of Deceit,* published in 1958. In twelve years and twenty-nine printings, the book sold a quarter-million copies in hardback and two million in paperback. Something of a media hound, Hoover sought to maintain the FBI's and his own public prestige by collaborating on the production of radio and television programs and Hollywood movies. These productions included *The FBI Story* (1959), starring James Stewart (1908–1997), and a popular television series, *The FBI,* that ran from 1965 to 1974. *Street with No Name* (1948), a full-length movie from Twentieth Century Fox, had the FBI's full cooperation.

and orders to investigate any individuals or groups it deemed possible subversives. HUAC soon compiled a list of roughly forty groups that it labeled communist fronts. (A front is an organization or group that serves as a disguise for secret and/or illegal activities or business dealings.) HUAC alleged that the listed groups, despite their sometimes patriotic names, were really organizations intent on promoting com-

A young J. Edgar Hoover. *Courtesy of the Library of Congress.*

By the early 1960s, Hoover's ability to seek out and expose hidden threats was well recognized. President John F. Kennedy (1917–1963; served 1961–63) ordered Hoover to target the Ku Klux Klan, a secret society and recognized hate group that promotes white supremacy and harasses African Americans and other minority groups. By then, Hoover was one of the most powerful figures in Washington, D.C., often appearing to be under the control of no one. Hoover's men monitored people who protested the Vietnam War (1954–75). They also watched the activities of civil rights leaders, such as Dr. Martin Luther King Jr. (1929–1968), who Hoover claimed had communist ties. Viewing these people as subversives, Hoover's men kept extensive files on them all. By the mid-1960s, Hoover's tactics of widespread surveillance, wiretapping, and maintaining detailed files on innocent citizens seemed a threat to personal liberties. As a result, Hoover's popularity with the public and with many government officials dropped sharply.

Hoover remained the director of the FBI until his death in 1972, a total of forty-eight years. In 1975 and 1976, a Senate-appointed committee (the Select Committee to Study Governmental Operations with Respect to Intelligence Activities) determined that Hoover's actions constituted more than harassment; he had violated citizens' constitutional rights of free speech and free assembly (the right to meet with other people and groups).

munist ideas. One of HUAC's most aggressive and probing members was a young Republican congressman from California, Richard M. Nixon (1913–1994), who would become president of the United States nearly twenty-five years later. Nixon had charged that his Democratic opponent in the 1946 congressional election, Jerry Voorhis (1901–1984), was a communist sympathizer.

The Hollywood Ten

In October 1947, HUAC opened an investigation of America's film industry. Hollywood had released several movies portraying Russia in a favorable light, such as *Song of Russia*. Also, some Hollywood artists were known as current or former members of the U.S. Communist Party. Ten of Hollywood's producers, directors, and screenwriters (most of the group were screenwriters) were called before the committee to explain their politics and reveal what organizations they were part of. Eight of the ten had communist affiliations. At the same time, fifty Hollywood directors, writers, and actors, outraged at the probing of individual Americans' beliefs, chartered a plane and headed for Washington, D.C. The famous fifty included Humphrey Bogart (1899–1957), Lauren Bacall (1924–), Ira Gershwin (1896–1983), Danny Kaye (1913–1987), and Frank Sinatra (1915–1998). They stopped along the way for press conferences in Kansas City, St. Louis, and Chicago. Their goal was to defend the Hollywood Ten's rights to free speech and free assembly (the right to meet with other people and groups).

The Hollywood Ten refused to answer HUAC's questions, calling the inquiry a clear violation of their constitutional rights. Ultimately all were convicted for contempt of court, or an act of disobedience against the court. After a U.S. circuit court of appeals in 1948 upheld the verdict, eight served one year in prison and two served six months. All were assessed $1,000 fines. None of them was able to get work after being released, because Hollywood's film producers had put all ten on a blacklist. (A blacklist is a list of names of people who are to be punished or boycotted.) The message was clear: Either cooperate with HUAC or risk being blacklisted. Some of the famous fifty retracted their support for the Hollywood Ten and said that the trip to Washington, D.C., was a mistake.

The blacklisting spread to radio and a new industry—television. Anyone found to be connected to a group that had anything to do with subversive activities, real or imagined, was blacklisted. For instance, if a group happened to have a communist as a member, everyone in the group could be blacklisted. The Red Scare had taken firm hold of the American public.

A fearful America

By spring 1948, Americans felt that if they were not constantly vigilant, the Cold War could be lost right on American soil. FBI director Hoover fueled fears by commenting that communism was not a political party (like the Democrats or the Republicans) but an evil way of life that could spread like a disease across America. Overseas, there were signs of communist aggression: The Soviets blockaded Berlin, which was located deep within Soviet-occupied East Germany. The only way to get food and supplies to Berliners living in the U.S., French, and British sectors of the city was by an American- and British-run airlift (see Chapter 3, Germany and Berlin). In China, a communist revolution that had been going on for many years began to look as though it would succeed. Led by Mao Zedong (1893–1976), whose army was supplied by the Soviets, the communists were gaining wide support from the Chinese people.

The Hollywood Ten and their attorneys: (bottom row, left to right) Herbert Biberman, attorney Martin Popper, attorney Robert W. Kenny, Albert Maltz, and Lester Cole; (middle row) Dalton Trumbo, John Howard Lawson, Alvah Bessie, and Samuel Ornitz; (top row) Ring Lardner Jr., Edward Dmytryk, and Adrian Scott. *Reproduced by permission of AP/Wide World Photos.*

Witnesses and spectators
await the start of House Un-
American Activities
Committee hearings on
October 20, 1947.
*Reproduced by permission of
the Corbis Corporation.*

Back in the United States in July 1948, after a year of investigation, twelve leaders of the American Communist Party were tried and convicted under the 1940 Smith Act. The Smith Act made it illegal to be part of an organization that supported the violent overthrow of the government. (In 1951, the Supreme Court upheld the constitutionality of the Smith Act in *Dennis v. the United States* and refused to overturn the convictions.) Also in mid-1948, Elizabeth Bentley (1908–1963), an American who had been spying for the Soviet Union, turned against the Soviets. She testified before a Senate subcommittee and HUAC, giving them information about a Washington-based spy ring of which she had been a part. One individual she implicated was Whittaker Chambers (1901–1961), a senior editor for *Time* magazine and a former communist.

The strange case of Alger Hiss

Chambers admittedly had been a communist through most of the 1920s and 1930s, but he denounced communism sometime in 1937 or 1938. During his years as a communist, he received and photographed secret U.S. government documents and passed the film on to the Soviets. In August 1948, Chambers went before HUAC. He testified that he knew of Communist Party members in high places in the U.S. government, including the State Department. The public as well as government leaders were particularly sensitive to and disturbed by accusations that communists had penetrated the highest ranks of government. Of all those Chambers named, most refused to respond to the charges and used the Fifth Amendment, which gives a person the right not to testify against oneself, when called before the HUAC. However, Alger Hiss (1904–1996), one of the people Chambers named, sternly denounced the charges. His adamant denial caught the attention of Congressman Nixon. Nixon firmly believed that those most guilty usually make the mistake of going overboard to deny any wrongdoing.

Hiss graduated from Harvard Law School in 1930. He served as a law clerk for Supreme Court justice Oliver Wendell Holmes (1841–1935) and also served in President Franklin D. Roosevelt's administration, joining the State Department in 1936. Hiss attended the Yalta Conference in 1945 (at which Roosevelt, Stalin, and Churchill discussed postwar plans), and that same year attended the United Nations (UN) organizing meeting in San Francisco. (The UN is a group of nations whose main goals are to maintain peace and security for its member nations, promote human rights, and address humanitarian needs.) Hiss left the State Department in 1946 to serve as president of the Carnegie Endowment for International Peace.

Despite his outstanding résumé, Hiss was called to testify in front of HUAC on August 5, 1948. Hiss again denied the charges made by Chambers. Hiss claimed he had never even seen Chambers. Nixon was not convinced. Called again before the HUAC on August 16, Hiss had to face Chambers in person. Hiss admitted that he knew Chambers, but said that he had known him by the name George Crosley. Chambers again asserted that Hiss had been a communist in the late 1930s. Hiss strongly denied the accusation one more time and then sued Chambers for libel. (Libel is an unjust published statement about a person intended to hurt or ruin the person's reputation.)

Accused U.S. communist Alger Hiss. *Reproduced by permission of Getty Images.*

In December 1948, HUAC called on Chambers at his farm, and he took the committee out to his garden. Hidden in a hollowed-out pumpkin were rolls of microfilm containing pictures of confidential government papers. Chambers claimed Hiss had given these to him in 1938 to be sent on to the Soviet Union. Nixon, relentlessly pursuing the case, believed the microfilm was evidence enough to convict Hiss. In summer 1949, Hiss was brought to trial on perjury charges (lying under oath) for denying he knew Chambers and for denying he gave away secrets to the Soviets. He could not be charged with spying, due to the statute of limitations, which states that certain crimes cannot be charged after a defined period of time has elapsed. The result was a hung jury, which is when a jury cannot reach a verdict.

In November 1949, Chambers gave the HUAC sixty-five pages of State Department documents allegedly copied by Hiss on a typewriter and several in Hiss's handwriting. Chambers claimed Hiss had given them to him in 1938. Hiss was brought to a retrial in late 1949, on the same perjury charges, and in January 1950 the jury found him guilty. He was sentenced to five years in prison and served three years and eight months. Hiss died in 1996 at the age of ninety-two, still proclaiming his innocence. However, when the U.S. National Security Agency released the decoded messages, they, along with documents released in the Soviet Union, appeared to point to Hiss, though there was not conclusive proof. The Hiss case aroused extreme emotions in the late 1940s and 1950s. Those convinced of his guilt berated those who thought he was innocent. It was a war of Cold War rhetoric, or bold words, within the United States. The winner in the whole episode was Richard Nixon, the California congressman. The public saw him as a young political warrior fighting the spread of communism in America.

Heightened apprehensions

Apprehensions about the security of the United States continued to grow and spread. In 1949, for example, the National Education Association, which represented public school teachers, declared it inappropriate for communists to teach in schools. Universities agreed that professors should not be communists and should be fired if they joined the Communist Party. Many states required loyalty oaths from public employees, who had to swear they were not part of any communist organization. Many people lost their jobs when they refused to take the oath on the grounds that it violated personal liberties.

Claims were also made that communists were influencing the civil rights movement among black Americans. The famous athlete Jackie Robinson (1919–1972), major league baseball's first African American player, testified before HUAC concerning claims that civil rights groups had a communist influence. Robinson denied this. The committee asked Robinson a hypothetical question: If World War III were to break out between the United States and the Soviet Union, would black Americans in the United States fight against the Soviets? Robinson stated he did not think it would be a problem for blacks to fight against communist countries.

The most chilling news to reach the American public came in September 1949, when President Truman revealed that the Soviet Union had tested an atomic bomb. The United States was no longer the only country that possessed the ultimate destructive weapon. Worse still, the Soviets had apparently built their bomb using technical information they received from spies within the Manhattan Project, a top-secret U.S. government program in which scientists designed and built the country's first atomic weapon. Americans realized with horror that their country had indeed been betrayed from within (see Chapter 6, Espionage in the Cold War).

President Truman appointed a high-level committee to reevaluate the security of the United States in light of the Soviet acquisition of the atomic bomb. In spring 1950, the committee issued its report. Known as NSC-68—short for National Security Council Document 68—the report stated that the communist Soviet Union posed a risk to all civilization. The report called for heightened U.S. intelligence-gathering around the world and recommended quadrupling the U.S. defense budget. Although Truman and Congress were not ready to take these new bold measures, the report could not be ignored; it was another troubling cloud hanging over the American public.

McCarthyism

By 1950, U.S. citizens had become accustomed to their fellow citizens being questioned about their allegiance to America. Many had been falsely accused of communist affiliations, sometimes by members of Congress or by leaders of organizations seeking to root out subversives. The accused were generally considered guilty until proven innocent. Most of them lost their jobs and friends.

No one better illustrated the actions of this troubled time than Senator Joseph R. McCarthy, a Republican from Wisconsin. McCarthy went on a four-year witch-hunt, hoping to expose American traitors—that is, communists. He manipulated the American public's fear of communism for his own political purposes (up to this point, his career in the U.S. Senate had been relatively uneventful). He made false accusations and claims to convince Americans that a massive communist conspiracy threatened to take over the country; he warned them that they would lose their democratic way of life. The term "McCarthyism" came into use by 1950 and is still in use in the twenty-first century. It is used to describe a political attitude of intolerance or hostility toward potentially subversive groups. In the 1950s, McCarthyism was characterized by slander, false public accusations that damage the reputations of those accused.

Elected to the U.S. Senate in 1946, McCarthy had led the voters to believe he flew dive-bombers in World War II and that he had been wounded in action. McCarthy had been in the Marine Corps but held a desk job as an intelligence officer. At that time, McCarthy went along as an observer on flights that held no danger and rode in the "tail gunner" (back) section. However, he made sure he was photographed sitting behind the aircraft's guns; he later used the photographs in his election campaign. His only injury during the war came onboard a ship when he missed a rung of a ladder during a party and broke his foot.

McCarthy was a weak senator for Wisconsin. In fact, he had developed a reputation as a troublemaker. He was up for reelection in 1952 but had little support from his state. Searching for an attention-grabbing issue, McCarthy decided to play on America's fear of communism. McCarthy made his famous kickoff speech in Wheeling, West Virginia, before the Women's Republican Club. He claimed the U.S. State Department was full of Communist Party members or those loyal to the communists. He dramatically held up a list that he claimed contained 205 names of State Department communists. (Sometime later, it was discovered that the list had been his laundry list.) McCarthy refused to reveal his sources and gave only a few names from the alleged list of 205. No one he named was ever proved guilty. However, he had struck a chord with the public with his strong stand against communism. Money poured in (and went to his personal bank account), and he received support letters from around the country.

McCarthy's strategy was attack followed by avoidance. He attacked by casting doubt on a person's political loyalties, forcing accused individuals to defend themselves publicly; then he avoided producing any real evidence. Yet he stayed on the attack by suggesting that anyone who criticized his tactics must be a communist. HUAC energetically investigated all those McCarthy named as suspects. Among those McCarthy attacked were Senate Majority Leader Scott Lucas (1892–1968) of Illinois; Senator Millard Tydings (1890–1961) of Maryland; Secretary of Defense George C. Marshall (1880–1959), a retired army general; and even President Truman himself. McCarthy's talent lay in at-

U.S. senator Joseph R. McCarthy of Wisconsin, who made it his life's work to root out supposed communists in the United States. *Courtesy of the Library of Congress.*

tacking in such a way that he repeatedly grabbed headlines. He became the center of Red Scare hysteria.

McCarthy was reelected to his senate seat in 1952. After Dwight D. Eisenhower (1890–1969; served 1953–61) was elected president in 1952, McCarthy was assigned to the unimportant Government Operations Committee; Eisenhower and other Republicans hoped that would keep him out of the spotlight. But McCarthy turned the insignificant position into something grander. He established the Permanent Subcommittee on Investigations, hired a bright young lawyer named Roy Cohn (1927–1986), and went after the State Department again. The subcommittee became known as the "McCarthy Committee." He almost destroyed the Voice of America, a broadcasting service that transmitted its democratic message to over eighty countries; McCarthy claimed that a communist plot within the State Department was influencing the programming. The McCarthy Committee also turned its attention to libraries, demanding that any book that seemed to support communism be burned. President Eisenhower, incensed by McCarthy's actions, nevertheless avoided public confrontations with him because of the strong support he enjoyed from the conservative wing of the party. Rampaging on, McCarthy planned to investigate the Central Intelligence Agency (CIA) but was not successful because the CIA would not cooperate with the hearings. Criticism of McCarthy began to rise in 1953. Famous television journalist Edward R. Murrow (1908–1965) convincingly contended that McCarthy was exploiting America's fears and intimidating countless honest U.S. citizens, causing viewers to change their minds about McCarthy. Finally, McCarthy pushed too far: He declared that the U.S. Army's base at Fort Monmouth, New Jersey, harbored a communist spy ring. No evidence was found. Ultimately, in the spring of 1954, army lawyer Joseph N. Welch (1890–1960) was able to bring McCarthy's long stream of unjustified attacks to an end by publicly exposing the lack of evidence behind his claims.

The Senate voted to censure, or officially reprimand, McCarthy, recognizing that his behavior from 1950 to 1954 had been highly dishonorable. While still in office, McCarthy died of an inflamed liver on May 2, 1957, at the age of forty-eight.

A Visit to the China Shop

An editorial cartoon depicts U.S. senator Joseph McCarthy of Wisconsin as a bull in a CIA china shop, with President Dwight D. Eisenhower and CIA director Allen Dulles hiding from the man who spent much of his Senate career accusing prominent Americans of being communists. *Reproduced by permission of the Corbis Corporation.*

The "Great Terror" of Stalin

The Red Scare and McCarthyism shook the foundation of individual liberties in America. Yet these troubles paled in comparison to what people in the Soviet Union and Eastern Europe endured under the rule of Soviet Communist Party leader Joseph Stalin. Stalin took control of the Soviet Union in 1924. To him, freethinking was intolerably threatening. He demanded that the people under his rule conform to the uniform thinking of the Communist Party, which Stalin alone dictated. Dissent, or public disagreement, was never allowed. Any dissenting person would be rooted out and most likely executed or, at the very least, sent to a labor camp, where the person would have to endure hard work under difficult conditions. When appointing officials, no matter how essential they were to the working of the party, Stalin considered no qualities or qualifications other than complete loyalty to him alone.

Violence defined the period of Stalin's reign. Beginning in 1929 through 1933 and resuming in 1937 until his death in 1953, Stalin directed purges that killed millions and sent many more millions to isolated, harsh labor camps. The purges were known as Stalin's "Great Terror." In the early 1930s, most of the people who had planned the 1917 revolution in Russia (the Bolsheviks) were killed for reasons no one but Stalin understood. In fact, most of those extinguished in the purges were supporters of Stalin, but Stalin devised elaborate false accusations, then extracted confessions to the false charges with threats of torture. The accused would be cruelly beaten, jailed in extremely hot and/or extremely cold cells, and threatened with the execution of their wives and children. When tried at Stalin's "show trials," most of the accused people were sentenced to death. A show trial occurs when an accused person is put on trial in a court of law but not given a chance to challenge the charges against him or her. The outcome is often determined beforehand, based on political factors rather than legal ones. Those who received prison sentences were, in fact, usually executed without delay. About fifty show trials occurred during Stalin's Great Terror. Yet millions of men, women, and children disappeared, going either to their deaths or to the labor camps.

By late 1938, roughly eight million were in the labor camps and one million in prison (based on the known capacity of the prisons and the fact that those prisons were over-crowded). Approximately two million died in the labor camps in 1937 and 1938. Political prisoners—also called "enemies of the people" or "politicals"—were mixed in with criminals. The millions of slave laborers in the labor camp system, which was known as the Gulag, became a necessary part of the Soviet economy. They worked always under inhumane conditions, erecting industrial and mining facilities, building and maintaining camps, manufacturing camp necessities, mining, lumbering, and doing various government projects.

By 1948, the communist governments in Eastern Europe were tightly controlled by Moscow. Stalin imposed absolute authority over the Soviet satellite countries, except Yugoslavia, which was under the leadership of Josip Tito (1892–1980). Between 1948 and Stalin's death in 1953, harsh treatment and threats of violence kept the people obedient to Stalin. He ordered more show trials in Hungary and Czechoslovakia. Roughly 150,000 Czech citizens became political prisoners.

In 1946, Stalin had launched a campaign against several film and theater people who he said went beyond the bounds set by the Communist Party. In early 1949, he followed up this campaign with a terrifying move against the often free-thinking Leningraders: Over two hundred were implicated in anti-Soviet activity aimed at undermining the Soviet Central Committee, which oversees the day-to-day activities of the Soviet Communist Party. The charges were made up to suit Stalin. All the accused people were shot in Leningrad. The massacre was followed by more violence, this time against acquaintances of the people just executed. The purges were bizarre—no real threats were being made against Stalin. The Soviet Union had recovered amazingly well from World War II, and there was strong stable support of Stalin. Yet Stalin turned to coercion and violence, as he had for the past quarter of a century. Stalin's pattern was apparently the only style of governing he knew.

After the Leningrad purge, Stalin concentrated on what he called "cosmopolitanism" or anti-Soviet foreign influence. He looked with suspicion on the Jews in the Soviet Union because most had relatives living in other countries. He contended that anti-Soviet foreign influence no doubt

flowed through the Jewish community. A number of prominent Jews, mostly Yiddish-language writers, were arrested
and shot. Just before his death, Stalin imagined yet another
plot against his government, the "doctors' plot." In January
1953, nine Moscow doctors, most of them Jews, were arrested and charged with scheming to kill Soviet leaders. In February, twenty-eight more doctors and their wives were arrested, imprisoned, and tortured. A show trial was under way

when Stalin suffered a fatal stroke on March 1 and died March 5, 1953. The "doctors' plot" trial immediately ceased.

It was widely accepted in Russia at the beginning of the twenty-first century that at least twenty million died during Stalin's reign. The total number of people who were "repressed" (which included death and exile) was approximately forty million, roughly half from 1929 to 1933 and the other half from 1937 to 1953.

For More Information

Books

Barson, Michael, and Steven Heller. *Red Scared! The Commie Menace in Propaganda and Popular Culture.* San Francisco: Chronicle Books, 2001.

Cohn, Roy. *McCarthy.* New York: New American Library, 1968.

Conquest, Robert. *The Great Terror: A Reassessment.* New York: Oxford University Press, 1990.

Hiss, Tony. *The View from Alger's Window: A Son's Memoir.* New York: Alfred A. Knopf, 1999.

"Hollywood Blacklist." In *Encyclopedia of the American Left.* 2nd ed. Edited by Mari Jo Buhle, Paul Buhle, and Dan Georgakas. New York: Oxford University Press, 1998.

Laqueur, Walter. *Stalin: The Glasnost Revelations.* New York: Charles Scribner's Sons, 1990.

Sherrow, Victoria. *Joseph McCarthy and the Cold War.* Woodbridge, CT: Blackbirch Press, 1999.

Volkogonov, Dmitri. *Stalin: Triumph and Tragedy.* New York: Grove Weidenfeld, 1991.

Web Sites

"HUAC and Censorship Changes." *Moderntimes Classic Film Pages.* http://www.moderntimes.com/palace/huac.htm (accessed on July 25, 2003).

"Senator Joe McCarthy—A Multimedia Celebration." *Webcorp.* http://www.webcorp.com/mccarthy/mccarthypage.htm (accessed on July 25, 2003).

United States Federal Bureau of Investigation. http://www.fbi.gov (accessed on July 25, 2003).

Espionage in the Cold War

6

"**E**spionage is a very serious matter for some, a deadly serious business. It violates international law and normal codes of civilized conduct, and yet it is virtually universal [everywhere] because it is considered a matter of vital national importance to states [countries]. Espionage generates its own rules." This is how Soviet affairs expert and former U.S. State Department official Raymond L. Garthoff describes the espionage game in his book *A Journey through the Cold War.*

Espionage, or more simply, spying, is the gathering and analyzing of information about enemies or potential enemies. The acquired information is called intelligence. Hence, agencies that gather such information are called intelligence-gathering agencies. Counterintelligence or counterespionage involves protecting a country and its agencies from spy activities carried out by enemies. The counterintelligence departments of intelligence agencies are always on the lookout for moles. Moles are double agents who betray the agency they work for. Quietly they funnel top-secret information to the enemy. For example, if an agent employed by the U.S. Central Intelligence Agency (CIA) was also secretly steal-

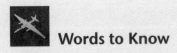

Words to Know

Capitalism: An economic system in which property and businesses are privately owned. Prices, production, and distribution of goods are determined by competition in a market relatively free of government intervention.

Central Intelligence Agency (CIA): A U.S. agency that gathers and interprets the meaning of information on foreign activities; it also carries out secret foreign operations.

Cold War: A prolonged conflict for world dominance from 1945 to 1991 between the two superpowers, the democratic, capitalist United States and the communist Soviet Union. The weapons of conflict were commonly words of propaganda and threats.

Communism: A system of government in which the nation's leaders are selected by a single political party that controls all aspects of society. Private ownership of property is eliminated and government directs all economic production. The goods produced and accumulated wealth are, in theory, shared relatively equally by all. All religious practices are banned.

Counterintelligence: Protection of a country and its agencies from spy activities carried out by enemies.

Espionage: Spying; the gathering and analyzing of information about enemies or potential enemies.

Federal Bureau of Investigation (FBI): The law enforcement agency of the U.S. Justice Department.

GRU: The Soviet military intelligence agency.

ing U.S. military documents and passing them to Soviet intelligence agents, he or she would be considered a mole.

Spying is considered one of the oldest professions, dating to biblical times. Historically it involved daring, adventure-seeking individuals who spied on nearby enemies, then informed their leaders of enemy activity. Large spy operations did not exist. In the United States, intelligence-gathering occurred as early as the American Revolution (1775–83) and during the Civil War (1861–65). Yet even by the beginning of the twentieth century, the only important intelligence operations were located on the European continent. There, as few as a thousand spies collected military intelligence on neighboring countries. With the advent of World War I (1914–18),

Intelligence: Information gathered through espionage activities.

KGB: The Soviet state security organization, 1917–2000. The KGB carried out thousands of murders under Soviet premier Joseph Stalin and was the most powerful Soviet intelligence agency. It handled all espionage operations, both foreign and domestic.

Military Intelligence, Department 5 (MI-5): Great Britain's counterintelligence agency; responsible for national security within that country's borders. Throughout the Cold War, it concentrated on Soviet spy networks operating inside Britain.

Military Intelligence, Department 6 (MI-6): Agency in Great Britain responsible for gathering intelligence worldwide; the British equivalent of the United States' CIA.

Moles: Double agents who betray the agency for whom they work.

National Security Agency (NSA): The United States' prime intelligence organization that listens to and analyzes foreign communications.

Reconnaissance: The act of surveying an area to gain information.

U-2: A U.S. espionage aircraft with a wingspan of 80 feet and a length of 50 feet that carried cameras capable of photographing a 120-mile-wide area.

VENONA: The code name for a program conducted by the U.S. Army's Signals Intelligence Service in 1943 to collect and break the cipher-coded messages of the Soviet KGB and GRU.

intelligence-gathering grew in importance. Code breaking, spy rings (a group of spies working together to achieve their goal), and espionage organizations supported by various governments became essential in guiding policies and strategies during the 1930s and during World War II (1939–45).

At the end of World War II, intelligence and counterintelligence organizations expanded rapidly. This expansion coincided with the beginning of the Cold War. The Cold War was a prolonged conflict for world dominance from 1945 to 1991 between the two superpowers, the democratic, capitalist United States and the communist Soviet Union. The weapons of conflict were commonly words of propaganda and threats. In the two world wars, armies fought on battle-

People to Know

Anthony F. Blunt (1907–1983): One of the KGB's famed Cambridge Spies.

Guy Burgess (1910–1963): One of the KGB's famed Cambridge Spies.

Winston Churchill (1874–1965): British prime minister, 1940–45, 1951–55.

Dwight D. Eisenhower (1890–1969): Thirty-fourth U.S. president, 1953–61.

Klaus Fuchs (1911–1988): British scientist who worked on the U.S. Manhattan Project and began passing detailed notes to the Soviets about the work being done on the development of a nuclear bomb.

Nikita S. Khrushchev (1894–1971): Soviet premier, 1958–64.

Donald Maclean (1913–1983): One of the KGB's famed Cambridge Spies.

Kim Philby (1911–1988): One of the KGB's famed Cambridge Spies.

Franklin D. Roosevelt (1882–1945): Thirty-second U.S. president, 1933–45.

Joseph Stalin (1879–1953): Dictatorial Russian/Soviet leader, 1924–53.

Harry S. Truman (1884–1972): Thirty-third U.S. president, 1945–53.

fields and oceans and in the sky, in plain sight of one another. In the Cold War, there was no established war zone, only regional flare-ups. Governments used spies who operated in the shadows to intercept enemy communications and learn about weapons strength, military movements, and potential targets. Putting all the information together, intelligence agencies attempted to determine immediate and future threats.

The United States and the Soviet Union emerged from World War II as the world's superpowers. Behind their suspicion of each other lay unreconcilable differences in political and economic philosophy. The United States operates under a democratic form of government and has a capitalist economy. In a democratic government, leaders are elected by a vote of the general population. In a capitalist economy, property and businesses are privately owned and are operated with relatively little government interference. U.S. citizens are guaranteed personal liberties such as freedom of speech and freedom to worship. The Soviet Union operated under a communist government. In a communist government, a single political party, the Communist Party, controls nearly all aspects of society. Leaders are selected by top party members. Private ownership of property and business is not allowed. Instead the government directs all economic production. The goods produced and wealth accumulated are, in theory, shared equally by all. Citizens are not guaranteed personal liberties, and religious practices are not tolerated.

The United States and its Western European allies greatly feared the spread of communism. They assumed that without

constant alertness, their democracies might give in to communist rule. Likewise, the Soviet Union feared that the capitalist nations wanted nothing more than to bring about the downfall of communism. Leaders from each nation deemed it necessary to know ahead of time what the other nation was plotting against them. Fear heightened in the United States during the late 1940s when Soviet espionage activities were discovered within the United States and Great Britain's borders. All around the world, espionage agencies were created to protect their respective nations through intelligence-gathering.

FBI director J. Edgar Hoover points to a map that shows the location of the bureau's agents. *Reproduced by permission of the Corbis Corporation.*

Espionage agencies

United States

In the United States, responsibility for gathering intelligence and carrying out spy operations, often called covert operations, in foreign countries fell to the CIA. Presi-

An FBI poster signed by
director J. Edgar Hoover
warns civilians against spies
and saboteurs. *Reproduced
by permission of the Corbis
Corporation.*

WARNING
from the
FBI

**The war against spies and saboteurs
demands the aid of every American.**

**When you see evidence of sabotage,
notify the Federal Bureau of Investigation at once.**

**When you suspect the presence of
enemy agents, tell it to the FBI.**

**Beware of those who spread enemy
propaganda! <u>Don't repeat vicious
rumors or vicious whispers.</u>**

Tell it to the FBI!

J. Edgar Hoover, *Director*
Federal Bureau of Investigation

The nearest Federal Bureau of Investigation office is listed on page one of your telephone directory.

dent Harry S. Truman (1884–1972; served 1945–53) disbanded the U.S. wartime military intelligence agency, the Office of Strategic Services (OSS) at the end of World War II. In July 1947, Congress passed the National Security Act, creating the CIA. The CIA reported national security information to the National Security Council (NSC), a newly created group in the executive branch of government. The NSC consisted of the president and the secretaries of state, defense, army, navy, and air force. In 1961, the CIA moved into its new headquarters in Langley, Virginia.

The Federal Bureau of Investigation (FBI) originated as the Bureau of Investigation under the Department of Justice in 1908. J. Edgar Hoover (1895–1972) took over the Bureau of Investigation in 1924 and created a force of rigorously trained agents. The bureau adopted its current name on July 1, 1932. After World War II, Hoover's FBI concentrated on protecting the United States from Soviet espionage within America's borders. The FBI dogged the American Communist Party and kept files on any American believed to have ties to the Communist Party or believed to be subversive, or have rebellious tendencies, toward the U.S. government.

The National Security Agency (NSA) was established in 1952 by a presidential directive. The forerunner of the NSA was the U.S. Army Signals Intelligence Service, which broke the Japanese military codes in World War II and thereby shortened the war. The NSA's role was to protect U.S. communications by creating code systems called ciphers or cryptosystems; it also broke enemy cryptosystems. NSA employees were known as the codemakers and codebreakers of the intelligence community.

In addition to the CIA, FBI, and NSA, the United States has an intelligence-gathering organization within each of the military services. Army Intelligence, Air Force Intelligence, Navy Intelligence, and Marine Corps Intelligence all are part of the U.S. intelligence community.

Great Britain

The Military Intelligence, Department 5 (MI-5) is Britain's counterintelligence agency. Established in 1909, MI-5 is responsible for national security within Great Britain's borders. Throughout the Cold War, it concentrated on Soviet spy networks operating inside Britain.

The Military Intelligence, Department 6 (MI-6) is the British equivalent of America's CIA. MI-6 gathers intelligence worldwide and is involved in all types of espionage against foreign enemies. The MI-6 grew out of the Secret Intelligence Service (SIS) established in 1911.

Soviet Union

From 1917 to 2000, the Soviet Union had two intelligence agencies: the KGB and the GRU. The KGB (the initials for the Russian translation of the Committee for State Security) was formed in December 1917 during the Bolshevik Revolution; it was originally called Cheka (see Chapter 1, Origins of the Cold War).

Cheka underwent numerous name changes until March 1954, when it took its final name, the KGB. Because of the many name changes, the term "KGB" is used generically to refer to the Soviet state security organization since its formation in 1917. The most dreaded of all intelligence organizations, the KGB carried out thousands of ruthless murders under Soviet premier Joseph Stalin (1879–1953). The KGB was the most powerful Soviet intelligence agency. It handled all espionage operations, both foreign and domestic. In 2000, the Russian Foreign Intelligence Service, the SVR, replaced the KGB.

The Soviet military intelligence agency was the GRU (the initials for the Russian translation of the Chief Intelligence Directorate of the General Staff of the Red Army). The GRU was formed in 1920. At times during the twentieth century, the Soviet military spies created their own espionage network apart from the KGB; at other times, the GRU found itself subordinate to the KGB. The GRU remained relatively intact in 2000.

VENONA

In 1995, four years after the end of the Cold War, the NSA broke a fifty-year silence on the VENONA project. VENONA documents were released for the general public to study. VENONA is the code name for a program conducted by the U.S. Army's Signals Intelligence Service in 1943 to collect and break the cipher-coded messages of the Soviet KGB and GRU. Cipher is a type of code system in which different letters or symbols replace the ordinary letters used to spell a word. Codebreakers who attempted to figure out the cipher were called cryptanalysts. (The prefix *crypt-* means hidden.) The VENONA documents revealed that by 1946 cryptanalysts had begun to succeed in deciphering the KGB and GRU mes-

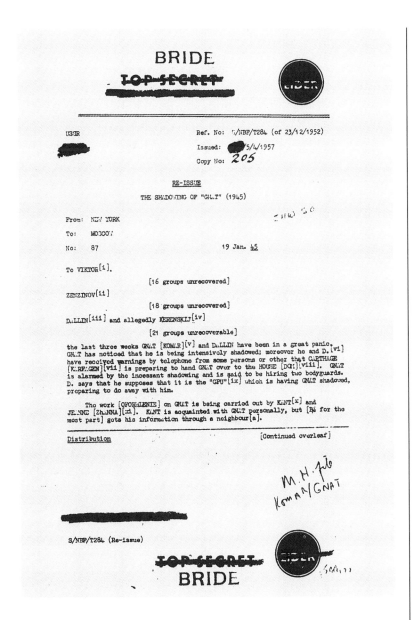

BRIDE

~~TOP SECRET~~

LIDER

U3ER

Ref. No: S/NBF/T284 (of 23/12/1952)

Issued: ██ 5/4/1957

Copy No: 205

RE-ISSUE

THE SHADOWING OF "GNAT" (1945)

From: NEW YORK

To: MOSCOW

No: 87   19 Jan. 45

To VIKTOR[i].

       [16 groups unrecovered]

ZENZINOV[ii]

       [18 groups unrecovered]

DALLIN[iii] and allegedly KERENSKIJ[iv]

       [21 groups unrecoverable]

the last three weeks GNAT [KOMAR][v] and DALLIN have been in a great panic. GNAT has noticed that he is being intensively shadowed; moreover he and D.[vi] have received warnings by telephone from some persons or other that CARTHAGE [KARFAGEN][vii] is preparing to hand GNAT over to the HOUSE [DOM][viii]. GNAT is alarmed by the incessant shadowing and is said to be hiring two bodyguards. D. says that he supposes that it is the "GPU"[ix] which is having GNAT shadowed, preparing to do away with him.

The work [OFORMLENIE] on GNAT is being carried out by KANT[x] and JEANNE [ZhANNA][xi]. KANT is acquainted with GNAT personally, but [B% for the most part] gets his information through a neighbour[a].

Distribution   [Continued overleaf]

M.H. ffb
Koman / GNAT

S/NBF/T284 (Re-issue)

~~TOP SECRET~~ LIDER

BRIDE

A decoded message from 1945 regarding a Soviet defector, intercepted through the VENONA project. *Courtesy of the National Security Agency Archives.*

---

sages intercepted by the Signals Intelligence Service in 1944 and 1945. Two communist defectors greatly aided this effort. (A defector is someone who renounces and leaves his or her native country.)

On September 5, 1945, Igor Gouzenko (1922–1985), a Russian GRU cipher clerk working at the Soviet embassy in Ottawa, Ontario, Canada, defected to Canada. He left the embassy with over one hundred documents stuffed in his

Decipher a Message

A cipher message is written with letters or symbols that replace only one letter of a word at a time. For example, "bab" might stand for the letter *s;* "tzy" might be the letter *a.* Hundreds of thousands of combinations are possible. An encrypted message is written in cipher rather than in plain text in order to conceal its meaning. (The prefix *crypt-* means hidden.) In World War II, the Germans used an electronic cipher machine called an Enigma to send messages. The Enigma looked like a typewriter, but when a letter key was hit, the machine automatically printed a cipher for the regular letter. During the war, U.S. intelligence agencies encrypted their messages to agents. A codebreaker was someone who used cryptanalysis to decode such messages.

Cold War spies carried tiny codebooks or "keylists" for deciphering messages. The books could be quickly disposed of in an emergency, even if it meant swallowing each tiny page. Below is an encrypted message and the key. Figure out the message.

Message: "cdexyzabcrstfghxyz, lmnzabijkopquvwyab rstfghxyz fghrstfghxyzmstqub rstyab lmnzabxyzqub yabxyzxyztoo."

Keylist: a = rst; b = cde; e = xyz; g = uvw; h = zab; i = ijk; l = mst; m = too; n = opq; r = fgh; s = yab; t = lmn; w = abc; y = qub.

Answer: "Beware, things are rarely as they seem."

---

shirt. Gouzenko's documents and his debriefing (interviews with him) yielded intelligence on Soviet cipher systems. Gouzenko also revealed names of individuals spying for the Soviets, in Canada and in the United States. Then, on November 7, Elizabeth Terrill Bentley (1908–1963), an American communist, defected to the FBI. Bentley had joined the Communist Party USA in 1938 and fallen in love with Jacob Golos, who was involved with Soviet intelligence. Golos trained her in the tricks and techniques of espionage. She then operated as a courier, or messenger, in various Soviet espionage networks in the United States. Bentley had become disenchanted with communism, and upon defection she implicated over one hundred people as spies for the Soviet Union. Many were employed in the U.S. government.

In 1946, with clues provided by Gouzenko and Bentley, Meredith Gardner (1913–2002), a brilliant cryptanalyst, began to crack a few Soviet cipher messages, including one that mentioned the atomic bomb. In October 1948, Gardner, who was employed by the U.S. Army Security Agency, began working with FBI special agent and Soviet expert Robert Lamphere (1918–2002). With continued help from Gouzenko, Gardner and Lamphere began to uncover a large number of Soviet espionage cases. The successes of VENONA alerted American, British, and Canadian leaders that Soviet espionage activities were being carried out within their borders. Between 1948 and 1951, a number of KGB agents were exposed. Intelligence gleaned from the messages unmasked the "Atomic Spies" and the "Cambridge Spies" and cast suspicion on the loyalties of Alger Hiss (1904–1996), who had left his position in the U.S. State Department in 1946 and subsequently been named as a communist sympathizer (see Chapter 5, Homeland Insecurities).

Atomic bombs and the Atomic Spies

The United States developed the world's first atomic bombs by mid-1945 through a concentrated top-secret project known as the Manhattan Project. The project brought together scientists from all around the nation. Also included were British and Canadian scientists, and German scientists who had escaped to the United States from Germany during World War II. They came to Los Alamos, New Mexico, in 1943 with the goal of making an atomic bomb. The two atomic bombs put together at Los Alamos were dropped on Hiroshima and Nagasaki, Japan, in August 1945.

Experts estimated that the Soviet Union was years behind the United States in atomic weapons development, and they predicted that the Soviets would not have the bomb until 1953 or 1954. Ominously, on September 3, 1949, a U.S. Air Force WB-29 weather reconnaissance aircraft flying a mission from Japan to Alaska detected high amounts of radiation in the atmosphere. The radiation was from an atomic bomb that the Soviet Union had successfully tested only a few days before, on August 29. Curiously, further study showed it was precisely the type of bomb that the United States had tested in New Mexico in mid-1945. With the Cold War raging, the implications were enormous: Now both the

Tradecraft

Tradecraft is the word spies use to refer to the tricks and techniques they use in their covert, or secret, operations. Although the advanced technology of satellites plays an integral part in espionage, human spies must still provide documents and samplings and use their judgment while conducting on-site sleuthing and when interpreting information.

Tradecraft remains just as important as it was in the twentieth century. Tricks and techniques are often handed down from one generation of spies to the next. For example, the "dead drop" used throughout Cold War spy operations was still in use in the twenty-first century. An inconspicuous signal, such as a piece of masking tape on a telephone pole or a certain type of soft drink can sitting on a rock, signaled that materials could be dropped for quick pickup or that a payment was waiting to be retrieved. Spies always received specific instructions about the dead drop site and a map with the most efficient way in and out of an area.

Tradecraft tools

- Lock picks: in the hands of an expert, a key ring holding several lock picks provided a swift entry through any door.

- Cameras: located in cigarette cases, purses, buttons, and watches. Spies in the 1990s sometimes wore a pair of ordinary-looking sunglasses with a tiny camera on the rim. The camera could be activated by a certain eye blink sequence.

- Radio transmitters: located in shoe heels, a false tooth, or a watch.

- Message carriers: hollow coins, shoe heels, shaving cans, hollow nails and bolts, umbrella handles, cuff links.

- Hidden weapons: knives and bullet-firing devices, located in lipstick holders, pipes, cigarettes, rings, umbrellas, or flashlights. When activated, a knife concealed in a shoe sole could pop out and make a spy's kick extremely dangerous.

United States and the Soviet Union had an atomic bomb; either country could devastate the other, but in doing so would risk an equally devastating retaliation. American scientists and the U.S. military quickly revised their predictions, stating that the Soviets would have several hundred atomic weapons by 1954. Yet they were puzzled by how fast the Soviet Union had developed its first bomb.

In August 1949, Lamphere alerted the British government and MI-6 that a British scientist had most likely passed

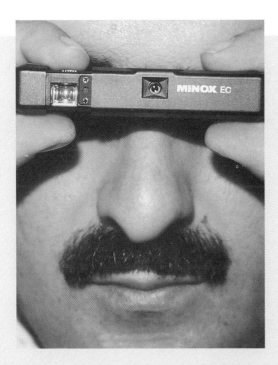

A miniature camera, one of the tools used by spies. *Photograph by Jeffrey L. Rotman. Reproduced by permission of the Corbis Corporation.*

- Messages: could be written in code, invisible ink (made visible with ultraviolet flashlights), or tiny microdots no bigger than a period at the end of a sentence.

- Listening devices: a "bug" in telephones, an audio surveillance device to allow eavesdropping on telephone conversations, tiny microphones placed in walls to eavesdrop on conversations.

- For the spy on the run: disguise kit with sunglasses, cigar, nose, wig, makeup; escape kits with compass, maps, flashlight, candles, a lighter (for warmth), escape knives, rubber gloves, chisels, and lock picks.

- The ultimate tradecraft tool: the "James Bond" spy car from the 1964 movie *Goldfinger.* The car, an Aston Martin, was fully loaded with machine guns, tire shredders, armor plating, and rotating tires. Although specifics are top-secret, the official vehicle for the U.S. president reportedly has some Bond-type protective features.

Learn more about tools of the trade at the International Spy Museum in Washington, D.C., or visit the Web site at http://www.spymuseum.org.

information about the development of the atomic bomb to the Soviets. Later, around the same time that the United States was investigating the suspicious radiation in the atmosphere, Lamphere was deciphering VENONA messages and uncovering information about Klaus Fuchs (1911–1988). Soon, Lamphere discovered that Fuchs was the suspected British scientist acting as a spy.

Born in Germany in 1911, Fuchs left his homeland in the mid-1930s for England. There, he found he could freely

FBI assistant director Hugh Clegg (left) and special agent Robert Lamphere return to the United States after spending two weeks questioning convicted atomic spy Klaus Fuchs in England in 1950. *Reproduced by permission of the Corbis Corporation.*

express his communist views. Communism appeared to him to be the answer to the world's problems. Fuchs finished a doctoral degree in physics and became a British citizen. By spring 1941, he was working on the "Tube Alloys" program, the British atomic bomb research project. In 1943, along with several other British scientists, he was transferred to Columbia University in New York City to work on the Manhattan Project. Soon, Fuchs was on his way to Los Alamos. A serious, intense researcher, Fuchs was never suspected to be passing detailed notes to a courier for the Soviets, Harry Gold (c. 1911–1972). Fuchs's notes answered specific questions from Soviet scientists on the methods of processing uranium and plutonium, the elements used in atomic bomb production. By the time the FBI confronted Fuchs with proof of his espionage activities, he was back in England. Fuchs confessed in January 1950 and was sentenced to fourteen years in prison. The Fuchs case revealed that the Soviets had penetrated deep into the Manhattan Project. The information the Soviets got from Fuchs and other "atomic spies" speeded up the development of the Soviet bomb by a few years.

From a photograph, Fuchs identified Gold as his courier. Gold, an American, was the son of poor Russian Jewish immigrants and was interested in the communist movement. Gold began espionage activities for the Soviets in 1935. Trained as a chemist, he began stealing industrial secrets from the Pennsylvania Sugar Company, where he worked. Arrested in 1950, Gold provided information to the FBI about other "atomic spies."

More intelligence from newly deciphered VENONA intercepts, combined with Gold's information, led to David

Greenglass (1922–). Greenglass was a highly skilled U.S. Army machinist, a type of tradesman much in demand at Los Alamos. Greenglass was sent to Los Alamos in 1943; apparently the fact that he and his wife, Ruth Greenglass (1925–), had joined the Young Communist League earlier in 1943 had not come forth. Until Ruth visited Los Alamos and informed him, Greenglass had no idea that the goal of the Manhattan Project was to develop an atomic bomb. His lack of knowledge was not unusual; very few of the thousands of workers involved in the project knew its ultimate objective. Ruth had received the information through David's sister, Ethel Rosenberg (1915–1953), and Ethel's husband, Julius Rosenberg (1918–1953).

Julius and Ethel Rosenberg, both natives of New York City, shared an active interest in politics. By 1942, they were full members of the American Communist Party. Julius soon pursued espionage activities. As David Greenglass confirmed in his June 1950 confession, the espionage soon became a family affair: Julius recruited David to supply information from Los Alamos. Besides atomic secrets, David provided scientific and technical information about the aircraft that would carry the bombs and about early work on spy satellites. Apparently Ethel typed many of the notes received from David before Julius passed the notes on to the KGB. For his part in the spy ring, David Greenglass was given a light sentence—ten years—because he provided the FBI with information about the Rosenbergs, his sister and brother-in-law. Also in exchange for his confession, Ruth was given immunity from prosecution.

The Rosenbergs were arrested in the summer of 1950, and in 1951 they were found guilty of conspiracy to commit espionage. Julius and Ethel staunchly proclaimed their innocence. They were both sentenced to die in the electric chair, a sentence carried out in 1953 at Sing Sing Prison in Ossining, New York. Many Americans believed that the Rosenbergs did not get a fair trial and that the sentence was much too harsh. Public protests against the executions sprang up around the country. However, information declassified, or made public, by the Russians in the 1990s confirmed that Julius had indeed passed Manhattan Project secrets to the Soviets.

The Cambridge Spies

In 1949, VENONA intercepts also uncovered the possibility that information had been transferred to the Soviets in 1944 and 1945 by a source in the British embassy in Washington, D.C. The spy's code name was Homer. Eventually Homer was identified as Donald Maclean (1913–1983), one of the four Cambridge Spies. The Cambridge Spies affected the course of World War II, aided Stalin's postwar dealings with British prime minister Winston Churchill (1874–1965) and American presidents Franklin D. Roosevelt (1882–1945; served 1933–45) and Harry S. Truman, and influenced the preparation of Soviet military strategies (including nuclear strategies) in the early years of the Cold War. There has probably never been a more successful spy ring in the history of espionage. Eventually they were all unmasked, but not one was caught. They were lucky, smart, determined idealists, those who put perfect ideas ahead of practical considerations. Except for Kim Philby (1911–1988), who accepted one pay-

Shadow, Ninja, Cloak, and Dagger

Espionage, or spying, involves gathering, analyzing, and communicating secret information, or as it is called in spy jargon, intelligence. The profession of spying has long recognized four spy types: shadow, ninja, cloak, and dagger. The shadow spy quietly collects information, generally at a distance from the action. Eavesdropping, tape recording, photography, film developing, and deciphering coded messages are part of shadow spying. Patience and perseverance are required. Shadow spies fit pieces of information together to understand and predict the plans and activities of foreign governments, intelligence agencies, and specific individuals.

Ninjas know no barriers. Seemingly invisible, with the slyness of a cat, ninjas move in and out of buildings without keys, find entrances into forbidden places, or slip in and out of personal relationships. Once they have collected the information they need, they move on. Vanishing into thin air is their specialty.

The cloak spy operates with an air of sophistication. The cloak spy is a smooth talker, self-assured, witty, and charming. Never one to stay in the shadows, this extrovert communicates easily and often is the most likable person in a group. He or she can glean information from a conversation without ever drawing suspicion. The cloak spy is sometimes in disguise. Simple sunglasses might be adequate, but cloak spies on the run can drastically change their physical appearance with makeup, false noses, false eyebrows, wigs, and clothes. A cloak spy always uses state-of-the-art communications tools, such as tiny cameras, recorders, transmitters, radios, and cipher keylists.

Once the sleuthing is finished and the gathered information is analyzed and communicated, dagger, the spy of action, moves in. The dagger's action plan is exacting and must be carried out quickly and decisively. The dagger carries the latest in defensive weapons and escape kits. This is the spy type who makes the raid, carries out the kidnapping, destroys an enemy's communications, or sabotages infrastructures such as bridges, roads, or airports. No need for dazzle or charm—the dagger is simply trouble.

ment from the Soviets in the mid-1950s when he was in dire financial straits, none of the Cambridge Spies received money for their services. The espionage work of the Cambridge Spies spanned half a century.

The saga of the Cambridge Spies began when the KGB formed a plan in the early 1930s to penetrate the British intelligence community. For the plan, the KGB looked to recruit bright young men in universities who hoped to have careers in the British government as diplomats or in the intelligence services. The KGB recruited four students from Trinity College at Cambridge University. All four knew each other at Trinity. They were Maclean, Philby, Anthony F. Blunt (1907–1983), and Guy Burgess (1910–1963).

The charming yet formal Blunt had developed a passion for communist ideology as a student. A discreet homosexual, he would eventually become the British royal family's art adviser; ironically, he was even knighted in 1956. Burgess, also a homosexual, led a rather outrageous lifestyle. Strikingly handsome, he could be charming too, but he was an alcoholic and unpredictable and frequently had to be bailed out of various indiscretions, or delicate situations. Maclean, serious and always tense, was a hard worker, but like Burgess, he drank heavily. Philby was the classic "cloak" spy—smooth, witty, self-assured. (See box.) Philby could always play the role necessary for the moment. He would serve the KGB for over fifty years.

The KGB brought the four young men along slowly in the 1930s, content to let them carry out small tasks to prove their usefulness to the Soviets. Blunt expanded his art history expertise. Maclean entered the British Foreign Service. Philby took a job as a reporter for the *London Times*.

During World War II, the Cambridge Spies began their intelligence work in earnest. Burgess and Philby served as agents in MI-6, Blunt served in MI-5, and Maclean worked in foreign British embassies, including the British embassy in Washington, D.C., beginning in 1944. Philby became an expert cryptanalyst at Britain's decoding center, Bletchley Park. All perfected their skills in passing secret documents to the Soviets. Most of the documents described military strategies of the World War II allies Great Britain and the United States. Maclean became a direct source to Stalin, informing him of communications between British prime minister Churchill and U.S. presidents Roosevelt and Truman.

At the end of World War II and the beginning of the Cold War, the Cambridge Spies continued their espionage activities for the Soviets. Maclean, still at the British embassy in Washington, D.C., kept Stalin informed on how the United States and Britain planned to unite Germany. Before the

Yalta, Potsdam, and Tehran conferences, in which the leaders of Great Britain, the United States, and the Soviet Union met to design a postwar world (see Chapter 1, Origins of the Cold War), Maclean told Stalin of the Western allies' plans. From February 1947 to September 1948, Maclean sat on the American-British-Canadian Combined Policy Committee (CPC) and on the Combined Development Trust (CDT). The purpose of the CPC and CDT was to share secrets on the development of atomic weapons. Never missing a meeting, Maclean was able to keep the Soviets up to date on British and American plans for military development of nuclear energy.

Meanwhile, Philby, an MI-6 agent, was sent to the Washington, D.C., British Foreign Office to serve as a link between MI-6 and the CIA. In this position, Philby had access to any FBI reports shared with the British. He was able to let Stalin know key U.S. strategies for the Korean War (1950–53), including the U.S. decision not to use nuclear weapons in Korea. Philby also became involved in the VENONA project. Burgess worked briefly as a British Broadcasting Corporation (BBC) radio broadcaster and in that post met many British politicians. He then served as secretary to the deputy British foreign minister, Hector McNeil, and was able to transmit top-secret British Foreign Office documents almost daily. He would later join Philby in Washington, D.C., as a secretary in the British Foreign Office. Blunt remained in Britain. In addition to advising the royal family on art, he recruited future Soviet agents and passed information from Philby and Burgess to the Soviets.

Burgess and Maclean gathered most of their material for the Soviets between 1939 and 1951; in 1951, they defected to the Soviet Union. Maclean may have provided the most valuable information of the four. His information covered Western foreign policy and military plans and capabilities.

Donald Maclean, one of the Soviet Union's Cambridge Spies. *Reproduced by permission of the Corbis Corporation.*

Philby, who became known as the "Master Spy" or the "Spy of the Century," produced intelligence for the longest period of time, from 1940 to 1963. In 1963, he defected to the Soviet Union. There, he spent the rest of his life as a KGB adviser, a trainer of spies, and a lecturer on espionage. At his death in 1988, he had given almost fifty years to the Soviet Union. In Philby's honor, the Soviet government issued a stamp with his picture on it.

Blunt, ever the English gentleman, remained in Great Britain. He was unmasked as a Soviet spy by a determined and suspicious MI-5 officer, Arthur Martin. The only way to obtain a confession was to offer Blunt immunity from prosecution. When confessing to Martin in 1964, Blunt revealed little information; all of it concerned other British moles who were dead or already known to British intelligence. He slyly managed to offer no new information. His undercover profession was not revealed to the public until 1979 by Prime Minister Margaret Thatcher (1925–), who stripped him of his knighthood. Blunt died quietly in England in 1983. Because of the Cambridge Spies' long-undetected activities, the U.S. intelligence community lost faith in British intelligence for several decades.

Ground-listening stations

Soviet premier and dictator Joseph Stalin died on March 5, 1953, but the Cold War did not come to an end. The United States and the Soviet Union were in a race for military superiority. Buildup of nuclear weapons and aircraft to carry those weapons was proceeding at full throttle in both countries; missiles were in the early stages of development. Each country was also intent on keeping track of the military activities of the other. Hence, the two superpowers intensified their espionage efforts.

The United States had allies geographically close to the Soviet Union, so U.S. intelligence was able to establish a series of ground-listening stations to monitor Soviet communications, radar signals, and Morse code messages. In May 1952, a listening station was set up in the village of Kirknewton, Scotland, near the capital city of Edinburgh. The U.S. ground stations intercepted communications dealing with the construction of Soviet radar systems and with Soviet aircraft movement. The stations were called SIGINT (short for signals intelligence) stations. Another station was established in Great Britain at a site known as Chicksands Priory. By the mid-1950s, several sites were operational in Turkey. These sites followed Soviet naval and air activity, including early missile testing. One of the most famous listening stations was in Berlin, Germany.

The Berlin tunnel

After World War II, Berlin had been divided into four sectors. The American, British, and French sectors were known as West Berlin, and the Soviet sector was known as East Berlin. There were no actual physical barriers between the sectors. Beneath East Berlin lay an underground junction of three major communication cables that connected the Soviet Union and East Germany. The British MI-6 came up with the bold idea of digging a tunnel from West Berlin to East Berlin for the purpose of tapping into the communication junction. America's CIA enthusiastically agreed at a London meeting. U.S. Army engineers began tunneling to a depth of 15 feet (4.6 meters) in early summer 1954. The project had to be carried out literally under the feet of East German guards and Soviet troops. The construction entrance to the tunnel had to be small so as not to attract attention, yet tons of earth had to be brought out. All the work had to be done as quietly as possible. Because the tunnel was packed with recording equipment, air-conditioning was installed to keep the ground above the tunnel from heating up. The tunnel was 300 yards (274 meters) long and 6 feet (1.8 meters) high. It was operational on February 25, 1955. Approximately six hundred tape recorders were used to record eight hundred reels of tape each day. Listening to the tapes back in Washington, D.C., were fifty CIA employees fluent in Russian and German. They eavesdropped on conversations and messages flowing between Moscow, the Soviet embassy in East Berlin, and the Soviet military headquarters near Berlin.

Unfortunately for the Western powers and unknown to the MI-6 and CIA, there had been a mole in the works

from the beginning. George Blake (1922–), supposedly an MI-6 agent, was in fact spying for the KGB and had been at the London meeting when the decision to build the tunnel was made. He told the Soviets about the tunnel, so they knew about it from the very start. On April 15, 1956, the East German police staged a discovery of the tunnel, pretending it was an accidental discovery so the CIA would still think information recorded over the last year was accurate. Much of what was on the tapes was disinformation—bogus, staged information. The CIA did not realize this until Blake was discovered and arrested in 1961. Blake had not only betrayed the tunnel operation but had identified many British agents spying in the Soviet Union. He was sentenced to forty-two years in prison, one year for each of the forty-two British agents doomed by his information. Blake managed to escape from prison in 1966 and defected to Moscow. Despite the Soviets' knowledge of the tunnel, declassified CIA documents made available in 1999 indicate that the CIA did obtain more than just disinformation from the tunnel tapes.

U-2 aircraft

Another variety of intelligence-gathering went on overhead, in the skies; it was called reconnaissance. Reconnaissance is the act of surveying an area to gain information. As early as 1948 and continuing in the 1950s, U.S. aircraft conducted photographic and electronic surveillance missions, flying as close as they could to the Soviet Union, along its borders, and occasionally venturing into Soviet airspace. On July 4, 1956, only a few months after the exposure of the Berlin tunnel, the United States began yet another daring espionage mission: development of the U-2 aircraft. It was a joint effort of the U.S. Air Force, the CIA, and the Lockheed Corporation. The U-2 had a wingspan of 80 feet (24.4 meters) and a length of 50 feet (15.2 meters); it cruised at 460 miles (740 kilometers) per hour, could fly 2,600 miles (4,183 kilometers) carrying a normal load without refueling, and carried cameras capable of photographing a 120-mile-wide (193 kilometer) area. The cockpit accommodated only one pilot. Taking espionage activities to new heights, the U-2 cruised at 68,000 to 75,000 feet (20,726 to 22,860 meters).

The United States' U-2 reconnaissance aircraft.
Reproduced by permission of the Corbis Corporation.

A military photographer takes pictures while in the cockpit. *Reproduced by permission of the Corbis Corporation.*

By the early 1950s, U.S. president Dwight D. Eisenhower (1890–1969; served 1953–61) understood how productive intelligence gathered by aircraft would be. In late 1955, he was presented with pictures taken by a U-2 flying over San Diego and pictures of one of his favorite golf courses there. They were amazingly detailed and clear. Although U.S. radar operators had been prewarned of the San Diego flight, they were unable to successfully track the aircraft. Impressed by this information, Eisenhower ordered reconnaissance flights over the Soviet Union. If the flights were detected, U-2 pilots would claim to be conducting high-altitude meteorologic studies. In truth, however, their mission was to photograph Soviet military bases, weapons stockpiles, missile launch test sites under construction, and Soviet industries. U-2s also flew reconnaissance missions over China, the Middle East, Indonesia, and other areas of interest to U.S. Cold War strategists.

The U-2 flights over the Soviet Union did not go undetected. The Soviets soon knew the U-2's speed, altitude,

Homing Pigeons

Although espionage and the latest technology went hand in hand in the mid-twentieth century, the humble homing pigeon remained a valuable part of covert operations during that time. These small, powerful birds flew great distances and had a remarkable knack of finding their way home.

Homing pigeons were the earliest spy planes of World War II and the first satellites of the 1950s. Soldiers and spies carried the birds hidden in clothes or packs, then released them for photography or sending messages. The homing pigeons flew with small, constantly clicking cameras strapped to their chests, photographing everything in their flight path. Homing pigeons also carried messages in leg canisters. The messages were reduced to tiny dots containing microphotography. Capable of flying in any weather, homing pigeons were sent on hundreds of thousands of missions during World War I and World War II and through the 1940s and

A soldier holds a homing pigeon during World War II. Homing pigeons were frequently used to deliver secret messages and carry cameras that continuously took reconnaissance photographs. *Reproduced by permission of the Corbis Corporation.*

1950s. An amazing 95 percent of the missions were completed, with the pigeons returning safely to their home base.

and range, but they did not know about the superb photographic abilities of the plane. The Soviets protested, but with their air defense missile systems reaching only 60,000 feet (18,288 meters), they could do little. The U-2 flights revealed Soviet missile capacity, information that helped Eisenhower in planning U.S. military strategy.

On May 1, 1960, pilot Francis Gary Powers (1929–1977) took off from Pakistan on a U-2 Soviet overflight. Tracked immediately by radar, the U-2 came over the Ural Mountains near Sverdlovsk. With their new S-75 antiaircraft defenses, the Soviets shot down the U-2. Powers was recovered alive, along with U-2 cameras. At first, Eisenhower used the preplanned excuse—that the pilot was conducting weather studies for the United States. But presented with clear evidence to the contrary, Eisenhower admitted that it was an espionage flight. However, he refused to apologize or say there would be no further spy flights. Outraged, Soviet premier Nikita Khrushchev (1894–1971) did not participate in an upcoming U.S.-Soviet summit. Relations between the two Cold War adversaries plummeted to new lows. Powers was sentenced to ten years in prison but was released in 1962 in exchange for Soviet spy Rudolf Abel (c. 1902–1971).

The U-2 remained an important tool in U.S. intelligence-gathering. It was a U-2 that took vitally important pictures of Soviet nuclear missiles being placed in Cuba, an island 90 miles (145 kilometers) off Florida's coast. The photographs led to a chilling encounter between the United States and the Soviet Union, a standoff that brought the world to the brink of nuclear war. Without the photos, however, the United States would have been unaware of a potential danger very close to home. (See Chapter 9, Cuban Missile Crisis.)

Human elements

By the end of the 1960s, new satellite reconnaissance systems in space would take photographs of military activity worldwide. Technological advances were rapid and produced astounding results. The U.S. CORONA project operated under the CIA and the U.S. Air Force. It was America's first imaging reconnaissance satellite program. The highly classified project spanned from 1959 to 1972, directed 145 satellite launches, and provided important intelligence for the U.S. government. Nevertheless, the human element, the human spy, remained invaluable to intelligence activities. It was the spy, the fearless mole deep within the enemy's territory, who brought back documents, made judgment calls, offered predictions, and advised leaders on foreign policy.

Why might a person become a spy?

Espionage is rarely a career choice made in high school or college. Spies are motivated by different factors, including patriotism, staunch political beliefs, ego, money, and failure to rise sufficiently in an intelligence agency position. Interestingly, most spies are volunteers, what the CIA calls "walk-ins." For whatever reason, someone with access to relatively high-level information walks into the offices of the CIA, FBI, MI-5, MI-6, KGB, or GRU and offers to obtain secret information. Sometimes spies become double agents, that is, they spy not only for their home country but for the enemy as well.

Oleg Penkovsky

Frequently, for any of the reasons that first motivated them to begin an espionage career, Soviet intelligence personnel working abroad suddenly "crossed over" or "turned" and began spying for the United States. One of the most valuable and prolific Soviet spies who volunteered to turn over information to the West was Oleg Penkovsky (1919–1963). Born in the Russian town of Ordzhonikidze, Penkovsky received his intelligence education at the France Military Academy from 1945 to 1948 and at the GRU's Military Diplomatic Academy from 1949 to 1953. He had attained the rank of colonel by 1950, and from 1955 to 1956 he served admirably as a GRU agent in Ankara, Turkey, his first foreign espionage assignment. He was preparing for a new GRU assignment in India when the KGB found out his father had fought against the Bolsheviks (Communists) and for the tsar in the Russian Revolution. Penkovsky's career still looked promising when he was designated head of the incoming class at the Military Diplomatic Academy. The head instructor job usually meant further promotion, but the KGB stepped in, and Penkovsky's career stalled. At the same time, he had become disillusioned with the brash Soviet premier, Nikita Khrushchev, especially Khrushchev's crude threats to dominate the world. Penkovsky decided to volunteer to the West.

After several unsuccessful attempts to indicate his willingness and ability to pass important Soviet information to the West, Penkovsky succeeded in establishing contact with Greville Wynne (1919–1990). Wynne was a representative of several British corporate industries and frequently traveled to Moscow on business. On April 6, 1961, in Moscow, Penkovsky passed his first package of information to Wynne. Two weeks later, Penkovsky headed a trade dele-

gation to London, where CIA and MI-6 agents were waiting to meet with him. From that time until October 12, 1962, Penkovsky provided thousands of documents and rolls of film from top-secret Soviet files. He took quantities of information out of KGB and GRU headquarters at night, photographed it at his small Moscow apartment, and then returned it the next day. He passed the material to Wynne on trips to London and Paris and in Moscow, sometimes handing over handfuls of film rolls.

Penkovsky also met clandestinely with Janet Chisholm, the wife of an MI-6 agent in Moscow. However, she was known to the KGB because of information George Blake, a Berlin mole, had provided. Penkovsky would hand boxes of candy to Chisholm, for her children, but under the candy was microfilm. Surveillance of Chisholm led to Penkovsky. By fall 1961, Penkovsky's trips out of Moscow ended, and by January 1962, he knew the KGB had him under surveillance. Nevertheless, he continued to place material in "dead drops," agreed-upon locations where his contacts could pick up the material later. On October 12, 1962, the KGB arrested Penkovsky, and he was ultimately sentenced to death.

Oleg Penkovsky reacts after receiving a death penalty sentence on May 11, 1963. He was convicted of collaborating with British intelligence. He was executed five days later. *Reproduced by permission of the Corbis Corporation.*

Penkovsky's information helped Presidents Eisenhower and Kennedy understand that much of Khrushchev's threatening speech was no more than bluffing. The CIA credited Penkovsky for turning over a massive amount of top-secret technical material concerning missiles, launch installations, and Soviet military theories and approaches. Penkovsky identified hundreds of KGB and GRU officers, including people stationed in Ceylon, India, Egypt, France, and Britain.

William Henry Whalen

William Henry Whalen, a U.S. Army lieutenant colonel, served in the army's Office of the Assistant Chief of Staff, Intelligence (OACSI) after World War II. Next, he was assigned to the Joint Chiefs of Staff Joint Intelligence Objective Agency (JIOA) and worked there from July 2, 1959, until July 5, 1960. In March 1959, Colonel Sergei A. Edemski, a Soviet military official, recruited Whalen. Whalen agreed to provide Edemski with sensitive U.S. military documents in exchange for cash, and he faithfully provided the material once a month in late 1959 and early 1960. Whalen met Edemski in an Alexandria, Virginia, shopping center parking lot for the handoffs. However, Edemski left the United States in the spring of 1960. In July 1960, Whalen suffered a heart attack and never returned to active army duty. He did, however, continue to wander through the Pentagon (he was still a recognizable face and security was more lax in those days), trying to access information, until 1963, when it became obvious he was under suspicion.

Whalen was indicted in July 1966, found guilty, and sentenced to fifteen years in prison. He had provided the Soviets with an impressive array of U.S. military manuals, as well as bulletins on the army's nuclear weapons and on air defense weapons. He also provided thousands of documents related to the Joint Chiefs of Staff. A U.S. Army deputy chief of staff concluded that Whalen had considerably compromised U.S. military capabilities in the event of a war with the Soviet Union.

"The game"

With the unmasking of famous moles such as the Cambridge Spies, George Blake, Oleg Penkovsky, and William Whalen, the U.S., British, Soviet, and French intelligence communities became convinced that more moles must be lurking within their agencies' counterintelligence divisions. Rampant suspicions and distrust gradually shifted the priorities of the intelligence agencies away from uncovering useful military and political intelligence. By the mid-1960s and well into the 1970s, intelligence agencies concentrated on "the game," which involved spies spying on each other (more than they spied on foreign enemy governments). This was well illustrated within the CIA: Allen Dulles (1893–1969), director of the CIA, appointed James Jesús Angleton (1917–1987) as head of the CIA's counterintelligence staff in 1954. Under Angleton's leadership, CIA human intelligence-gathering efforts against the Soviet Union came almost to a standstill by the mid-1960s. Just as Oleg Penkovsky had done in the early 1960s, other Soviet intelligence agents attempted to volunteer as CIA informers. However, Angleton was deeply—and unreasonably—suspicious that these potential informers were actually attempting to spy further for the Soviets. These suspicions prevented the CIA from taking advantage of the Soviet spies' knowledge. The tangled espionage-counterespionage web did not begin to straighten out until Angleton's departure from the CIA in 1974.

By the mid-1970s, the CIA again focused on extracting military and government information about U.S. enemies. For example, the CIA worked with "turned" GRU agents Colonel Anatoli Nikolaevich Filatov and Aleksandr Dmitrievich Ogorodnik, both of whom provided a variety of Soviet military secrets and Soviet diplomatic reports.

Unlikely pair of spies

Through the later 1960s and 1970s, the CIA, KGB, and GRU received an abundant amount of intelligence from U.S. and Soviet satellites orbiting Earth. From April 1975 until their arrest in January 1977, Christopher Boyce (1953–) and Andrew Daulton Lee (1952–) provided the Soviets with secrets about America's most advanced satellite programs. Boyce, a twenty-two-year-old college dropout, worked for the space technology corporation TRW in a low-paying, low-level job. However, he worked inside TRW's so-called Black Vault, monitoring top-secret communications from CIA-TRW satellites. His buddy Lee was most interested in procuring enough marijuana to satisfy his cravings. The two teamed up to make extra cash.

Beginning in mid-1975, Boyce transferred detailed information on three satellite systems, code-named Rhyolite, Argus, and Pyramider, to the KGB. Serving as courier for Boyce, Lee delivered the technical information, primarily to the Soviet embassy in Mexico City, Mexico. Pyramider provided a means of communication for CIA agents abroad; agents relayed messages to each other on this system. The agents' names and all their communications were exposed by Boyce's deception. KGB officials were so impressed with Boyce that they offered to pay for his undergraduate and graduate school tuition so he could eventually work for the CIA or within the U.S. State Department. He could then become a KGB mole. But before Boyce could attend his first class at the University of California, Riverside, the unpredictable and careless Lee ruined their spy career by attracting the attention of the Mexican police as he dropped off a package of information. Both were arrested, tried, and convicted. Lee received life imprisonment, but was paroled in 1998; Boyce received forty years in prison, but was released in 2003. Boyce claimed that his actions stemmed from his opposition to the Vietnam War (1954–75).

Soviet spy Christopher Boyce is returned to prison after escaping in 1981. He had originally been arrested in 1977 for providing the Soviets with secrets about U.S. satellites. *Reproduced by permission of the Corbis Corporation.*

1985: Year of the spy

The U.S. press labeled 1985 the "year of the spy." Arrests by the FBI during that year terminated many prolific espionage careers. The first arrest came in May. Subsequently, November proved fascinating as the activities of spy after spy came to an end.

The Walker spy ring

In the 1960s, the U.S. Navy encrypted (coded) all of their radio communications (see box). The NSA supplied the codes. Each month, the navy sent its fleet the codes for use that month. The codes were in codebooks called "keylists." To encrypt and decipher (decode) messages, cryptographic machines had to have their dials set each month according to the keylist of the month. The keylists told the navy communication specialists how to set the dials.

John A. Walker Jr. (1938–) was a watch officer for the U.S. Navy's Atlantic Fleet submarine command based in Norfolk, Virginia. His duties included monitoring encrypted messages for the fleet's submarines. Those submarines were stationed in various locations, from the Mediterranean Sea to the Arctic Ocean. One day in April 1968, Walker, who was experiencing family difficulties and financial problems, put a keylist in his pocket and walked out of the communications room. He drove four hours to the Soviet embassy in Washington, D.C., then burst into the embassy and demanded to see the officer in charge of security. The KGB officer paid Walker between $1,000 and $2,000 for that keylist and informed him they could do business again in the future. At that point, Walker asked for a regular salary—an unusual request for someone planning to work an undercover job. Though he was surprised, the KGB officer agreed to pay Walker $500 to $1,000 a week for the keylists. Until his retirement in August 1976, Walker continuously supplied the KGB with the keylists to a wide variety of cryptographic machines onboard the Atlantic Fleet. He then recruited a fellow navy radioman, Jerry A. Whitworth (1939–). Whitworth served between 1975 and 1983 in naval communications on the West Coast and on three different ships. All the while, he provided Walker with cryptographic materials. Walker also recruited his brother Arthur around 1980 and his own son, Michael, in late 1982. Michael had already joined the navy, and by 1984 he was stationed on the USS *Nimitz*. On the *Nimitz*, Michael had access to "burnbags," garbage bags that contained classified messages. Michael carried the bags to the furnace and had plenty of time to rummage through them. When his father was arrested by the FBI on the night of May 19, 1985, Michael had just made a dead drop of a grocery bag full of documents from the *Nimitz*. The Walkers—John, Arthur, and Michael—and Whitworth all received prison sentences for their espionage activities. They were betrayed by John's ex-wife Barbara, who at the time had no idea her son Michael was involved.

Soviet KGB general Boris Aleksandrovich Solomatin (1924–) was the KGB head of Anti-American operations during the Walker period of activity. According to the *Court TV's Crime Library* Web site, Solomatin called Walker the "most important" spy. He said that Walker was "the equivalent of a seat inside your Pentagon where we could read your most vital secrets." If the United States and the Soviet Union had gone to war during the Walkers' activity, the encryption materials would have allowed the Soviets access to all U.S. naval communications and movements.

Oleg Gordievsky

Oleg Gordievsky (1938–), son of a KGB officer, was groomed from an early age for KGB service. He received his first foreign assignment in 1966. A bright and trusted KGB agent, Gordievsky was placed in charge of KGB operations in Great Britain, Australia, New Zealand, and all of Scandinavia in 1972. The KGB did not know that Gordievsky had become highly disillusioned with the Soviets over their treatment of Czechoslovakia in 1968.

From 1972 until 1985, Gordievsky served the KGB in both London and Moscow, but during that time, he was one of the most daring types of spies, a double agent. While working as a top spy for the KGB, he also kept the British intelligence services informed of all KGB activities in Great Britain. In 1985, CIA mole Aldrich Ames (1941–) tipped the KGB about Gordievsky. Gordievsky was brought back to Moscow, but the British were able to rescue him, secretly whisking him out of Moscow and back to safety in Britain.

Gordievsky greatly aided the United States in 1985 by helping the presidential administration understand the new Soviet premier, Mikhail Gorbachev (1931–). Gordievsky told President Ronald Reagan (1911–; served 1981–89) and Reagan's advisers that the Soviets had become very paranoid, fearing the United States might indeed start a nuclear war. He suggested they back off and moderate their language toward the Soviets. Since taking office in 1981, Reagan had consistently used brash and harsh language concerning the Soviet Union. Nevertheless, Reagan was shocked that the Soviets thought he might really start a nuclear war. Reagan called for a face-to-face summit in November 1985 to establish better relations with Gorbachev.

Vitaly Yurchenko

One of the strangest spy stories of 1985 began in early August when KGB officer Vitaly Yurchenko defected to the CIA at the American embassy in Rome, Italy. The defection lasted only three months. On November 2 in Washington, D.C., while dining with a CIA official, Yurchenko bolted away through the restaurant's kitchen and disappeared onto the crowded streets. (As of December 2002, the restaurant where Yurchenko bolted still served a platter of pigs' feet with a "Yurchenko Shooter," a shot of Russian vodka.) After leaving the restaurant, Yurchenko walked to the Soviet embassy on Wisconsin Avenue about a mile away. There he claimed that he had been drugged and kidnapped by the CIA and held in Fredericksburg, Virginia. On November 6, he was flown back to Moscow.

Vitaly Yurchenko, the KGB officer who defected to the United States and then changed his mind three months later. *Photograph by Doug Mills. Reproduced by permission of the Corbis Corporation.*

Yurchenko's strange tale about being drugged by the CIA may have saved his life; otherwise he most likely would have been executed for defecting to the United States. In reality, during his three months with the CIA, Yurchenko answered many perplexing questions and helped settle controversies concerning various persons suspected of selling information to the Soviets; he also confirmed CIA suspicions about moles located in Canada and Germany. Yurchenko's information brought about several arrests, including the arrest of Ronald Pelton, a disgruntled former NSA employee. Pelton had sold Soviet agents his recollections of classified information dating from 1980 to 1985. He was arrested on November 24, 1985.

Larry Wu-Tai Chin

On November 22, 1985, another spy career came to an end when the FBI arrested Larry Wu-Tai Chin (1923–1986), a Chinese American mole who spied for China for decades.

Chin had uncovered intelligence for the Communist People's Republic of China (PRC) for at least thirty years. Chin began employment with the U.S. Army Liaison Mission in China in 1943. He transferred to the Foreign Broadcast Information Service (FBIS) in Okinawa in 1952, to Santa Rosa, California, in 1961, and to northern Virginia in 1970. He retired from the FBIS in 1981. Reportedly, he was paid several hundred thousand dollars for his many years of funneling information to the PRC. In February 1986, Chin was convicted of espionage crimes, but he committed suicide in his prison cell before he was sentenced.

Jonathan Pollard

Another November arrest was that of Jonathan Jay Pollard (1954–), who carried out intelligence activities for Israel's Defense Ministry, in its Office of Scientific Liaison (code name Lakam). This office was not just concerned with the sharing of scientific studies; it was also involved in intelligence operations.

In 1983, U.S. president Reagan had signed an agreement with Israel, a strong U.S. ally, to hand over to Israel all information the United States acquired regarding Israel's national security. However, there were limits to what the United States would share. Israel had from time to time requested information the United States refused to provide. Pollard, a civilian naval intelligence employee, provided a way for Israel to acquire documents that the United States did not want Israel to have. Although he was paid for the documents he provided, Pollard apparently was also genuinely motivated to provide the Israelis with information he believed they needed for their national security.

Between July 1984 and his arrest on November 21, 1985, he provided a large amount of raw intelligence material from the Anti-Terrorist Alert Center (ATAC) Threat Analysis Division, Naval Investigation Service, where he was a watch officer. A sampling included information on air defense systems and chemical warfare production related to Tunisia, Libya, Iraq, and Syria; Soviet shipments of arms to Arab states; and detailed information on the way the United States collects its intelligence information. Never before in U.S. intelligence history had someone stolen so much top-secret information in such a short time. U.S. officials considered all the information to be highly damaging to the U.S. intelligence community, especially the information on how the United States collects intelligence.

Pollard's arrest proved extremely embarrassing to the Israeli government, which quickly labeled Pollard's activities as a "rogue operation" that Israel had not controlled. In a U.S. court, Pollard received the harshest sentence possible: life in prison. By the late 1990s, there was considerable pressure from many mainstream Jewish organizations in the United States and Israel to free Pollard. The groups believed Pollard's actions had provided much-needed information to Israel. The Israeli government, supporting this point of view, officially acknowledged that Pollard was an Israeli agent and then attempted to have him released to Israel. Yet because of the highly sensitive and damaging intelligence Pollard disclosed, the United States had not acted to alter his sentence as of 2003.

1990 to 2001

A Russian coup on a statue

On August 20, 1991, as the Cold War came to an end (see Chapter 15, End of the Cold War), tens of thousands of Moscow residents gathered around a massive 12-ton (11-metric ton) bronze statue of Feliks Dzerzhinski (1877–1926), which had stood for many, many years outside KGB headquarters. Dzerzhinski was the brutal chief of the early KGB (or Cheka, as it was then called). Shouting "Iron Felix" and "Down with the KGB," the crowd watched as two huge construction cranes removed the statue. The removal of the statue symbolically marked the end of the old KGB. By the end of 1991, reorganization of the KGB would be complete. With Soviet premier Boris Yeltsin (1931–) now in charge, the Federal Agency for Government Communications and Information (FAPSI) and the Russian Foreign Intelligence Service (SVR) were established, replacing various divisions of the KGB. FAPSI was in charge of cryptographic analysis and SIGINT communications. SVR was in charge of fighting terrorism; gathering political, economic, and scientific intelligence; and preventing drug trafficking. Russia's SVR and the United States' CIA agreed to possible cooperation in several of these areas. The GRU remained basically intact but was under new leadership.

Three mole arrests: Sombolay, Ames, and Hanssen

In the United States, the intelligence community would face three highly publicized mole arrests: Albert Sombolay in March 1991, Aldrich Ames on February 23, 1994, and Robert Hanssen on February 18, 2001. Sombolay, a specialist 4th class with the Army Artillery, was stationed in Baumholden, Germany, at the start of the Persian Gulf War (1991). The U.S. goal in the Gulf War was to liberate the tiny oil-rich nation of Kuwait, which had been invaded by Iraq. Born in Zaire, Africa, Sombolay had become a U.S. citizen in 1978 and joined the U.S. Army in 1985. He was sent to Germany in December 1990. From Germany, Sombolay provided to the Jordanian embassy in nearby Brussels, Belgium, information on U.S. troop deployment, military identification cards, and information on chemical warfare. The U.S. Army Military Intelligence arrested Sombolay in March 1991. His only motive for the espionage was money.

Jubilant Russians step on the head of the toppled statue of KGB founder Feliks Dzerzhinski in 1991. *Photograph by Alexander Zemlianichenko. Reproduced by permission of AP/Wide World Photos.*

Aldrich Ames, known as Rick, was a CIA agent whose chief purpose over the years was to penetrate Soviet intelligence by recruiting foreigners to be moles for the CIA inside the Soviet Union. Instead, Ames was the most damaging mole the CIA ever suffered. In the mid-1980s, using his intimate knowledge of those spying for the United States inside the Soviet Union, he single-handedly destroyed CIA covert operations in that country. He sold to the KGB the names of twenty-four men and one woman, all Russians spying for the United States. All of them were arrested, and many of them were executed. Ames put dozens of other CIA officers in the Soviet Union at risk. For this, he was paid $2 million, and another $2 million was kept in Moscow for him.

Not until the early 1990s did the CIA seriously suspect and look for a mole. Assuming he would never be caught, Ames carried on with his espionage activities. By October 1992, Ames had come under increased CIA surveillance. It was not until February 1994 that the CIA felt it had enough evidence to arrest Ames and his wife, Maria del Rosario Casas. Offering full cooperation, Ames kept bargaining until his wife got only a five-year sentence and he got a life sentence without parole, rather than death. Moscow intelligence officials publicly lamented the arrest of Ames and their loss of a key information source. Ames remains a huge embarrassment to the CIA.

Robert Philip Hanssen

Robert Philip Hanssen (1944–) was sworn into the FBI on January 12, 1976, and remained an FBI agent for twenty-five years. Apparently Hanssen was the exception to the rule that spies do not grow up planning to be spies. It seems Hanssen had decided to become a spy in his teen years or even earlier. From childhood through college, he subscribed to *MAD* magazine and devoured the "Spy vs. Spy" feature. Unsettled during his college years, Hanssen attended dental school for a short while before switching to Northwestern University and graduating with a master's degree in business administration (MBA).

Hanssen married Bonnie Wauck in August 1968, and they had six children together. They were devoted Roman Catholics and belonged to a very conservative Catholic group,

Opus Dei. By the late 1970s, Hanssen was assigned to the elite New York City FBI office. Money was very tight for the family. It was at this time that Hanssen made contact with Russian agents in New York. He purportedly gave them worthless information but was paid $20,000, perhaps to encourage his activities. Bonnie discovered him counting the cash in the basement. She marched Hanssen to their Opus Dei priest, who told Hanssen to give the money to charity and be done with such activity. Bonnie, too, demanded that he stop his espionage activities.

At the FBI, Hanssen was recognized for his brilliant mind, but he had few interpersonal skills. He was seen as a loner and an arrogant person. Nevertheless, he continued to receive important assignments. In 1983, he was assigned to the Soviet Analytical Unit in Washington, D.C., and his personnel classification was somewhere above Top-Secret. Yet his salary failed to provide a decent living for his family. On October 4, 1985, Hanssen "turned." He revealed to the KGB the names of three of its officers who were working for the United States as double agents. Over the next five years, he delivered to the KGB thousands of secret documents, including some that contained information on nuclear weapons placement and satellite positions. In return, he received hundreds of thousands of dollars. Hanssen continued funneling information right up until his arrest by FBI agents at a drop site on February 18, 2001. Hanssen was sentenced to life in prison without parole, but an annual $38,000 widow's pension was arranged for his wife.

Robert Philip Hanssen, an FBI employee who became a Soviet informant.
Reproduced by permission of the Corbis Corporation.

Vasili Mitrokhin—KGB archivist

Vasili Mitrokhin (1922–), a longtime archivist for the KGB, compiled his own private record of the KGB's foreign operations. In 1956, Mitrokhin was assigned to check and seal three hundred thousand files in the KGB archive. For almost thirty years, Mitrokhin copied KGB documents by hand. At first, he wrote notes on scraps of paper, threw them in the wastebasket, then retrieved them later. After a while, he put his notes on regular paper and stuffed his trouser pockets. KGB guards never stopped Mitrokhin. On the weekends, he and his family would travel to a family home in the country. There, Mitrokhin hid much of his material under the floorboards.

Mitrokhin retired from the KGB in 1984 after thirty years of work in the KGB archives. In 1992, he defected to Britain with his family. Mitrokhin brought with him his KGB files, which he believed were a part of Soviet history that needed to be preserved and shared. His files covered the entire Cold War and went back as far as 1918. In a book published in 1999 by Christopher Andrew and Mitrokhin, *The Sword and the Shield,* the FBI called the Mitrokhin files the "most complete and extensive intelligence ever received from any source."

For More Information

Books

Aldrich, Richard J. *The Hidden Hand: Britain, America, and Cold War Secret Intelligence.* London: John Murray, 2001.

Andrew, Christopher, and Oleg Gordievsky. *KGB: The Inside Story of Its Foreign Operations from Lenin to Gorbachev.* New York: HarperCollins, 1990.

Andrew, Christopher, and Vasili Mitrokhin. *The Sword and the Shield: The Mitrokhin Archive and the Secret History of the KGB.* New York: Basic Books, 1999.

Earley, Pete. *Confessions of a Spy: The Real Story of Aldrich Ames.* New York: Berkley Books, 1997.

Earley, Pete, and Gerald Shur. *WITSEC: Inside the Federal Witness Protection Program.* New York: Bantam, 2002.

Garthoff, Raymond L. *A Journey through the Cold War: A Memoir of Containment and Coexistence.* Washington, DC: Brookings Institution Press, 2001.

Gates, Robert M. *From the Shadows: The Ultimate Insider's Story of Five Presidents and How They Won the Cold War.* New York: Simon and Schuster, 1996.

Havill, Adrian. *The Spy Who Stayed Out in the Cold: The Secret Life of FBI Double Agent Robert Hanssen.* New York: St. Martin's Press, 2001.

Isaacs, Jeremy, and Taylor Downing. *Cold War: An Illustrated History, 1945–1991.* Boston: Little, Brown, 1998.

Mahoney, M. H. *Women in Espionage: A Biographical Dictionary.* Santa Barbara, CA: ABC-CLIO, 1993.

Oberdorfer, Don. *From the Cold War to a New Era: The United States and the Soviet Union, 1983–1991.* Baltimore, MD: Johns Hopkins University Press, 1998.

Philby, Kim. *My Silent War: The Soviet Master Agent Tells His Own Story.* New York: Grove Press, 1968.

Platt, Richard. *Spy.* New York: Alfred A. Knopf, 1996.

Richelson, Jeffrey T. *A Century of Spies: Intelligence in the Twentieth Century.* New York: Oxford University Press, 1995.

Web Sites

Central Intelligence Agency. http://www.cia.gov (accessed on August 11, 2003).

Court TV's Crime Library. http://www.crimelibrary.com (accessed on August 11, 2003).

Federal Bureau of Investigation. http://www.fbi.gov (accessed on August 11, 2003).

International Spy Museum. http://spymuseum.org (accessed on August 11, 2003).

National Security Agency. http://www.nsa.gov (accessed on August 11, 2003).

"Secret, Lies, and Atomic Spies." *Nova Online.* http://www.pbs.org/wgbh/nova/venona (accessed on August 11, 2003).

"The VENONA Home Page." *National Security Agency.* http://www.nsa.gov/docs/venona (accessed on August 11, 2003).

A Worldwide Cold War

7

"**Y**ou have to take chances for peace just as you must take chances for war.... If you are scared to go to the brink, you are lost." As noted in Ronald E. Powaski's *Cold War: The United States and the Soviet Union, 1917–1991,* these are the words of John Foster Dulles (1888–1959), secretary of state for President Dwight D. Eisenhower (1890–1969; served 1953–61). During the Cold War, Dulles orchestrated a strategy known as "brinkmanship." Brinkmanship is the practice of forcing a confrontation in order to achieve a desired outcome; in the Cold War, brinkmanship meant using nuclear weapons as a deterrent to communist expansion around the world. Communism is a system of government in which a single political party controls almost all aspects of society. All property is owned by the government, which controls all industrial production; wealth is, in theory, shared equally by all. Religious practices are not tolerated under communist governments.

Dulles was a hard-line anticommunist; he viewed the Soviet Union, China, and other communist governments as enemies of democracy, government run by citizens who are

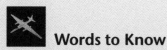

Words to Know

Brinkmanship: An increased reliance on nuclear weapons as a deterrence to threats of communist expansion in the world; an international game played between the Soviet Union and the United States of who has the highest number of and the most powerful weapons with which to threaten the enemy.

Capitalism: An economic system in which property and businesses are privately owned. Prices, production, and distribution of goods are determined by competition in a market relatively free of government intervention.

Cold War: A prolonged conflict for world dominance from 1945 to 1991 between the two superpowers, the democratic, capitalist United States and the communist Soviet Union. The weapons of conflict were commonly words of propaganda and threats.

Communism: A system of government in which the nation's leaders are selected by a single political party that controls all aspects of society. Private ownership of property is eliminated and government directs all economic production. The goods produced and accumulated wealth are, in theory, shared relatively equally by all. All religious practices are banned.

Nation-building: Installing friendly governments wherever feasible around the world by the United States and the Soviet Union.

North Atlantic Treaty Organization (NATO): A peacetime alliance of the United States and eleven other nations, and a key factor in the attempt to contain communism; the pact meant that the United States became the undisputed global military leader.

Southeast Asia Treaty Organization (SEATO): An alliance of nations created to combat the expansion of communism in the Southeast Asian region, specifically Vietnam, Cambodia, and Laos. Member nations included the United States, Great Britain, France, New Zealand, Thailand, Australia, Pakistan, and the Philippines.

Third World: Poor underdeveloped or economically developing nations in Africa, Asia, and Latin America. Many were seeking independence from political control of Western European nations.

Warsaw Pact: A mutual military alliance between the Soviet Union and the Eastern European nations under Soviet influence, including East Germany.

represented by elected officials. Dulles asserted that President Harry S. Truman's (1884–1972; served 1945–53) containment policy had been too reactionary, meaning that Truman only reacted to communist threats and never went on the offensive. Containment was a key U.S. Cold War policy intended to restrict the territorial growth of communist rule. Dulles wanted the United States to take the initiative, freely using the threat of nuclear war, perhaps even liberating Eastern Europe from Soviet control. Dulles's position reflected the prevailing mood of the American public in the early 1950s.

In 1953, following the end of Truman's presidency in January, the death of Soviet premier Joseph Stalin (1879–1953) in March, and the end of the Korean War (1950–53) in June, the Cold War took on a new look, with new superpower leaders. Although the Cold War spread around the globe, the United States and the Soviet Union had at least begun talking, and a fairly stable military balance had been established in Europe. The United States stood behind the Western European countries, and the Soviet Union controlled the Eastern European countries. Ironically, the stability in Europe was made possible by the presence of nuclear weapons. Each superpower's arsenal of weapons ensured that in the event of an attack and counterattack, both the Soviet Union and the United States—along with much of the rest of the world—would be devastated. Neither superpower desired such an outcome. So even as the Soviet Union and the United States continued arms buildup, talks between the two helped lessen the tensions of the period and fears of nuclear war.

The superpowers tried to keep pace with each other in weapons production, but in economic terms, it was no contest: The capitalist West was far more prosperous than the communist East. This was especially apparent in Europe. In a capitalist economy, property and businesses are privately owned. In a marketplace operating relatively free of govern-

People to Know

Jacobo Arbenz Guzmán (1913–1971): Guatemalan president, 1950–54.

Carlos Castillo Armas (1914–1957): Guatemalan president, 1954–57.

John Foster Dulles (1888–1959): U.S. secretary of state, 1953–59.

Dwight D. Eisenhower (1890–1969): Thirty-fourth U.S. president, 1953–61.

Nikita S. Khrushchev (1894–1971): Soviet premier, 1958–64.

Georgy M. Malenkov (1902–1988): Soviet premier, 1953–55.

Mohammad Mosaddeq (1880–1967): Iranian premier, 1951–53.

Ngo Dinh Diem (1901–1963): Republic of Vietnam president, 1954–63.

Joseph Stalin (1879–1953): Dictatorial Russian/Soviet leader, 1924–53.

Harry S. Truman (1884–1972): Thirty-third U.S. president, 1945–53.

Soviet premier Georgy M. Malenkov. *Courtesy of the Library of Congress.*

ment regulation, competition determines prices of goods, production levels, and how goods are distributed. The stark contrast in prosperity between East and West contributed to a decline in Communist Party support throughout Western Europe. Communist rule was increasingly associated with political purges, labor camps, and show trials, none of which appealed to people in the free (democratic) and capitalist nations of Western Europe.

New leaders

Only a few weeks after Dwight D. Eisenhower was inaugurated as the thirty-fourth U.S. president in January 1953, Soviet premier Stalin died. The new Soviet premier was Georgy Malenkov (1902–1988). Nikita Khrushchev (1894–1971) became the secretary general—the new Soviet Communist Party leader. With Stalin gone, the Soviet Union changed from a dictatorship to an authoritarian government in which centralized power rested with the Soviet Communist Party. (In an authoritarian government, a ruling political party assumes full governmental authority, demands complete obedience of its citizens, and is not legally accountable to the people.)

Malenkov wanted to focus on internal Soviet issues. Stalin had previously declared that capitalism and communism could not peacefully coexist in the world. In contrast, Malenkov declared that peaceful solutions could end international Cold War problems. In early April, shortly after taking office, he called for talks to reduce military forces in Europe. In response, in a speech on April 16, President Eisenhower expressed interest in discussing arms reduction. However, Eisenhower gave Malenkov a number of conditions: He said that Malenkov would need to allow free elections in Eastern Europe, stop supporting communist revolutionary movements in Asia, permit on-site inspections as part of nuclear disarmament, and accept West Germany's membership in the North Atlantic Treaty Organization (NATO). (NATO is a military defense alliance of several Western European nations, the United States, and Canada.) On May 11, British prime minister Winston Churchill (1874–1965), who had been reelected in 1951, proposed that the world leaders hold a meeting to resolve Cold War tensions. However, U.S. secretary of state Dulles and West German chancellor Konrad Adenauer (1876–1967) argued against such a meeting. They claimed the Soviets were likely not sincere in pursuing peaceful coexistence, but merely trying to weaken the West. With the strong anticommunist mood in the United States, which was spurred by U.S. senator Joseph McCarthy (1908–1957) of Wisconsin, Dulles did not want the federal administration to appear weak in dealing with the communists. The idea of arms reduction talks soon faded away.

Senator McCarthy and the hunt for communists at home

Senator McCarthy and his supporters stepped up anticommunist rhetoric, or overblown, dramatic statements or speeches, in the United States (see Chapter 5, Homeland Insecurities). Under their strong influence, Eisenhower signed an executive order in April 1953 giving heads of federal agencies authority to fire employees whom they suspected of disloyalty to the country. Although no one was actually charged with spying or subversion (an attempt to overthrow or undermine an established political system), hundreds of federal employees lost their jobs. Caught in the purge were some of the top political analysts who monitored China and the Soviet Union, people who were needed for developing an informed foreign policy. Also among those fired from their public service jobs was the father of the atomic bomb, J. Robert Oppenheimer (1904–1967). He had supposedly associated with communists and strongly opposed the development of the hydrogen bomb. A later investigation revealed no disloyalty on the part of Oppenheimer. (In fact, in 1963, U.S. president Lyndon B. Johnson [1908–1973; served 1963–69] presented an Atomic Energy Commission award to Oppenheimer in recognition of his service to the nation.)

Future Soviet leader Leonid Brezhnev (seated, far right) and other Soviet officials meet at a Warsaw Pact conference. *Reproduced by permission of the Corbis Corporation.*

In April 1954, Senator McCarthy launched a televised investigation of supposed communist subversion in the U.S. Army. However, the public and members of Congress had finally had enough of McCarthy's unfounded accusations. The Republicans in the Senate passed a resolution officially criticizing McCarthy for denying citizens their constitutional right of a fair public trial to answer the accusations McCarthy was making with little evidence. As a result, McCarthy was not allowed to conduct any more inquiries, but the influence of his earlier actions would last for years.

The Warsaw Pact

In Berlin in January 1954, the foreign ministers of the United States, France, Britain, and the Soviet Union met to discuss the reunification of Germany. However, each country still had differing concerns and points of view on how to build a postwar Germany, so no agreements could be reached. Further, the Soviets insisted that NATO be abolished, and the United States insisted on free elections throughout Germany. Separately, the three Western allies agreed to give West Germany full national sovereignty and the opportunity to rearm. West Germany would join NATO in 1955. The Soviets responded to the expansion of NATO by creating the Warsaw Pact in 1955. The pact set up a mutual military alliance between the Soviet Union and the Eastern European nations under Soviet influence, including East Germany.

The New Look—brinkmanship

During the Berlin conference, on January 12, 1954, Secretary of State Dulles announced a new U.S. military strategy in the fight against communism. In response to communist aggression of any kind, he said, the United States would retaliate with a massive nuclear attack. The strategy was designed to prevent war by threatening the ultimate war. This strategy was referred to as an "asymmetrical response." ("Asymmetrical" means out of proportion or unequal.) In other words, the U.S. reaction would potentially be much harsher than the original aggression. The Soviets or any other aggressor would pay heavily for even minor hostile actions. Former president Truman had favored a containment policy, calling for military responses tailored to the nature of each hostile action—that is, calling for the U.S. response to be at the same general level as the hostile action. The new strategy introduced by Dulles increased secret operations and promoted more-aggressive diplomatic activity, such as directly confronting countries that allowed growth of internal communist influences and threatening economic sanctions.

Dulles argued that focusing on nuclear capability would be much cheaper than maintaining the massive conventional air and ground forces that were called for in National Security Council Document 68 (NSC-68). Truman had adopted the NSC-68 strategy in 1950. But for Eisenhower, the U.S. economy was a priority, and less spending appealed to him. Dulles's strategy, which included a major reduction in conventional forces, was one way to reduce spending. The U.S. military budget dropped from over $41 billion in Truman's last annual budget proposed for 1954 to less than $31 billion, the amount requested by Eisenhower for 1955, a 25-percent decrease. The number of army personnel dropped from 1.5 million to 1 million. The air force became much more prominent, playing a key role in the new massive retaliation strategy. The B-52, the nation's first intercontinental jet bomber capable of delivering nuclear bombs on Soviet targets, became the backbone of the strategic air power. Planning emphasized development of long-range intercontinental ballistic missiles and intermediate-range missiles, all armed with nuclear warheads, as well as smaller-scale tactical nuclear weapons for the army and navy. (Tactical weapons allow for more flexible maneuvering of military forces.) By December 1954, NATO's tactical nuclear weapons supplementing conventional forces (troops, ships, and airplanes) included atomic cannons and small nuclear missiles. The brinkmanship strategy, featuring a scaled-down but much more powerful military, was called the New Look.

Though it saved NATO members money by requiring fewer conventional forces, the new U.S. policy made Western European nations uneasy. The original goal of ninety-six NATO military divisions was reduced to twenty-five by late 1954. Fewer ground forces in Europe could make the West unable to respond to small incidents with anything less than U.S. nuclear retaliation. Therefore, one of the weaknesses of brinkmanship was that it gave the U.S. president fewer options for responding to hostile actions. To Europeans and many Americans, too, nuclear war seemed a drastic response to a localized hostile action. The United States tried to ease their worries by continuing to arm NATO forces with tactical nuclear weapons and maintaining U.S. troops in West Germany.

Khrushchev considered the new U.S. strategy very aggressive and threatening to Soviet interests. However, Khrushchev was interested in reviving the Soviet industrial and agricultural economy rather than pursuing massive funding for conventional arms. Like Eisenhower and Dulles, he decided to concentrate on development of nuclear ballistic missiles, a much less expensive option than development of conventional arms. As a result, Khrushchev significantly increased the Soviet nuclear weapons program. By 1955, the Soviets had over three hundred atomic and thermonuclear

weapons and intercontinental bombers. Soon the United States feared the Soviets had many more nuclear arms than they actually did. Nevertheless, when conflicts arose, both the Soviet Union and the United States could threaten each other with nuclear war. The strength of both countries deterred them from actually starting a war; whoever fired first would not only destroy the other but be destroyed itself.

U.S. secretary of state John Foster Dulles (far right) meets with British foreign minister Harold Macmillan (far left) and French foreign minister Antoine Pinay on November 8, 1955.
Reproduced by permission of the Corbis Corporation.

The Third World

Europe remained divided along East-West lines: Western European countries were backed by the United States, and the Soviet Union oversaw the Eastern European countries. "Nation-building," installing friendly governments willing to join in combating or promoting communism, became a key strategy for the United States and the Soviet Union during this Cold War period. Third World countries were key targets for nation-building. (The term "Third World" refers to poor underdeveloped or developing nations in Africa, Asia, and Latin America; most Third World countries have economies primarily based on agriculture, with few other industries.) Another major U.S. strategy was to create military defense alliances around the borders of the Soviet Union. For example, the United States made defense agreements with South Korea and with the Republic of China (ROC) on Taiwan; the agreements were patterned after NATO in Europe. The United States would eventually have formal agreements to defend forty-five nations around the world.

The U.S. Central Intelligence Agency (CIA), led by Allen Dulles (1893–1969), the brother of John Foster Dulles, would play a key role in nation-building. Less expensive than military operations and less open to congressional and public review, the CIA supported friendly leaders and their governments through secret operations; they also supported the overthrow of unfriendly governments. Various extreme methods, even assassination plots against foreign leaders, were planned. Historians later presumed that targets included Cuban president Fidel Castro Ruz (1926–), China's premier Zhou Enlai (1898–1976), and Congo prime minister Patrice Lumumba (1925–1961). To identify possible communist influences, the CIA also infiltrated various kinds of organizations, including student groups and church groups.

The U.S. policy of nation-building was not always welcomed by Third World countries. Most Third World countries were or had been European colonies. But colonialism was coming to an end. (Colonialism is control over an economically weaker country and/or its citizens. Most often colonialism refers to Western European nations exercising control over various Third World countries.) Nationalist movements were gaining strength: Third World countries increasingly sought independence from foreign control. Nationalism refers to the strong loyalty of a person or group to its own country.

Driven by poverty and despair, people in Third World countries often wanted to overthrow local rulers who controlled the countries' wealth; generally the wealth was benefiting a controlling colonialist power, or a capitalist country. Seeing an opportunity to weaken colonialist powers such as France, communist leaders stepped in to help. In the early twentieth century, communists in China and Russia had aligned themselves with the peasants and common workers. Communist political ideas were in general supportive of the common people; therefore, the communists were already inclined to help Third World countries in the mid-twentieth century. In 1955, Soviet Communist Party leader Khrushchev and Soviet premier Nikolay Bulganin (1895–1975), who replaced Georgy Malenkov, visited India, Burma, and Afghanistan to offer economic aid to the nationalist movements there.

Since India had gained independence from British colonial rule in 1947, it chose a path of neutrality (not aligning with either the Soviet Union or the United States). As a result, it became a Third World leader. In 1955, India and twenty-eight other neutral countries attended a conference in Southeast Asia; they held another meeting in 1961 in Belgrade, Yugoslavia. They formed a bloc, or group, of countries that agreed to focus on economic development, not Cold War politics. Many U.S. businesses began locating offices and industrial factories in neutral Third World countries, providing much-needed jobs. However, many Third World nations would equate the growing U.S. presence with the earlier hated European colonialism.

Because the communists often assisted nationalist movements, the United States had difficulty distinguishing nationalist ideologies from communism. The United States sometimes perceived nationalist movements as communist-inspired revolutions. Land reform, a common feature of nationalist movements, often involved confiscation of large foreign land holdings, which were then parceled out to citizens for small farming operations. American corporations sought U.S. government support in defending their extensive holdings in Third World nations. In an effort to keep perceived revolutionary movements in check, President Eisenhower established the Inter-American Development Bank in 1959 to provide economic assistance to governments that remained friendly to the United States. In 1961, President John F. Kennedy (1917–1963; served 1961–63) followed this policy with the formation of the Alliance for Progress program.

Another complicating factor for the United States was that longtime colonial powers, such as Britain and France, were also longtime friends of the United States. Therefore, the U.S. government felt compelled to defend colonial holdings. A dilemma existed: If the United States supported a nationalist movement, it would be criticized by allies and hardline anticommunists. If it did not support these movements, the nationalists would likely find support from the Soviets, America's Cold War enemy.

The Middle East

As part of the New Look strategy, the Eisenhower administration decided to counter Soviet-supported nationalist movements with CIA covert operations, particularly in Third World countries in the Middle East. The Middle East is a vast region including parts of southwestern Asia, southeastern Europe, and northern Africa. It includes Turkey to the north, Iran to the east, and Sudan to the south. It also includes Egypt, Iraq, Saudi Arabia, Israel, Syria, Jordan, Yemen, Lebanon, Cyprus, Oman, Bahrain, Qatar, and United Arab Emirates. Iran provides one example of covert CIA activity: In 1951, Iranian premier Mohammad Mosaddeq (1880–1967) nationalized the Anglo-Iranian Oil Company, a British-owned company, so that profits would not go to a foreign-held company but would stay within Iran. In response, international oil companies boycotted (joined together and refused to buy) Iranian oil. In reaction to the boycott, on May 28, 1953, Mosaddeq appealed to Eisenhower for help. In his message, Mosaddeq commented that he would have to go to the Soviets if the United States did not help. Already leery of Mosaddeq's control of Iranian oil, which was critically needed by Western nations, Eisenhower declined Mosaddeq's request. In July, Mosaddeq dissolved the Iranian parliament and established relations with the Soviets. The CIA went into action in August to orchestrate a change in government by bringing in the shah, Mohammad Reza Pahlavi (1919–1980), to restore a monarchy, or rule by a single person, friendly to the United States and Western Europe. On August 19, 1953, the CIA paid antigovernment rioters to take to the streets and force a coup d'état, an illegal or forceful change of government. After several hundred deaths, Mosaddeq resigned, and the shah ultimately became the ruler.

The United States provided military and economic aid to the new Iranian government in 1954. That year, an international oil consortium, or business alliance, was established, replacing the earlier exclusively British control of Iranian oil. American oil companies owned 40 percent of the new Iranian operations. The Iranian army would become the best equipped and largest in the Middle East. The United States was particularly pleased with the regime change because Iran shared a long border with the Soviet Union. This potentially blocked a possible Soviet expansion of influence in the direction of the oil-rich Persian Gulf.

Latin America

Latin America was another Third World region of concern to the U.S. administration during the Cold War period. Latin America includes the entire Western Hemisphere south of the United States. It includes Central and South America as well as Mexico and the islands of the West Indies. The rapidly growing population in Latin America suffered greatly from poverty, disease, and illiteracy in the mid-twentieth century. A small upper class controlled the governments, armies, and most wealth. For landless peasants, the ideas of communism, in contrast to the existing governmental systems, could be appealing. To prevent the spread of such ideas and a full-blown communist revolution, the U.S. government often felt it must support the ruling elite.

For example, in Guatemala, 2 percent of the population owned 70 percent of the nation's wealth. In 1953, President Jacobo Arbenz Guzmán (1913–1971), the popularly elected leader of Guatemala, began a program of land reform to ease some of his country's poverty. The reform program included nationalizing 234,000 acres of uncultivated land owned by the Boston-based United Fruit Company. Arbenz provided payment to the company for the land, but the company was unhappy with the payment it received. The company appealed to the Eisenhower administration for help. Since Arbenz's support base included the Guatemalan Communist Party, Secretary of State John Foster Dulles claimed that Arbenz posed a communist threat to the region. (Coincidentally, Dulles had performed legal work earlier for United Fruit Company.)

As a result of Dulles's input, Eisenhower authorized a CIA overthrow of the Guatemalan government. The United

U.S. secretary of state John Foster Dulles. *Reproduced by permission of the Corbis Corporation.*

States trained and armed a small group of Guatemalan political exiles in neighboring countries. Suspecting a U.S.-led coup attempt, Arbenz sought help from the Soviet Union. The Soviets arranged shipments of arms to Guatemala from Czechoslovakia. Claiming Soviet interference in the Western Hemisphere, the U.S.-trained army launched an attack against the Guatemalan army under air cover flown by CIA pilots. On June 27, 1954, Arbenz fled the country. Carlos Castillo Armas (1914–1957), one of the soldiers supported by the United States, established a military junta (a group of military leaders in political control). Castillo banned all political opposition parties, then imprisoned suspected political opponents and killed many of them. Castillo also ended the land reform program and gave United Fruit Company its land back.

Guatemala would serve as a U.S. base for future operations in the region. Although the United States claimed the uprising was the will of the Guatemalan people, many Latin Americans were dismayed by the covert military force the United States used to overthrow a legally elected government. However, some Latin American leaders who were friendly with the United States took the action in Guatemala as a strong and welcome signal that they could count on U.S. help to protect them from internal uprisings. The United States worked with harsh and dictatorial regimes in Latin America—Fulgencio Batista (1901–1973) in Cuba; Anastasio Somoza (1896–1956) and sons Luis Anastasio Somoza (1922–1967) and Anastasio Somoza (1925–1980) of Nicaragua; and Alfredo Stroessner (1912–) in Paraguay—because these regimes shared the U.S. government's anticommunist views. The United States preferred to support strong central governments, even brutal ones, rather than let communist influences take hold in struggling Latin American countries.

Indochina

Indochina is a peninsula in Southeast Asia that extends from the southern border of China into the South China Sea. It includes, among other countries, Vietnam, Cambodia, and Laos. Because these three countries had good natural resources, especially rubber and rice, they became French colonies in the nineteenth century. In 1947, the French began fighting communist revolutionary Ho Chi Minh (1890–1969) and his Vietminh army. Over ninety thousand French troops were killed in a seven-year period. Then, in early 1954, French forces in northern Vietnam were put on the defensive by the Vietminh forces. On April 26, approximately fifteen thousand French troops became trapped at a garrison at Dien Bien Phu. France desperately appealed to the United States for military help. In deciding whether to provide assistance, Eisenhower considered the popular "domino theory"—that if Vietnam fell to communism, other countries would follow. First would be Burma, Thailand, and the rest of Indochina. Next would be Japan, Taiwan, and the Philippines, and finally Australia and New Zealand. The president considered a plan that would use both conventional and nuclear weapons against Vietminh positions surrounding the French troops. However, the American public did not want to see U.S. forces sent to a far-off war so soon after the Korean War (see Chapter 2, Conflict Builds). Therefore, Eisenhower chose not to respond, and the French forces surrendered at Dien Bien Phu on May 7, 1954.

At the urging of Britain and France, the United States joined in a conference about Vietnam in Geneva, Switzerland, that also included China and the Soviet Union. On May 8, the day after the fall of the French at Dien Bien Phu, the issue of Indochina was raised. By July, a settlement had seemingly been reached, ending the Vietnamese conflict. France agreed to recognize the independence of Vietnam, Cambodia, and Laos. Vietnam was divided in two at the seventeenth parallel. The communists would control the north half; they established the Democratic Republic of Vietnam. In the south was a government aligned with the West called the Republic of Vietnam. The Geneva agreement called for national elections throughout Vietnam, as well as in Laos and Cambodia, in two years. It also prohibited any of the three countries from joining military alliances or allowing foreign military bases within their borders. Despite the agreement, the United States objected to communist control of the north and refused to observe the ban on military assistance to South Vietnam. The United States was eager to provide economic and covert support. Like the United States, the communists in northern Vietnam would defy the agreement, refusing to allow the national elections. The Soviet Union and communist China supplied the Vietminh army with weapons.

To combat the expansion of communism in the region, in September 1954 the United States led the creation of a Southeast Asian alliance patterned after NATO. It was called the Southeast Asia Treaty Organization (SEATO). Member nations included the United States, Great Britain, France, New Zealand, Thailand, Australia, Pakistan, and the Philippines. Since the Geneva settlement banned Vietnam, Cambodia, and Laos from joining alliances, SEATO extended protections to those countries without their signatures. By November, U.S. military advisers were training a South Vietnamese army called the Army of the Republic of Vietnam (ARVN). For the next five years, U.S. aid to South Vietnam would total $1.2 billion, financing 80 percent of the military expenses and almost half of the country's nonmilitary government spending.

The Geneva settlement called for public elections in all of Vietnam by 1956, but the United States opposed such elections, fearing a communist victory. Instead a tightly controlled public election was held in October 1955, in South Vietnam only. The referendum led to a 98 percent voter approval of the Republic of Vietnam's government, with Ngo Dinh Diem (1901–1963) as its president. Formal U.S. recognition came quickly to Diem, even though he had little popular support. His support came mostly from the small landlord class, the military, and his own corrupt bureaucracy. Because of this weak support, Diem moved to eliminate all political opposition. In reaction, the Vietminh, still located in pockets of southern Vietnam, began a military resistance movement with the goal of reunifying Vietnam under a communist government.

The Far East

The easternmost part of Asia is often referred to as the Far East. Included under this general term are China, Korea,

Japan, Taiwan, Hong Kong, and eastern Siberia. By late 1953, the United States withdrew its Seventh Fleet from the Taiwan Strait, where ships had been sent during the Korean War to guard against any possible invasion of Taiwan by the People's Republic of China (PRC), the communist government that had been controlling Mainland China since 1949. The PRC feared that the removal of the Seventh Fleet meant Chinese nationalists, who controlled Taiwan and its surrounding is-

Representatives from the eight member nations of the Southeast Asia Treaty Organization (SEATO) meet in September 1954.
Reproduced by permission of the Corbis Corporation.

lands, had U.S. approval to invade Mainland China. It was no secret that Taiwan's president, Chiang Kai-shek (1887–1975), had hopes of militarily retaking Mainland China. The United States and the PRC made no progress in establishing formal relations at the 1954 Geneva conference, and on September 3, 1954, the PRC began bombarding two islands held by Taiwan, Jinmen (Quemoy) and Mazu (Matsu). Two U.S. soldiers were killed. The PRC also attacked the Tachen Islands and captured the island of Ichiang. In October, the PRC established stronger ties with the Soviets. As part of a formal Sino-Soviet (Sino means "Chinese") agreement, the PRC regained control of Manchuria, and the Soviets agreed to financially assist PRC industrialization programs.

Given China's aggression against Taiwan and strengthening relationship with the Soviets, the U.S. Joint Chiefs of Staff recommended to President Eisenhower a full military response including use of atomic weapons. Eisenhower, however, was unwilling to go to war with the PRC over the small islands. Instead, the United States signed a mutual defense treaty with Taiwan on November 23, 1954. Approved by the U.S. Senate on February 9, 1955, the treaty promised U.S. military support to Taiwan in exchange for Chiang's agreement to drop any plans of invading China. The PRC nevertheless viewed this pact with great suspicion and still saw Taiwan as a threat; therefore, the PRC's hostile actions continued. In January 1955, Congress had also passed the Taiwan Resolution, authorizing Eisenhower to use whatever force he felt necessary to protect Taiwan and its islands. Given that broad authority, Eisenhower threatened to use nuclear weapons to resolve the crisis if the PRC did not halt its bombardments in the Taiwan Strait. This act of brinkmanship forced the PRC to reconsider its position, and in April 1955 PRC foreign minister Zhou Enlai indicated an interest in discussing solutions to the Taiwan crisis; the following month, a cease-fire, or an ending of all hostilities, went into effect. Even though the two countries had no formal relations, they began meetings in Geneva. The discussions dragged on, and the crisis faded away for the time being.

The key victim of the Taiwan Strait crisis was the Communist Party cause. A lack of Soviet support during the crisis greatly bothered the PRC communists. Their disillusionment with the Soviet Union would become a major factor in a later political split between the two countries, the two largest communist nations in the world. It also led the PRC to greatly accelerate its nuclear weapons program, because leaders there felt they could not rely on Soviet protection.

A Cold War thaw

As their relationship with the PRC deteriorated, the Soviets sought to improve relations with the West. For example, on May 15, 1955, the United States and the Soviet Union reached an agreement over the future of Austria. The agreement removed all postwar occupation forces of the Soviet Union, the United States, France, and Britain. It established Austria as a fully independent and neutral country.

With both the United States and the Soviet Union having successfully tested powerful hydrogen bombs, Eisenhower and Khrushchev wished to limit the escalating arms race and reduce tensions. The two met in Geneva on July 18, 1955. It was the first meeting of superpower leaders since the Potsdam Conference ten years earlier. Little progress toward arms control was made, but having such talks was considered a good sign. The Soviets proposed to close all foreign military bases operated by the United States and the Soviet Union. They also suggested banning the use of nuclear weapons for offensive first strikes and restricting the size of armed forces in smaller nations. The United States believed such restrictions would inhibit the rearming of West Germany and jeopardize the future of NATO, potentially limiting U.S. military presence and the general military strength of the alliance. The reunification and rearming of post–World War II (1939–45) Germany continued to be a central sticking point between the two superpowers. The Soviets also proposed replacing NATO and the Warsaw Pact with an all-Europe security agreement. Germany would be unarmed, reunified, and neutral. Because of the wounds Germany inflicted on the Soviets in World War II, the Soviets could not accept a reunified, well-armed Germany made stronger by an alignment with the West. If Germany could not remain unarmed, the Soviets stated, then they would strongly prefer two separate countries: East Germany and West Germany. East Germany, under Soviet influence, would serve as a cushion between West Germany and the Soviet-controlled countries of Eastern Europe.

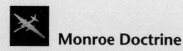

Monroe Doctrine

The Cold War was not the beginning of global competition between Russia and the United States. They had crossed paths in their efforts to expand in the early nineteenth century. This interaction led to the establishment of a major U.S. foreign policy that would last into the Cold War over a century later.

In 1821, Tsar Alexander I (1777–1825) of Russia claimed the lands of Alaska and part of the Pacific Northwest. The Russian claim extended southward into an area the United States believed it had already acquired in a treaty with Spain. In addition, Russia had formed an alliance with two other European nations, and fears rose among the British and Americans that this alliance might try to gain control of some of Spain's former colonies in Latin America. The colonies had recently gained their independence from Spain. The young United States, having just defeated Great Britain in the War of 1812, wanted to rid the Western Hemisphere of European influence. Seeking new trade opportunities and territories for future expansion, it debated what to do.

Finally, U.S. secretary of state John Quincy Adams (1767–1848) recommended that President James Monroe (1758–1831; served 1817–25) announce a policy prohibiting further establishment of European colonies in the Western Hemisphere. On December 2, 1823, in the president's annual address to Congress, Monroe pronounced a new policy that has guided the nation ever since—the Monroe Doctrine. Monroe stated that the United States would stay out of European internal affairs and wars; that the Western Hemisphere was closed to further colonization by European nations, including Russia; and that the United States would not interfere with existing colonies. Lastly—and most significantly for the later Cold War era—Monroe stated that any attempt by a European na-

The West rejected the Soviets' proposals to disband NATO and reunify a weakened Germany. They feared the Soviets were merely trying to weaken Western alliances with false promises of peaceful coexistence and then turn around and attack later. The United States would only accept a reunified Germany if nationwide free elections were allowed; there was no doubt that such elections would align Germany with the West. Eisenhower countered the Soviet military proposals with a proposal of arms control; however, the Soviets found Eisenhower's plan unacceptable. The proposed plan, "Open Skies," called for extensive aerial inspections. The Soviets

HANDS OFF!

A political cartoon from the early 1900s shows President Theodore Roosevelt standing behind a cannon with a "Monroe Doctrine" sign on it, yelling "Hands Off!" to a European king who is attempting to make claims to the Spanish colony of Santo Domingo. The Monroe Doctrine declared the United States would not tolerate interference from European nations in North and South America. *Reproduced by permission of the Corbis Corporation.*

tion to control a nation in the Western Hemisphere would be considered a hostile act. In the Cold War, the Monroe Doctrine would support efforts by the United States to combat Soviet communist influences in Latin America. Following the announcement of the Monroe Doctrine, Russia shifted the southern boundary of its claim farther north, and the perceived threat against the former Spanish colonies never materialized. Russia sold the territory of Alaska to the United States in 1867 for $7.2 million. From that point through the Cold War era, the entire Western Hemisphere was under U.S. influence, meaning the United States was willing to challenge any new European influence in the broad region.

feared that aerial inspections would reveal all Soviet military installations and make them vulnerable to U.S. nuclear missile attack.

Although the most concrete result of the conference consisted of cultural exchanges, involving the fine arts of theater, dancing, writing, etc., the conference did establish a friendlier spirit and for a time lessened fears of nuclear war. The period is often referred to as a Cold War thaw, because relations between the United States and the Soviet Union gradually began to warm. The Geneva conference revealed

U.S. president Dwight D. Eisenhower (left) shakes hands with Soviet leader Nikita Khrushchev in Geneva in 1955. *Reproduced by permission of the Corbis Corporation.*

two major Cold War facts: A nuclear stalemate had been reached between the United States and the Soviet Union, and the West no longer expected to militarily win the Cold War in the event of a "hot" war.

The Cold War thaw allowed Khrushchev to turn to Soviet domestic issues. In February 1956, he gave an epic speech, the "Crimes of Stalin" speech, to the Twentieth Congress of the Soviet Communist Party. By denouncing the activities of former Soviet premier Joseph Stalin, Khrushchev attacked his most serious opponents in the Soviet Communist Party, who still preferred Stalin's hard-line policies. Khrushchev described the torture and executions of many innocent people and the self-glorification that Stalin sought. Stalin's behavior, Khrushchev contended, was counter to communist principles. According to Khrushchev, Stalin served the Soviet Union poorly. Khrushchev pointed to a new direction for the Soviet Union: He would accept different forms of socialism, or a state-controlled society, such as the communist government led by Josip Tito (1892–1980) in Yugoslavia; it remained independent of Soviet control. Unlike Stalin, Khrushchev also claimed that communism and capitalism could peacefully coexist; conflict was not necessarily inevitable, as Stalin had preached. Khrushchev's speech seemed to suggest that expansion would no longer be a communist goal. By mid-1956, members of the Eisenhower administration were cautiously hopeful that a new era might be beginning, with the Soviets gradually relaxing their control of Eastern Europe.

For More Information

Ambrose, Stephen F. *Eisenhower: The President.* London: Allen and Unwin, 1984.

Collier, Christopher. *The United States in the Cold War*. New York: Benchmark Books/Marshall Cavendish, 2002.

Fried, Richard M. *Nightmare in Red: The McCarthy Era in Perspective*. New York: Oxford University Press, 1990.

Gleijeses, Piero. *Shattered Hope: The Guatemalan Revolution and the United States, 1944–1954*. Princeton, NJ: Princeton University Press, 1991.

Hahn, Peter L. *The United States, Great Britain & Egypt, 1945–1956: Strategy and Diplomacy in the Early Cold War*. Chapel Hill: University of North Carolina Press, 1991.

Marks, Frederick W., III. *Power and Peace: The Diplomacy of John Foster Dulles*. Westport, CT: Praeger, 1993.

Mayers, David A. *Cracking the Monolith: U.S. Policy Against the Sino-Soviet Alliance, 1949–1955*. Baton Rouge: Louisiana State University Press, 1986.

Powaski, Ronald E. *The Cold War: The United States and the Soviet Union, 1917–1991*. New York: Oxford University Press, 1998.

Rabe, Stephen G. *Eisenhower and Latin America: The Foreign Policy of Anticommunism*. Chapel Hill: University of North Carolina Press, 1988.

Ulam, Adam B. *The Rivals: America and Russia Since World War II*. New York: Penguin Books, 1976.

Where to Learn More

Books

Barson, Michael, and Steven Heller. *Red Scared! The Commie Menace in Propaganda and Popular Culture*. San Francisco: Chronicle Books, 2001.

Brubaker, Paul E. *The Cuban Missile Crisis in American History*. Berkeley Heights, NJ: Enslow, 2001.

Ciment, James. *The Young People's History of the United States*. New York: Barnes and Noble Books, 1998.

Collier, Christopher. *The United States in the Cold War*. New York: Benchmark Books/Marshall Cavendish, 2002.

FitzGerald, Frances. *Way Out There in the Blue: Reagan, Star Wars, and the End of the Cold War*. New York: Simon & Schuster, 2000.

Gaddis, John L. *We Now Know: Rethinking Cold War History*. New York: Oxford University Press, 1997.

Gates, Robert M. *From the Shadows: The Ultimate Insider's Story of Five Presidents and How They Won the Cold War*. New York: Simon & Schuster Trade Paperback, 1997.

Glynn, Patrick. *Closing Pandora's Box: Arms Races, Arms Control, and the History of the Cold War*. New York: Basic Books, 1992.

Grant, R. G. *The Berlin Wall*. Austin, TX: Raintree Steck-Vaughn, 1999.

Herring, George C. *America's Longest War: The United States and Vietnam, 1950–1975*. 2nd ed. New York: Knopf, 1988.

Huchthausen, Peter A., and Alexander Hoyt. *October Fury.* Hoboken, NJ: Wiley, 2002.

Isaacs, Jeremy, and Taylor Downing. *Cold War: An Illustrated History, 1945–1991.* Boston: Little, Brown, 1998.

Jacobs, William Jay. *Search for Peace: The Story of the United Nations.* New York: Atheneum, 1996.

Keep, John L. H. *A History of the Soviet Union, 1945–1991: Last of the Empires.* New York: Oxford University Press, 1995.

Kelly, Nigel. *Fall of the Berlin Wall: The Cold War Ends.* Chicago: Heineman Library, 2001.

Kort, Michael G. *The Cold War.* Brookfield, CT: Millbrook Press, 1994.

LaFeber, Walter. *America, Russia, and the Cold War, 1945–1996.* 8th ed. New York: McGraw-Hill, 1997.

Parrish, Thomas. *Berlin in the Balance, 1945–1949: The Blockade, the Airlift, the First Major Battle of the Cold War.* Reading, MA: Addison-Wesley, 1998.

Parrish, Thomas. *The Cold War Encyclopedia.* New York: Henry Holt, 1996.

Pietrusza, David. *The End of the Cold War.* San Diego, CA: Lucent, 1995.

Sherrow, Victoria. *Joseph McCarthy and the Cold War.* Woodbridge, CT: Blackbirch Press, 1999.

Sibley, Katherine A. S. *The Cold War.* Westport, CT: Greenwood Press, 1998.

Smith, Joseph. *The Cold War, 1945–1991.* 2nd ed. Malden, MA: Blackwell, 1998.

Stein, Conrad. *The Korean War: "The Forgotten War."* Springfield, NJ: Enslow, 1994.

Walker, Martin. *The Cold War: A History (Owl Book).* New York: Henry Holt, 1995.

Magazines

Hoover, J. Edgar. "How to Fight Communism." *Newsweek,* June 9, 1947.

Levine, Isaac Don. "Our First Line of Defense." *Plain Talk,* September 1949.

"X" (George F. Kennan). "The Sources of Soviet Conduct." *Foreign Affairs,* July 1947.

Novels

Brunner, Edward. *Cold War Poetry.* Urbana: University of Illinois Press, 2000.

Clancy, Tom. *The Hunt for Red October.* New York: Berkley Publishing Group, 1985.

Clancy, Tom. *Red Storm Rising.* New York: Berkley Publishing Group, 1987.

Clancy, Tom, and Martin Greenberg. *Tom Clancy's Power Plays: Cold War.* New York: Berkley Publishing Group, 2001.

George, Peter. *Dr. Strangelove, or How I Learned to Stop Worrying and Love the Bomb.* New York: Bantam Books, 1964.

Le Carre, John. *Spy Who Came in from the Cold.* New York: Coward, Mc-Cann & Geoghegan, 1978.

Littell, Robert. *The Company: A Novel of the CIA.* New York: Overlook Press, 2002.

Web Sites

The Atomic Archive. http://www. atomicarchive.com (accessed on September 26, 2003).

CNN Interactive: The Cold War Experience. http://www.CNN.com/SPECIALS/cold.war (accessed on September 26, 2003).

"Cold War History: 1949–1989." *U.S. Air Force Museum.* http://www.wpafb.af.mil/museum/history/coldwar/cw.htm (accessed on September 26, 2003).

The Dwight D. Eisenhower Library and Museum. http://www.eisenhower.utexas.edu (accessed on September 26, 2003).

George Bush Presidential Library and Museum. http://bushlibrary.tamu.edu (accessed on September 26, 2003).

Gerald R. Ford Library and Museum. http://www.ford.utexas.edu (accessed on September 26, 2003).

International Spy Museum. http://spymuseum.org (accessed on September 26, 2003).

John F. Kennedy Library and Museum. http://www.cs.umb.edu/jfklibrary/index.htm (accessed on September 26, 2003).

Lyndon B. Johnson Library and Museum. http://www.lbjlib.utexas.edu (accessed on September 26, 2003).

The Manhattan Project Heritage Preservation Association, Inc. http://www.childrenofthemanhattanproject.org (accessed on September 26, 2003).

National Atomic Museum. http://www.atomicmuseum.com (accessed on September 26, 2003).

National Security Agency. http://www.nsa.gov (accessed on September 26, 2003).

President Mikhail Sergeyevich Gorbachev. http://www.mikhailgorbachev.org (accessed on September 26, 2003).

The Richard Nixon Library and Birthplace. http://www.nixonfoundation.org (accessed on September 26, 2003).

Ronald Reagan Presidential Library. http://www.reagan.utexas.edu (accessed on September 26, 2003).

"Secrets, Lies, and Atomic Spies." *Nova Online.* http://www.pbs.org/wgbh/nova/venona (accessed on September 26, 2003).

Truman Presidential Museum & Library. http://www.trumanlibrary.org (accessed on September 26, 2003).

U.S. Central Intelligence Agency (CIA). http://www.cia.gov (accessed on September 26, 2003).

Woodrow Wilson International Center for Scholars. *The Cold War International History Project.* http://wwics.si.edu/index. cfm?fuseaction= topics.home &topic_id=1409 (accessed on September 26, 2003).

Index

A

Abel, Rudolf, *1:* 150
ABM. *See* Antiballistic missiles (ABM)
Abrahamson, James A., *2:* 353 (ill.)
Acheson, Dean, *1:* 23, 45–46, 95
Adams, John Quincy, *1:* 186
Adenauer, Konrad, *1:* 67, 171; *2:* 306
AEC. *See* Atomic Energy Commission (AEC)
Afghanistan
    Carter, Jimmy, and, *2:* 335–36, 337
    Central Intelligence Agency and, *2:* 340
    Gorbachev, Mikhail, and, *2:* 335–36
    Reagan, Ronald, and, *2:* 340, 355
    Soviet Union and, *2:* 335–36, 337, 351, 355–56
Africa, *2:* 206–8, 325–27. *See also* Middle East; specific countries

African Americans, *2:* 279 (ill.)
    Black Power and, *2:* 276, 281–82
    economy and, *2:* 278, 281, 282
    freedom and, *2:* 275–76
    military draft and, *2:* 285
    racism and, *2:* 275–76, 278–83, 285
    Red Scare and, *1:* 115
    segregation and, *2:* 278–79, 281
    separatism and, *2:* 281
    violence and, *2:* 281–82
Agent Orange, *2:* 283
Agnew, Spiro, *2:* 310
Alexander I, *1:* 186
Alien Registration Act. *See* Smith Act
Allende Gossens, Salvador, *2:* 308
Alliance for Progress, *1:* 177; *2:* 252, 262–63
Allied Control Council, *1:* 56, 60–61
Allies
    definition of, *1:* 2
    peace treaty and, *2:* 364

Italic type indicates volume number; illustrations are marked by (ill.).

World War II and, *1:* 8–18, 48,
55, 105
All-Russian Communist Party. *See*
Communist Party
Ames, Aldrich, *1:* 157, 162
Anastasio Somoza, Luis, *1:* 180
Andropov, Yuri, *2:* 344, 348, 349
Andrus, Cecil, *2:* 322 (ill.)
Angleton, James Jesús, *1:* 154
Angola, *2:* 308, 326–27
Antiballistic missiles (ABM), *2:*
247, 258, 303
Anti-Radical Division, *1:* 102–3.
See also Federal Bureau of In-
vestigation (FBI)
ANZUS Pact, *1:* 50
Arabs, *2:* 328–30. *See also* specific
countries
Arbenz Guzmán, Jacobo, *1:* 169,
179–80
Argentina, *2:* 324
Armistice of Panmunjan, *1:* 50 (ill.)
Arms race. *See* Nuclear weapons,
race for
Armstrong, Neil A., *2:* 199, 199
(ill.)
Arzamas-16, *1:* 89–90
Aswan High Dam, *2:* 203
Asymmetrical response, *1:* 173–75
Atomic bombs. *See also* Nuclear
weapons
definition of, *1:* 80, 88
development of, *1:* 9, 80–84,
87, 88–91; *2:* 244
hydrogen bombs and, *1:* 92–95
testing of, *1:* 13–14, 43, 79–80,
85–86, 90, 91, 115
use of, *1:* 17, 86–88, 135; *2:*
219, 241
Atomic Energy Commission
(AEC), *1:* 80, 92, 93–94; *2:*
242–43
"Atoms for Peace," *2:* 241
Attlee, Clement, *1:* 3, 15, 16 (ill.),
86
Australia, *1:* 50
Austria, *1:* 185
Azerbaijan (Iran), *1:* 20

B

B-28 bombs, *2:* 242–43, 243 (ill.)

B-47 aircraft, *2:* 237 (ill.)
B-52 aircraft, *2:* 238, 242–43
Baby boom, *2:* 286–87
Back channel negotiations, *2:*
300, 301
Baghdad Pact, *2:* 202, 204. *See
also* Central Treaty Organiza-
tion (CENTO)
Balaguer, Joaquín, *2:* 265
Ballistic Missile Early Warning
Systems (BMEWS), *2:* 239
(ill.), 240
Baltic States, *1:* 7; *2:* 361–62, 367,
369
Ban the Bomb marches, *2:* 245–46
Baruch, Bernard, *1:* 3, 22
Basic Principle of Relations be-
tween the United States and
Soviet Union, *2:* 304
Batista y Zaldívar, Fulgencio, *1:*
180; *2:* 208, 215, 258
Bay of Pigs, *2:* 214, 217–18, 218
(ill.), 252, 258–59
BBC, *1:* 143
Begin, Menachem, *2:* 329 (ill.),
329
Belarus, *2:* 370, 373
Belgium, *1:* 37; *2:* 207–8
Benes, Edvard, *1:* 34–35, 35 (ill.)
Bentley, Elizabeth Terrill, *1:* 112,
134
Beria, Lavrenty, *1:* 81, 89–90, 91
Berlin, *1:* 58 (ill.), 59 (ill.), 61
(ill.), 64 (ill.), 67 (ill.), 73
(ill.), 75 (ill.), 76 (ill.). *See also*
Berlin Wall; East Berlin; West
Berlin
airlift, *1:* 37, 56, 62–66, 64 (ill.),
111
blockades in, *1:* 37, 56, 62–66,
64 (ill.), 67 (ill.), 111
communism in, *1:* 57, 73
détente and, *2:* 306
division of, *1:* 37, 55–56, 68,
145
economy of, *1:* 55–56, 65–66,
68–69; *2:* 200
espionage and, *1:* 145–46
government of, *2:* 210, 212,
259–60
harassment in, *1:* 61
Kennedy, John F., and, *1:*
72–73, 76–77; *2:* 259–60

Khrushchev, Nikita S., and, *1:*
69–71, 73; *2:* 200–201,
259–60
nuclear weapons and, *1:* 62,
64–65, 70
reunification of, *1:* 77
Soviet Union and, *1:* 61–62,
65–66, 111
transportation and, *1:* 68–69,
70, 71
tunnel in, *1:* 145–46, 146 (ill.)
World War II and, *1:* 57
Berlin Wall, *1:* 73 (ill.), 75 (ill.),
76 (ill.)
construction of, *1:* 71–75; *2:*
260
crossing, *1:* 75–76
definition of, *1:* 56; *2:* 252
fall of, *1:* 75, 77; *2:* 355, 363
significance of, *1:* 76–77
as Wall of Shame, *1:* 76
Bevin, Ernest, *1:* 18–19
Big Three, *1:* 2, 9–18, 14 (ill.), 29,
30 (ill.). *See also* Grand Al-
liance
Bishop, Maurice, *2:* 341
Black Muslims, *2:* 281
Black Panthers, *2:* 281–82
Black Power, *2:* 276, 281–82
Black Saturday, *2:* 228
Blacklists, *1:* 110
Blake, George, *1:* 145–46, 152
Blake, Gordon, *2:* 225
Blunt, Anthony F., *1:* 128, 142,
143, 144
BMEWS. *See* Ballistic Missile Early
Warning Systems (BMEWS)
Boeing Aircraft, *2:* 238
Boland Amendments, *2:* 332
Bolshevik Revolution. *See also*
Bolsheviks
communism and, *1:* 2, 3–5, 6–7
economy and, *1:* 6
freedom and, *1:* 100–101
KGB (Soviet secret police) and,
1: 132
Lenin, Vladimir I., and, *1:* 6–7
Red Scare and, *1:* 101–3
Wilson, Woodrow, and, *1:* 4–5
Bolsheviks, *1:* 2, 3–5, 6–7, 120. *See
also* Bolshevik Revolution
Bonn (West Germany), *1:* 67
Books, *1:* 118

Boyce, Christopher, *1:* 154–55,
155 (ill.)
Brandt, Willy, *2:* 299, 305–6, 306
(ill.)
Brazil, *2:* 263–64, 324
Bretton Woods Conference, *1:* 13
Brezhnev Doctrine, *2:* 298, 300,
358
Brezhnev, Leonid, *1:* 172 (ill.); *2:*
305 (ill.), 331 (ill.)
Africa and, *2:* 325–27
Brezhnev Doctrine and, *2:* 300
Carter, Jimmy, and, *2:* 316, 330
Czechoslovakia and, *2:* 268
death of, *2:* 348
détente and, *2:* 310, 311
Dubcek, Alexander, and, *2:* 268
election of, *2:* 255–56
Ford, Gerald, and, *2:* 314
health of, *2:* 349
Helsinki Accords and, *2:* 314
human rights and, *2:* 323–24
nation building and, *2:* 325–27
Nixon, Richard M., and, *2:* 273,
304, 307
nuclear weapons and, *2:*
256–58, 304, 305, 323, 330,
336–37
Strategic Arms Limitation Talks
(SALT) and, *2:* 304, 323, 330
Brinkmanship
asymmetrical response and, *1:*
173–75
definition of, *1:* 167, 168
Eisenhower Doctrine and, *2:*
203–5
Eisenhower, Dwight D., and, *2:*
203–4
Kennedy, John F., and, *2:* 256
New Look and, *1:* 173–75
nuclear weapons and, *1:* 167,
168, 169, 184
British Broadcasting Corporation
(BBC), *1:* 143
Brown, Harold, *2:* 321, 322 (ill.)
*Brown v. Board of Education of
Topeka, 2:* 278–79
Brussels Pact, *1:* 37
Brzezinski, Zbigniew, *2:* 321,
327–28, 335
Bulganin, Nikolay, *1:* 177; *2:* 197
Bulgaria, *1:* 18
Bundy, McGeorge, *2:* 221

Burgess, Guy, *1:* 128, 142, 143
Bush, George, *2:* 363 (ill.)
  Baltic States and, *2:* 369
  China and, *2:* 362
  Cold War and, *2:* 347
  democracy and, *2:* 369
  economy and, *2:* 362
  election of, *2:* 356
  Germany and, *2:* 363–64
  Gorbachev, Mikhail, and, *2:*
    347, 356–57, 362–64, 368,
    369, 372
  Iran-Contra scandal and, *2:*
    332–33
  Iraq and, *2:* 365
  Kissinger, Henry, and, *2:* 356
  North Atlantic Treaty Organiza-
    tion (NATO) and, *2:* 363–64
  nuclear weapons and, *2:*
    356–57, 362, 368, 369–70,
    372
  Reagan, Ronald, and, *2:* 256
  Soviet collapse and, *2:* 369–70
  Soviet Union and, *2:* 369–70
  Strategic Air Command (SAC)
    and, *2:* 369
  Strategic Arms Reduction Talks
    (START) and, *2:* 357
  Yeltsin, Boris, and, *2:* 369
Bush, Vannevar, *1:* 83
Byrnes, James, *1:* 3, 16, 18, 20, 31

C

Cambodia, *1:* 181–82; *2:* 327, 328
Cambridge Spies, *1:* 135, 140–44
Cameras, *1:* 136, 137 (ill.)
Camp David, *2:* 201, 328–30, 329
  (ill.)
Campaign for Nuclear Disarma-
  ment (CND), *2:* 245–46
Candy, *1:* 66
Capitalism
  Cold War and, *1:* 25, 60
  communism and, *1:* 19, 23–24,
    25, 29, 33, 129, 169–70, 188;
    2: 215–16, 352
  definition of, *1:* 28, 56, 126,
    168; *2:* 192, 214, 298, 320,
    348
  democracy and, *2:* 299, 320

  economy and, *1:* 4, 27, 28, 56,
    58, 104, 126, 168, 169–70; *2:*
    192, 214, 216, 298, 299, 320,
    348, 372–73
  Germany and, *1:* 58–59
  Gorbachev, Mikhail, and, *2:*
    352
  Great Depression and, *1:* 104
  imperialism and, *2:* 208, 215
  Khrushchev, Nikita S., and, *1:*
    188
  Marshall Plan and, *1:* 31–32
  nation building and, *1:* 177,
    178–79
  property and, *1:* 4, 27, 28, 56,
    58, 101, 126, 128, 168, 169;
    2: 192, 214, 216, 298, 299,
    320, 348
  Russia and, *2:* 373
  Soviet Union and, *2:* 304, 352,
    361, 367–68
  Yeltsin, Boris, and, *2:* 367–68
Carmichael, Stokely, *2:* 276, 281
Cars, *1:* 137
Carter Doctrine, *2:* 336
Carter, Jimmy, *2:* 322 (ill.), 329
  (ill.), 331 (ill.)
  Afghanistan and, *2:* 335–36,
    337
  Africa and, *2:* 325–27
  Brezhnev, Leonid, and, *2:* 316,
    330
  Brown, Harold, and, *2:* 321
  Brzezinski, Zbigniew, and, *2:*
    321
  cabinet of, *2:* 321–22
  Camp David Accords and, *2:*
    328–30
  Carter Doctrine and, *2:* 336
  Central Intelligence Agency
    and, *2:* 322
  China and, *2:* 301, 327–28, 336
  containment and, *2:* 327
  Deng Xiaoping and, *2:* 328
  détente and, *2:* 322–23, 335–36
  dictatorship and, *2:* 322–23,
    324, 330–31
  Egypt and, *2:* 328–30
  election of, *2:* 315, 321, 335,
    337–38
  foreign affairs experience of, *2:*
    321
  Gromyko, Andrey, and, *2:* 326

human rights and, *2:* 315–16, 323–25

Iran and, *2:* 334–35

Israel and, *2:* 328–30

Latin America and, *2:* 324

military draft and, *2:* 336

Nicaragua and, *2:* 330–31

nuclear weapons and, *2:* 315, 323, 330, 336, 337

Pakistan and, *2:* 336

Palestine and, *2:* 328

Panama and, *2:* 263

Sakharov, Andrey, and, *2:* 315, 324

South Korea and, *2:* 324

Soviet Union and, *2:* 335–36

Strategic Arms Limitation Talks (SALT) and, *2:* 323, 330, 336

Third World and, *2:* 325

Trilateral Commission and, *2:* 321

Vance, Cyrus, and, *2:* 321

Casey, William, *2:* 332–33

Castillo Armas, Carlos, *1:* 169, 180

Castro Ruz, Fidel, *2:* 209 (ill.), 216 (ill.), 227 (ill.)

Bay of Pigs and, *2:* 217–18

Cuban Missile Crisis and, *2:* 229

Cuban Revolution and, *2:* 208–9, 214–16, 258

Dominican Republic and, *2:* 264

Khrushchev, Nikita S., and, *2:* 217

nation building and, *1:* 176

Panama and, *2:* 263

Soviet Union and, *2:* 209–10, 217, 258

Castro Ruz, Raúl, *2:* 219

Casualties. *See* Death

CDT. *See* Combined Development Trust (CDT)

Ceausescu, Nicolae, *2:* 360

CENTO. *See* Central Treaty Organization (CENTO)

Central Intelligence Agency (CIA)

Afghanistan and, *2:* 340

Bay of Pigs and, *2:* 217–18, 259

Carter, Jimmy, and, *2:* 322

Chile and, *2:* 308

Congo and, *2:* 208

Cuba and, *2:* 209, 217–18, 259

definition of, *1:* 126

espionage and, *1:* 34, 143, 145–46, 154, 158, 162

formation of, *1:* 34, 129–30

imperialism and, *2:* 208, 209, 217–18, 259, 269–70, 308, 322

Iran and, *2:* 332, 333

Iran-Contra scandal and, *2:* 332

location of, *1:* 131

McCarthy, Joseph R., and, *1:* 118

moles and, *1:* 154

nation building and, *1:* 176, 178, 179–80

reconnaissance and, *1:* 147, 150

Red Scare and, *1:* 118

U-2 and, *1:* 147

Vietnam War and, *2:* 269–70

Central Treaty Organization (CENTO), *2:* 204. *See also* Baghdad Pact

Chambers, Whittaker, *1:* 101, 112–13, 113–14

Chamoun, Camille N., *2:* 204

Chang Chu-Chung, *1:* 40 (ill.)

Charter of Paris, *2:* 366

Chechnya, *2:* 375, 375 (ill.)

Checkpoint Charlie, *1:* 75–76, 76 (ill.), 76–77

Cheka. *See* KGB (Soviet secret police)

Chemical warfare, *2:* 283–84, 290

Cheney Award, *1:* 66

Cheney, Richard, *2:* 356

Chernenko, Konstantin, *2:* 344, 345, 348, 349, 350

Chiang Kai-shek, *1:* 40 (ill.)

civil war and, *1:* 38, 41

government of, *1:* 46, 184; *2:* 205

Chief Intelligence Directorate of the General Staff of the Red Army. *See* GRU (Soviet military intelligence agency)

Children, *1:* 64 (ill.), 66

Chile, *2:* 264, 308, 324

China, *2:* 295 (ill.). *See also* People's Republic of China (PRC); Republic of China (ROC); Taiwan

Bretton Woods Conference and, *1:* 12

Brezhnev Doctrine and, *2:* 300

Bush, George, and, *2:* 362

Carter, Jimmy, and, *2:* 301, 327–28, 336

civil war in, *1:* 38–42, 111; *2:* 327

Communist Party in, *1:* 38–42, 111; *2:* 294–95

Cultural Revolution in, *2:* 266–67, 276, 277, 293–95, 295 (ill.)

democracy and, *2:* 362

détente and, *2:* 297

economy of, *1:* 52; *2:* 206

Egypt and, *2:* 202

Eisenhower, Dwight D., and, *1:* 184

espionage and, *1:* 158–59

Gorbachev, Mikhail, and, *2:* 356

Great Leap Forward and, *2:* 206

Ho Chi Minh and, *1:* 42

Kennedy, John F., and, *2:* 266

Kissinger, Henry, and, *2:* 300–301, 302

Korean War and, *1:* 46, 47, 48

Marshall, George C., and, *1:* 40–41

military and, *1:* 52

most-favored-nation trade status of, *2:* 336, 362

Nationalists in, *1:* 38–42

Nixon, Richard M., and, *2:* 300–302, 311, 312

nuclear weapons and, *1:* 185; *2:* 206, 246–47, 258, 266, 300, 373

Red Guard in, *2:* 266, 267 (ill.), 294, 295, 295 (ill.)

Red Scare and, *1:* 111

Soviet Union and, *1:* 40–42, 52, 111, 184–85; *2:* 205–6, 265–66, 300–301, 301–2, 327, 356

Stalin, Joseph, and, *1:* 40, 42

Taiwan and, *1:* 50, 183–85; *2:* 205, 266, 301

Tiananmen Square, *2:* 295 (ill.), 362

Truman, Harry S., and, *1:* 40, 42

United Nations and, *2:* 266, 327

Vietnam and, *1:* 42; *2:* 328

Vietnam War and, *2:* 270–71, 290, 301

World War II and, *1:* 12, 39

Chisholm, Janet, *1:* 152

Chou Enlai, *1:* 176, 184

Christmas bombing, *2:* 313

Churchill, Winston, *1:* 14 (ill.), 30 (ill.)

Big Three and, *1:* 2, 9–10, 29

elections and, *1:* 15, 171

espionage and, *1:* 140, 142

Iron Curtain and, *1:* 20–21

nuclear weapons and, *1:* 171

United Nations and, *1:* 12

Yalta agreements and, *1:* 2, 10, 11, 105

CIA. *See* Central Intelligence Agency (CIA)

Ciphers

Cambridge Spies and, *1:* 142

SIGINT and, *2:* 224

tradecraft and, *1:* 137

U.S. Navy and, *1:* 155–57

VENONA and, *1:* 127, 132–35

World War II and, *1:* 131

CIS. *See* Commonwealth of Independent States (CIS)

Civil rights. *See also* Freedom; Human rights

Civil Rights Act of 1964, *2:* 254, 282

Hoover, J. Edgar, and, *1:* 109

loyalty programs and, *1:* 107

Red Scare and, *1:* 110, 113, 115, 172

Civil Rights Act of 1964, *2:* 254, 282

Clark, Tom Campbell, *1:* 107

Cleaver, Eldridge, *2:* 281

Clegg, Hugh, *1:* 138 (ill.)

Clifford, Clark, *1:* 22; *2:* 273

Clifton, Chester, *1:* 72

Cloaks, *1:* 141

CND. *See* Campaign for Nuclear Disarmament (CND)

Coal, *1:* 64, 65, 65 (ill.)

Cohn, Roy, *1:* 118

Cold War, *1:* 106 (ill.)

balance in, *1:* 169; *2:* 374

beginning of, *1:* 1–3, 20, 23–24

Berlin airlift and, *1:* 66

capitalism and, *1:* 25, 60

causes of, *1:* 23–24, 29

communism and, *1:* 25, 60, 105

costs of, *2:* 372–73

death in, *2:* 372

definition of, *1:* 1–2, 28, 56, 80, 100, 126, 168; *2:* 192, 234, 252, 276, 298, 320, 348

democracy and, *1:* 25, 60, 105; *2:* 347

détente and, *2:* 297–300

economy and, *1:* 24–25

Eisenhower, Dwight D., and, *1:* 52

end of, *1:* 66, 160; *2:* 347, 351, 355, 357, 370–72

espionage and, *1:* 24, 127–29, 129–32

fear and, *1:* 105, 128–29

freedom and, *2:* 347

Germany and, *1:* 60–61

Khrushchev, Nikita S., and, *1:* 52

as Long Peace, *2:* 374

name of, *1:* 2–3

nuclear weapons and, *2:* 233–35

origins of, *1:* 3–25

peace and, *2:* 374

Red Scare and, *1:* 114

Stalin, Joseph, and, *1:* 25, 52

thaw of, *1:* 187–88; *2:* 192–93, 297–300

Truman, Harry S., and, *1:* 24, 25, 52

Colonialism. *See also* Imperialism

Africa and, *2:* 206–8

containment and, *2:* 206

France and, *2:* 206, 268–69

Great Britain and, *2:* 202, 206

Indochina and, *2:* 268–69

Middle East and, *2:* 202

Monroe Doctrine and, *1:* 186–87

nation building and, *1:* 176–78

Portugal and, *2:* 206

Combined Airlift Task Force, *1:* 65

Combined Development Trust (CDT), *1:* 143

Combined Policy Committee (CPC), *1:* 143

Comecon. *See* Council of Mutual Economic Assistance (Comecon)

Cominform. *See* Communist Information Bureau (Cominform)

Committee for State Security. *See* KGB (Soviet secret police)

Committee of 100, *2:* 245–46

Committee on the Present Danger, *2:* 338

Committee to Reelect the President (CREEP), *2:* 310

Commonwealth of Independent States (CIS), *2:* 370, 374–76

Communism. *See also* Communist Party

in Berlin, *1:* 57, 73

Bolshevik Revolution and, *1:* 2, 3–5, 6–7

capitalism and, *1:* 19, 23–24, 25, 29, 33, 129, 169–70, 188; *2:* 215–16, 352

Cold War and, *1:* 25, 60, 105

collapse of, *2:* 347, 357–60

in Cuba, *2:* 216–17

Cultural Revolution and, *2:* 277, 293–94

definition of, *1:* 2, 28, 56, 80, 99, 100, 126, 168; *2:* 192, 214, 234, 252, 276, 298, 320, 348

democracy and, *1:* 100–101, 128–29, 167–68; *2:* 215–16, 267–68, 319, 347

dictatorship and, *2:* 263

in East Germany, *1:* 30–31

in Eastern Bloc, *1:* 105

economy and, *1:* 2, 3, 27–29, 28, 56, 57, 80, 99, 100, 126, 128, 167, 168, 169–70; *2:* 192, 214, 215, 234, 251, 252, 262, 276, 290–92, 298, 299, 319–20, 348, 352

elections and, *1:* 2, 3, 27, 28, 56, 57, 80, 99, 100, 105, 126, 128, 168; *2:* 192, 214, 215, 234, 251, 252, 276, 298, 320, 348

fear of, *1:* 99–100; *2:* 372

freedom and, *1:* 5, 20–21, 77, 99, 100–101; *2:* 292

freedom of speech and, *2:* 292

freedom of the press and, *2:* 292

Fuchs, Klaus, and, *1:* 137–38

Gold, Harry, and, *1:* 138

Gorbachev, Mikhail, and, *2:* 352, 358

Great Depression and, *1:* 104

Greenglass, David, and, *1:* 139

Greenglass, Ruth, and, *1:* 139

Helsinki Accords and, *2:* 314, 315

Hoover, J. Edgar, on, *1:* 111

imperialism and, *2:* 254, 261–62, 268, 300, 307–8

in Indochina, *1:* 42

Johnson, Lyndon B., and, *2:* 270, 283

Kennedy, John F., and, *2:* 251–54, 262, 269

Khrushchev, Nikita S., on, *2:* 191

labor and, *1:* 104

Nixon, Richard M., and, *2:* 251, 311–12

in Poland, *1:* 57

property and, *1:* 2, 3, 7, 27–29, 28, 56, 57, 80, 99, 100, 104, 126, 128, 167, 168; *2:* 192, 214, 215, 234, 251, 252, 276, 298, 299, 319–20, 347, 348

Reagan, Ronald, and, *2:* 338

religion and, *1:* 2, 3, 28, 56, 80, 99, 100, 126, 128, 167, 168; *2:* 192, 214, 234, 252, 276, 292, 298, 320, 348

Rosenberg, Ethel, and, *1:* 139

Rosenberg, Julius, and, *1:* 139

in Soviet Union, *1:* 27–29; *2:* 299

teachers and, *1:* 115

in Third World, *1:* 176–78; *2:* 193

in Vietnam, *1:* 42

Vietnam War and, *2:* 283, 284, 290

in Yugoslavia, *1:* 51

Communist Information Bureau (Cominform), *1:* 33

Communist Party. *See also* Communism

Bolshevik Revolution and, *1:* 2, 4–5

in China, *1:* 38–42, 111; *2:* 294–95

coup attempt by, *2:* 368–69

Cultural Revolution and, *2:* 294–95

in Czechoslovakia, *1:* 32, 34–35, 37; *2:* 359–60

democracy and, *2:* 267–68

in East Germany, *2:* 358–59

elections and, *1:* 27

formation of, *1:* 2, 3, 7

in France, *1:* 31

Gorbachev, Mikhail, and, *2:* 347, 360–62, 367–68, 372

in Hungary, *2:* 358

in Italy, *1:* 31

Khrushchev, Nikita S., and, *1:* 170, 188; *2:* 241, 254–55, 260

Lenin, Vladimir I., and, *1:* 3, 101

in Poland, *1:* 11, 12–13; *2:* 357–58

in Romania, *2:* 360

in Russia, *1:* 3, 101; *2:* 369, 373

in Soviet Union, *1:* 120, 121, 170, 188; *2:* 241, 254–55, 260, 338, 347, 348–49, 360–62, 367–69, 372

Stalin, Joseph, and, *1:* 120, 121

Taiwan and, *1:* 184–85

Yeltsin, Boris, and, *2:* 369

Conference on Security and Co-operation in Europe (CSCE), *2:* 348, 365–66

Congo, *2:* 207–8, 326–27

Congress of People's Deputies, *2:* 360–61

Conservative Party, *1:* 15

Containment

Africa and, *2:* 325–27

Carter, Jimmy, and, *2:* 327

colonialism and, *2:* 206

definition of, *1:* 28

economy and, *1:* 28, 31–32, 35–36, 49–50, 51

Eisenhower, Dwight D., and, *2:* 202

Four Point Program and, *1:* 49–50

Germany and, *1:* 58

Iran and, *2:* 334

Kennan, George, and, *1:* 35–36

Korean War and, *1:* 46

Marshall Plan and, *1:* 31–32
Middle East and, *2:* 202
military and, *1:* 36, 44–45,
    48–49, 50
National Security Council
    (NSC) and, *1:* 28, 32, 44–45
North Atlantic Treaty Organiza-
    tion (NATO) and, *1:* 28, 168;
    2: 348
NSC-68 and, *1:* 28, 44–45
nuclear weapons and, *1:* 32, 92,
    93
politics and, *1:* 36
Reagan, Ronald, and, *2:* 340–41
Rio Pact and, *1:* 36
Southeast Asia Treaty Organiza-
    tion (SEATO) and, *1:* 168
strength and, *1:* 93
Truman, Harry S., and, *1:*
    29–30, 168–69, 173–74
Contras, *2:* 331–32, 332–33
Conventional Forces in Europe
    (CFE) treaty, *2:* 355, 365–66
CORONA, *1:* 150
Council of Foreign Ministers, *1:*
    17–18
Council of Mutual Economic As-
    sistance (Comecon), *1:*
    33–34
Counterculture, *2:* 276, 286–88
Counterintelligence, *1:* 125, 126
Country Joe and the Fish, *2:* 288
Country wall, *1:* 74. *See also*
    Berlin Wall
Cox, Edward, *2:* 311 (ill.)
Cox, Tricia, *2:* 311 (ill.)
CPC. *See* Combined Policy Com-
    mittee (CPC)
CREEP. *See* Committee to Reelect
    the President (CREEP)
"Crimes of Stalin," *1:* 188; *2:*
    192–93
Cruise missiles, *2:* 330
CSCE. *See* Conference on Security
    and Cooperation in Europe
    (CSCE)
Cuba, *2:* 218 (ill.), 220 (ill.), 223.
    See also Cuban Missile Crisis
    Bay of Pigs, *2:* 214, 217–18, 218
        (ill.), 252, 258–59
    Central Intelligence Agency
        (CIA) and, *2:* 209, 217–18,
        259

communism in, *2:* 216–17
Czechoslovakia and, *2:* 221
dictatorship and, *2:* 208, 215
economy of, *2:* 208, 209–10,
    215, 216–17
Eisenhower, Dwight D., and, *2:*
    208–10, 216–17, 258
elections in, *2:* 216
imperialism and, *2:* 217–19
nation building and, *1:* 180
nuclear weapons and, *2:*
    219–20, 248, 265
Operation Mongoose and, *2:*
    219
revolution in, *2:* 208–9,
    214–16, 258
Soviet Union and, *2:* 209–10,
    216, 217, 219–21, 258, 273,
    310
submarine base in, *2:* 310
Cuban Missile Crisis, *2:* 220 (ill.),
    223 (ill.), 227 (ill.)
    announcement of, *2:* 226–27
    Black Saturday, *2:* 228
    blockade and, *2:* 214, 225–26,
        227–29, 260
    definition of, *2:* 214, 252
    Ex-Comm and, *2:* 221–25
    installation of missiles, *2:*
        219–20, 260
    intelligence and, *1:* 150; *2:*
        221–25, 223 (ill.), 260
    Kennedy, John F., and, *2:*
        213–14, 221–27, 228, 229,
        260
    Khrushchev, Nikita S., and, *2:*
        219–20, 226, 227, 228, 229,
        260
    National Security Agency (NSA)
        and, *2:* 221, 224
    National Security Council
        (NSC) and, *2:* 221–25
    negotiations concerning, *2:*
        228–29, 260
    nuclear war and, *2:* 213–14,
        222, 226–28, 230, 239, 241,
        252, 254, 372
    Organization of American
        States (OAS) and, *2:* 226
    Strategic Air Command (SAC)
        and, *2:* 225
    Turkey and, *2:* 228, 229,
        229–30, 260

U.S. Air Force and, *2:* 225
United Nations and, *2:* 226, 227
Cultural Revolution, *2:* 266–67, 276, 277, 293–95, 295 (ill.)
Culture, *2:* 276, 286–88, 292–93, 338
Currency, *1:* 62
Czech National Committee, *1:* 34
Czechoslovakia, *2:* 359 (ill.)
    Communist Party in, *1:* 32, 34–35, 37; *2:* 359–60
    Cuba and, *2:* 221
    Czech National Committee and, *1:* 34
    democracy and, *2:* 359–60
    economy of, *2:* 267
    Egypt and, *2:* 202
    elections in, *2:* 360
    Germany and, *1:* 34
    Mao Zedong and, *2:* 300
    Marshall Plan and, *1:* 34
    Prague Spring and, *2:* 252, 267–68
    Soviet Union and, *1:* 34; *2:* 268
    Warsaw Pact and, *2:* 268

D

Daggers, *1:* 141
Davidenko, Viktor, *1:* 95
De Gaulle, Charles, *2:* 299, 306
Dead drops, *1:* 136, 152
Death. *See also* Execution
    Berlin airlift and, *1:* 63
    Berlin Wall and, *1:* 74
    in Cold War, *2:* 372
    in Great Terror, *1:* 120, 121, 123
    in Korean War, *1:* 48; *2:* 372
    in Vietnam War, *2:* 271, 273, 283–84, 290, 313, 372
    in World War II, *1:* 17, 57, 87–88
Declaration of Human Rights, *2:* 315
Declaration on Liberated Europe, *1:* 9
DEFCON, *2:* 226–27, 227–28, 229, 241
Defection, *1:* 163–64
Defense Condition. *See* DEFCON

Democracy
    Bush, George, and, *2:* 369
    capitalism and, *2:* 299, 320
    China and, *2:* 362
    Cold War and, *1:* 25, 60, 105; *2:* 347
    communism and, *1:* 100–101, 128–29, 167–68; *2:* 215–16, 267–68, 319, 347
    Communist Party and, *2:* 267–68
    Czechoslovakia and, *2:* 359–60
    definition of, *1:* 4; *2:* 192, 214, 276, 298, 320
    East Germany and, *2:* 358–59
    Eastern Bloc and, *2:* 357–60
    economy and, *2:* 262
    elections and, *1:* 4, 27, 58, 128, 167–68; *2:* 192, 214, 216, 276, 298, 299, 320
    freedom and, *1:* 5, 27, 100–101, 103, 104–5, 107–12, 128; *2:* 275–77
    freedom of speech and, *2:* 275–77
    Germany and, *1:* 58–59
    Gorbachev, Mikhail, and, *2:* 347
    Hungary and, *2:* 358
    imperialism and, *2:* 254, 261–62, 307–8
    Latin America and, *2:* 262, 263, 339
    perestroika and, *2:* 358
    Poland and, *2:* 357–58
    racism and, *2:* 282–83
    Reagan, Ronald, and, *2:* 315
    Red Scare and, *1:* 108–9
    religion and, *1:* 4, 101; *2:* 192
    Russia and, *2:* 373
    Soviet Union and, *2:* 347, 360–61, 367–68
    Yeltsin, Boris, and, *2:* 367–68
Democracy in America, 1: 1
Democratic National Committee (DNC), *2:* 298, 299, 310
Democratic Party, *1:* 48, 106–7
Democratic People's Republic of Korea (DPRK). *See* North Korea
Democratic Republic of Congo. *See* Congo

Democratic Republic of Vietnam, *1:* 42, 181

Deng Xiaoping, *2:* 321, 327–28

Denmark, *2:* 243

Dennis v. United States, 1: 112

De-Stalinization, *2:* 192–93, 265–66

Détente
Afghanistan and, *2:* 335–36
Brezhnev, Leonid, and, *2:* 310, 311
Carter, Jimmy, and, *2:* 322–23, 335–36
China and, *2:* 297
Cold War and, *2:* 297–300
definition of, *2:* 297, 298, 320
election of 1976 and, *2:* 314–15
Europe and, *2:* 299, 305–6, 337
Ford, Gerald, and, *2:* 311, 314, 315
Helsinki Accords and, *2:* 299–300, 313–14
Kissinger, Henry, and, *2:* 310, 311, 315
Nixon, Richard M., and, *2:* 310, 311, 314
Reagan, Ronald, and, *2:* 315, 338
Soviet Union and, *2:* 297–98, 304–5, 310, 311
Strategic Arms Limitation Talks (SALT) and, *2:* 297–98, 304–5
Vietnam War and, *2:* 312
Watergate scandal and, *2:* 299, 310–11
West Berlin and, *2:* 306

Dictatorship
Carter, Jimmy, and, *2:* 322–23, 324, 330–31
Chile and, *2:* 308
communism and, *2:* 263
Cuba and, *2:* 208, 215
Cultural Revolution and, *2:* 266–67, 293–95
Great Terror and, *1:* 120–23
Guatemala and, *1:* 180
Latin America and, *2:* 308, 324, 330–31, 339–40
Nicaragua and, *2:* 330–31
Reagan, Ronald, and, *2:* 339–40
U.S. protests and, *2:* 268, 275–77, 279, 280–81

Dies Committee. *See* House Un-American Activities Committee (HUAC)

Dies, Martin, *1:* 101, 104–5

DNC. *See* Democratic National Committee (DNC)

Dobrynin, Anatoly, *2:* 215, 226, 228–29

Dr. Strangelove, 2: 236, 236 (ill.)

Dominican Republic, *2:* 264–65

Double agents. *See* Moles

DPRK. *See* North Korea

Draft, *2:* 284–85, 336

Duarte, José Napoleón, *2:* 339

Dubcek, Alexander, *2:* 252, 253, 267–68

Dulles, Allen, *1:* 119 (ill.), 154, 176; *2:* 208

Dulles, John Foster, *1:* 175 (ill.), 180 (ill.)
asymmetrical response and, *1:* 173–74
brinkmanship and, *1:* 167–69
nation building and, *1:* 179
nuclear weapons and, *1:* 171

Dumbarton Oaks Conference, *1:* 12

Dzerzhinski, Feliks, *1:* 160, 161 (ill.)

E

East Berlin, *1:* 72 (ill.), 73 (ill.), 75 (ill.), 76 (ill.). *See also* Berlin
as capital city, *1:* 68
détente and, *2:* 306
government of, *1:* 69–71; *2:* 201
Soviet Union and, *1:* 69–71

East Germany, *1:* 60 (ill.)
communism in, *1:* 30–31
Communist Party in, *2:* 358–59
democracy in, *2:* 358–59
economy of, *1:* 68–69, 71, 73; *2:* 260
elections in, *2:* 359, 363
formation of, *1:* 30–31, 38, 55, 68
Gorbachev, Mikhail, and, *2:* 358–59
government of, *1:* 68
independence of, *2:* 201

Ostopolitik and, *2:* 305–6
refugees from, *1:* 68–69, 71, 73
Soviet Union and, *1:* 68, 69–71;
   2: 358–59
"Easter Parade," *1:* 66
Eastern Bloc. *See also* Iron Curtain
   composition of, *1:* 105
   democracy in, *2:* 357–60
   Great Terror in, *1:* 121
   Khrushchev, Nikita S., and, *2:*
      193–96
   reform in, *2:* 268
   Soviet Union and, *2:* 193–96,
      349
Economy
   African Americans and, *2:* 278,
      281, 282
   Alliance for Progress and, *2:*
      262–63
   of Berlin, *1:* 55–56, 65–66,
      68–69; *2:* 200
   Bolshevik Revolution and, *1:* 6
   Bush, George, and, *2:* 362
   capitalism and, *1:* 4, 27, 28, 56,
      58, 104, 126, 168, 169–70; *2:*
      192, 214, 216, 298, 299, 320,
      348, 372–73
   of China, *1:* 52; *2:* 206
   Cold War and, *1:* 24–25
   Commonwealth of Indepen-
      dent States (CIS) and, *2:* 370
   communism and, *1:* 2, 3,
      27–29, 28, 56, 57, 80, 99,
      100, 126, 128, 167, 168,
      169–70; *2:* 192, 214, 215,
      234, 251, 252, 262, 276,
      290–92, 298, 299, 319–20,
      348, 352
   containment and, *1:* 28, 31–32,
      35–36, 49–50, 51
   of Cuba, *2:* 208, 209–10, 215,
      216–17
   of Czechoslovakia, *2:* 267
   democracy and, *2:* 262
   of East Germany, *1:* 68–69, 71,
      73; *2:* 260
   of Germany, *1:* 57, 58–59; *2:*
      372
   global, *1:* 12, 13, 23–24, 25, 32
   Gorbachev, Mikhail, and, *2:*
      362
   of Great Britain, *1:* 17
   Great Depression and, *1:* 103–4

of Japan, *1:* 42; *2:* 372
Khrushchev, Nikita S., and, *2:*
   292
Marshall Plan and, *1:* 28, 31–32
Marxism and, *1:* 6
military and, *1:* 173–74; *2:* 275,
   277–78, 290
military-industrial complexes
   and, *2:* 275, 277–78, 290
Molotov Plan and, *1:* 28, 32–34
of Nicaragua, *2:* 332
Roosevelt, Franklin D., and, *1:*
   5, 12–13, 103–4
of Russia, *2:* 373
of Soviet Union, *1:* 17, 174–75;
   2: 277, 278, 290–92, 303,
   304, 337, 338, 343, 347–52,
   361, 362, 367–68
Third World and, *2:* 252, 254,
   307
of United States of America, *1:*
   17; *2:* 304, 338–39, 362,
   372–73
of West Germany, *1:* 62–66,
   67–68, 68–69
Yeltsin, Boris, and, *2:* 373
Yugoslavia and, *1:* 51
Edemski, Sergei A., *1:* 153
Egypt, *2:* 202–3, 204–5, 309–10,
   328–30
Einstein, Albert, *1:* 81, 94; *2:* 244
Eisenhower Doctrine, *2:* 192,
   203–5
Eisenhower, Dwight D., *1:* 119
   (ill.), 188 (ill.)
   brinkmanship and, *2:* 203–4
   Camp David and, *2:* 201
   China and, *1:* 184
   Cold War and, *1:* 52
   containment and, *2:* 202
   Cuba and, *2:* 208–10, 216–17,
      258
   Egypt and, *2:* 203
   Eisenhower Doctrine and, *2:*
      203–4
   election of, *1:* 48, 118, 170
   espionage and, *1:* 152; *2:* 198,
      240
   France and, *1:* 181
   Jordan and, *2:* 204
   Khrushchev, Nikita S., and, *1:*
      185–88; *2:* 193, 200–201,
      205, 210–12, 240

Korean War and, *1:* 48

Lebanon and, *2:* 204

loyalty programs and, *1:* 171

Malenkov, Georgy M., and, *1:* 170–71

McCarthy, Joseph R., and, *1:* 118

missiles and, *2:* 198–99

Mosaddeq, Mohammed, and, *1:* 178

nation building and, *1:* 177, 178–80

nuclear energy and, *2:* 241

nuclear weapons and, *1:* 70, 170–71; *2:* 200–201

Open Skies and, *1:* 186–87

reconnaissance and, *1:* 148, 150; *2:* 211–12

Suez War and, *2:* 203

Taiwan and, *1:* 184

Vietnam and, *1:* 181–82; *2:* 283

West Berlin and, *1:* 70

Elections

  of 1948, *1:* 107

  of 1952, *1:* 48, 117, 118

  of 1960, *1:* 70; *2:* 212, 251

  of 1964, *2:* 270

  of 1968, *2:* 273, 312

  of 1972, *2:* 312

  of 1976, *2:* 314–15

  of 1980, *2:* 335, 337–38

  of 1984, *2:* 344–45

  of 1996, *2:* 373

  of 2000, *2:* 373

  communism and, *1:* 2, 3, 27, 28, 56, 57, 80, 99, 100, 105, 126, 128, 168; *2:* 192, 214, 215, 234, 251, 252, 276, 298, 320, 348

  Communist Party and, *1:* 27

  in Cuba, *2:* 216

  in Czechoslovakia, *2:* 360

  democracy and, *1:* 4, 27, 58, 128, 167–68; *2:* 192, 214, 216, 276, 298, 299, 320

  in East Germany, *1:* 68; *2:* 359, 363

  in Great Britain, *1:* 15

  in Hungary, *2:* 358

  in Poland, *2:* 357–58

  Red Scare and, *1:* 106

  in Russia, *2:* 373

in Soviet Union, *1:* 52; *2:* 255–56, 360–61

in Vietnam, *1:* 182

in West Germany, *1:* 67, 173

Yalta agreements and, *1:* 105

El Salvador, *2:* 331, 339

Elsey, George, *1:* 22

Empire Ken, *2:* 203 (ill.)

Enola Gay, *1:* 87–88

"Enormous," *1:* 90–91

Espionage, *1:* 136, 137 (ill.), 146 (ill.), 149 (ill.). *See also* Intelligence; Moles; Reconnaissance

  Ames, Aldrich, and, *1:* 162

  Berlin tunnel and, *1:* 145–46, 146 (ill.)

  Boyce, Christopher, and, *1:* 154–55

  Cambridge Spies and, *1:* 135, 140–44

  Central Intelligence Agency (CIA) and, *1:* 34, 143, 145–46, 154, 158, 162

  China and, *1:* 158–59

  Churchill, Winston, and, *1:* 140, 142

  Cold War and, *1:* 24, 127–29, 129–32

  definition of, *1:* 125–26

  Eisenhower, Dwight D., and, *1:* 152; *2:* 198, 240

  execution and, *1:* 140, 152, 158, 162

  Federal Bureau of Investigation (FBI) and, *1:* 131, 143, 163

  Gorbachev, Mikhail, and, *1:* 157

  Gordievsky, Oleg, and, *1:* 157

  Great Britain and, *1:* 127, 131, 136–38, 140–44, 145–46, 151–52, 157

  GRU (Soviet military intelligence agency) and, *1:* 154

  Hanssen, Robert Philip, and, *1:* 162–63

  Hiss, Alger, and, *1:* 44, 135

  history of, *1:* 126–27

  human element of, *1:* 150–51

  Israel and, *1:* 159–60

  Jordan and, *1:* 161

  Kennedy, John F., and, *1:* 152

KGB (Soviet secret police) and, *1:* 140, 141–42, 144
Khrushchev, Nikita S., and, *2:* 240
Korean War and, *1:* 143
Lee, Andrew Daulton, and, *1:* 154–55
listening stations and, *1:* 144–45
Manhattan Project and, *1:* 88–89, 90–91, 115, 128, 138, 139
media and, *1:* 143
military and, *1:* 131
Military Intelligence, Department 5 and, *1:* 142
Military Intelligence, Department 6 and, *1:* 142, 143, 145–46, 152
National Security Agency (NSA) and, *1:* 131
nuclear weapons and, *1:* 9, 14, 19, 43, 88–89, 90–91, 108, 115, 128, 135–40, 143; *2:* 197–98
Philby, Kim, and, *1:* 140–41, 142, 143, 144
photography and, *1:* 137 (ill.), 147–50; *2:* 198, 222
Pollard, Jonathan Jay, and, *1:* 159–60
radio and, *1:* 143
Reagan, Ronald, and, *1:* 157
reconnaissance and, *1:* 147–50
Red Scare and, *1:* 44, 107, 112, 113–14
Roosevelt, Franklin D., and, *1:* 140, 142
satellites and, *1:* 150, 154–55
Sombolay, Albert, and, *1:* 161
Soviet Union and, *1:* 9, 14, 19, 43, 60, 88–89, 90–91, 127, 132, 136–45, 146, 148–50, 151, 152, 153, 154–58, 160, 162, 163–64
Stalin, Joseph, and, *1:* 140, 142–43
tradecraft of, *1:* 136–37, 141
Truman, Harry S., and, *1:* 140, 142
types of, *1:* 141
U-2 aircraft and, *1:* 127, 147–50; *2:* 211, 240, 310
U.S. Army and, *1:* 145–46, 153, 161

U.S. Navy and, *1:* 155–57
VENONA, *1:* 127, 132–35, 133 (ill.), 138, 140, 143
Walker spy ring and, *1:* 155–57
West Germany and, *1:* 60
World War I and, *1:* 126–27, 149
World War II and, *1:* 127, 131, 140, 142–43, 149; *2:* 224
Wu-Tai Chin, Larry, and, *1:* 158–59
Yurchenko, Vitaly, and, *1:* 158
Estonia, *2:* 361–62, 369
Ethiopia, *2:* 325–26, 326 (ill.)
Ethnic conflict, *2:* 315, 324, 374–76. *See also* Racism
Europe, *1:* 106 (ill.); *2:* 371 (ill.). *See also* specific countries and regions
détente and, *2:* 299, 305–6, 337
peace and, *2:* 364–67
European Recovery Program for Western Europe. *See* Marshall Plan
Ex-Comm, *2:* 221–25
Execution. *See also* Death
Cuban Revolution and, *2:* 208
Cultural Revolution and, *2:* 266–67, 294
espionage and, *1:* 140, 152, 158, 162
Great Terror and, *1:* 120, 121, 188; *2:* 192
KGB (Soviet secret police) and, *1:* 127, 132
Executive Order 9835, *1:* 107

F

FAPSI. *See* Federal Agency for Government Communications and Information (FAPSI)
Far East, *1:* 182; *2:* 265. *See also* specific countries
Farouk (king of Egypt), *2:* 202
Farrell, Thomas, *1:* 79–80
Fat Man, *1:* 85, 87–88, 90, 91
FBI. *See* Federal Bureau of Investigation (FBI)
Fear
Cold War and, *1:* 105, 128–29
of communism, *1:* 99–100; *2:* 372

McCarthyism and, *1:* 101, 116, 118

of nuclear war, *2:* 372, 374

Red Scare and, *1:* 11, 105

Fechter, Peter, *1:* 74

Federal Agency for Government Communications and Information (FAPSI), *1:* 160

Federal Bureau of Investigation (FBI), *1:* 130 (ill.). *See also* Intelligence

definition of, *1:* 126

espionage and, *1:* 131, 143, 163

formation of, *1:* 131

freedom and, *1:* 108–9

propaganda and, *1:* 108

Red Scare and, *1:* 100, 107, 108

Federal Republic of Germany. *See* East Germany

Fifth Amendment, *1:* 110, 113

Filatov, Anatoli Nikolaevich, *1:* 154

First Lightning, *1:* 90

Fission, *1:* 80, 81, 87

Ford, Gerald R., *2:* 310–11, 314, 315

Forester's Cabin, *1:* 90

Forrestal, James V., *1:* 22

Four Point Program, *1:* 49–50

Four-power Allied Control Council, *1:* 15

France

Berlin airlift and, *1:* 63

colonialism and, *2:* 206, 268–69

Communist Party in, *1:* 31

détente and, *2:* 306

Egypt and, *2:* 203

Germany and, *1:* 59

Indochina and, *1:* 42, 50, 181–82

North Atlantic Treaty Organization (NATO) and, *2:* 203, 306

nuclear weapons and, *2:* 247, 373

Suez War and, *2:* 203

Vietnam and, *1:* 42, 181–82; *2:* 283

Western European Union (WEU) and, *1:* 37

World War II and, *1:* 3; *2:* 364

Freedom. *See also* Civil rights; Human rights; specific freedoms

African Americans and, *2:* 275–76

Cold War and, *2:* 347

communism and, *1:* 5, 20–21, 77, 99, 100–101; *2:* 292

democracy and, *1:* 5, 27, 100–101, 103, 104–5, 107–12, 108–9, 128; *2:* 275–77

Federal Bureau of Investigation (FBI) and, *1:* 108–9

in Poland, *2:* 193–94

racism and, *2:* 275–76, 282–83

Red Scare and, *1:* 103, 104–5, 107–12

in Soviet Union, *2:* 292, 348, 351, 357, 367

Stalin, Joseph, and, *1:* 100, 120

Freedom of assembly, *1:* 109, 110

Freedom of religion, *1:* 128

communism and, *1:* 2, 3, 28, 56, 80, 99, 100, 126, 128, 167, 168; *2:* 192, 214, 234, 252, 276, 292, 298, 320, 348

democracy and, *1:* 4, 101, 128; *2:* 192

in Soviet Union, *2:* 357

Freedom of speech

communism and, *2:* 292

democracy and, *1:* 128; *2:* 275–77

glasnost and, *2:* 351

Hollywood Ten and, *1:* 110

Hoover, J. Edgar, and, *1:* 109

Freedom of the press, *2:* 252, 267–68, 292

Frei Montalvá, Eduardo, *2:* 264

Friedrichstrasse Crossing. *See* Checkpoint Charlie

Fuchs, Klaus, *1:* 90–91, 128, 137–38

Fusion, *1:* 88

G

Gardner, Meredith, *1:* 134–35

Garthoff, Raymond L., *1:* 125

General Intelligence Division, *1:* 103. *See also* Federal Bureau of Investigation (FBI)

Generation gap, *2:* 287

Georgia (USSR), *2:* 362

German Democratic Republic. *See* West Germany

Germany, *1:* 59 (ill.), 60 (ill.), 61
  (ill.). *See also* East Germany;
  West Germany
  Bush, George, and, *2:* 363–64
  capitalism and, *1:* 58–59
  Cold War and, *1:* 60–61
  containment and, *1:* 58
  Czechoslovakia and, *1:* 34
  democracy and, *1:* 58–59
  division of, *1:* 30–31, 38,
    66–69, 172–73
  economy of, *1:* 57, 58–59; *2:*
    372
  France and, *1:* 59
  Gorbachev, Mikhail, and, *2:*
    363–64
  government of, *1:* 15, 30–31,
    55, 57–59
  Great Britain and, *1:* 58–59
  money in, *1:* 62
  Nazi-Soviet Non-Aggression
    Pact and, *1:* 6–8
  North Atlantic Treaty Organiza-
    tion (NATO) and, *2:* 363–64
  nuclear weapons and, *1:* 81–82,
    85; *2:* 200–201, 364
  reparations and, *1:* 15–17, 57,
    58
  reunification of, *1:* 172–73,
    185–86; *2:* 201, 363–64
  Soviet Union and, *1:* 6–8, 29,
    57; *2:* 363–64
  transportation and, *1:* 68–69
  World War II and, *1:* 2, 3, 7–8,
    8–9, 10, 11, 15–17, 29, 55,
    56–57, 58–59; *2:* 364
Ghana, *2:* 255
Ginzburg, Vitali, *1:* 95
Glasnost, *2:* 348, 351, 367
Glenn, John H., Jr., *2:* 198
Gold, Harry, *1:* 91, 108, 138
Goldwater, Barry, *2:* 270
Golos, Jacob, *1:* 134
Gomulka, Wladyslaw, *2:* 193–94
Good Neighbor policy, *2:* 265
Gorbachev, Mikhail, *2:* 351 (ill.),
  354 (ill.), 363 (ill.)
  Afghanistan and, *2:* 355–56
  Bush, George, and, *2:* 347,
    356–57, 362–64, 368, 369,
    372
  capitalism and, *2:* 352
  China and, *2:* 356

communism and, *2:* 352, 358
Communist Party and, *2:* 347,
  360–62, 367–68, 372
Conventional Force Talks in
  Europe and, *2:* 355
coup attempt on, *2:* 368–69
democracy and, *2:* 347
East Germany and, *2:* 358–59
economy and, *2:* 362
election of, *2:* 350–51, 373
espionage and, *1:* 157
Estonia and, *2:* 361–62
freedom of religion and, *2:* 357
glasnost and, *2:* 348, 351, 367
Intermediate-range Nuclear
  Force (INF) treaty and, *2:* 372
Iraq and, *2:* 365
Lithuania and, *2:* 362, 367
military and, *2:* 355–56
Nobel Peace Prize for, *2:* 361
North Atlantic Treaty Organization (NATO) and, *2:* 363–64
nuclear weapons and, *2:* 351,
  352–55, 356–57, 364, 368,
  369–70, 372
perestroika and, *2:* 348, 351,
  361
Poland and, *2:* 358
Reagan, Ronald, and, *2:*
  352–56, 372
resignation of, *2:* 370
Shevardnadze, Eduard, and, *2:*
  351
Shultz, George, and, *2:* 352
Soviet collapse and, *2:* 367–69,
  370, 372
Soviet republics and, *2:* 361–62,
  367–68, 369, 370, 372
Strategic Arms Reduction Talks
  (START) and, *2:* 357, 372
Strategic Defense Initiative
  (SDI) and, *2:* 352, 354
Thatcher, Margaret, and, *2:* 352
United Nations and, *2:* 355,
  365
Yeltsin, Boris, and, *2:* 367–68,
  373
Gordievsky, Oleg, *1:* 157
Gottwald, Klement, *1:* 34–35
Goulart, João Belchio Marques, *2:*
  264
Gouzenko, Igor, *1:* 133–34, 135

Government Operations Committee, *1:* 118
Grand Alliance, *1:* 8–18. *See also* Big Three
Great Britain
    Berlin airlift and, *1:* 62–65
    Big Three and, *1:* 2, 9–10, 13
    Bretton Woods Conference and, *1:* 12
    colonialism and, *2:* 202, 206
    economy of, *1:* 17
    Egypt and, *2:* 202, 203
    elections in, *1:* 15
    espionage and, *1:* 127, 131, 136–38, 140–44, 145–46, 151–52, 157
    Germany and, *1:* 58–59
    Grand Alliance and, *1:* 8–9
    Greece and, *1:* 23
    Grenada and, *2:* 341
    intelligence and, *1:* 127
    Iran and, *1:* 20
    Jordan and, *2:* 204
    Middle East and, *2:* 202
    nuclear weapons and, *1:* 138; *2:* 245–46, 373
    Soviet Union and, *1:* 18–19
    Suez War and, *2:* 203
    Turkey and, *1:* 23
    Western European Union (WEU) and, *1:* 37
    World War II and, *1:* 2, 3, 8–11, 12, 13, 15, 17, 86; *2:* 364
Great Depression, *1:* 5, 103–4
Great Leap Forward, *2:* 206
Great Society, *2:* 254, 272, 282
Great Terror, *1:* 120–23, 188; *2:* 192–93
Greece, *1:* 2, 23
Green Berets, *2:* 256, 269
Greenglass, David, *1:* 91, 108, 138–40
Greenglass, Ruth, *1:* 91, 139
Greenland, *2:* 243
Grenada, *2:* 340 (ill.), 340–41
Gromyko, Andrey, *2:* 259 (ill.)
    Angola and, *2:* 326
    Carter, Jimmy, and, *2:* 326
    Cuban Missile Crisis and, *2:* 224–25
    Iran and, *1:* 20
    Kennedy, John F., and, *2:* 224–25
    replacement of, *2:* 351
    Strategic Arms Limitation Talks (SALT) and, *2:* 323
    Vance, Cyrus, and, *2:* 323
Groves, Leslie R., *1:* 79, 81, 83, 89
GRU (Soviet military intelligence agency)
    definition of, *1:* 126
    espionage and, *1:* 154
    formation of, *1:* 132
    Penkovsky, Oleg, and, *1:* 151, 152
    Yeltsin, Boris, and, *1:* 160
Guantánamo naval base, *2:* 210
Guatemala, *1:* 179–80
Gulag, *1:* 120–21. *See* Labor camps
Gulf of Tonkin Resolution, *2:* 270
Guyana, *2:* 265

H

Haile Selassie (emperor of Ethiopia), *2:* 325
Hair, 2: 287
Hall, Theodore Alvin, *1:* 90–91
Halvorsen, Gail S., *1:* 66
Hanssen, Robert Philip, *1:* 162–63, 163 (ill.)
Harriman, William Averell, *1:* 22, 25
Hatch Act, *1:* 104
Hatch, Carl A., *1:* 104
Havel, Václav, *2:* 360
Head Start, *2:* 282
Helsinki Accords, *2:* 299–300, 313–14, 315
Hidden weapons, *1:* 136
Hiroshima
    bombing of, *1:* 86–87, 88, 135; *2:* 219, 241
    death in, *1:* 17, 87
Hiss, Alger, *1:* 114 (ill.)
    conviction of, *1:* 101, 114
    espionage and, *1:* 44, 135
    Red Scare and, *1:* 44, 113–14
Hitler, Adolf, *1:* 8 (ill.)
    defeat of, *1:* 48
    military campaigns of, *1:* 6, 105
    nuclear weapons and, *1:* 81–82
Ho Chi Minh, *1:* 42, 181; *2:* 269, 283
Hollywood Ten, *1:* 100, 110, 111 (ill.)

Holmes, Oliver Wendell, *1:* 113
Holton, Gerald, *2:* 246
Homing pigeons, *1:* 149 (ill.), 149
Honecker, Erich, *2:* 358–59
Hoover, J. Edgar, *1:* 109 (ill.), 129
    (ill.), 130 (ill.)
  civil rights and, *1:* 109
  on communism, *1:* 111
  death of, *1:* 109
  freedom and, *1:* 108–9
  House Un-American Activities
    Committee (HUAC), and, *1:*
    108
  Kennedy, John F., and, *1:* 109
  King, Martin Luther, Jr., and, *1:*
    109
  Masters of Deceit, 1: 108
  propaganda and, *1:* 108
  Red Scare and, *1:* 103, 107, 108,
    111
  Roosevelt, Franklin D., and, *1:*
    108
  Vietnam War and, *1:* 109
Hopkins, Harry, *1:* 12
Hot Line Agreement, *2:* 230,
    241–44
House Un-American Activities
    Committee (HUAC), *1:* 112
    (ill.)
  Chambers, Whittaker, and, *1:*
    113, 114
  definition of, *1:* 100
  function of, *1:* 100
  Hiss, Alger, and, *1:* 113
  Hollywood Ten and, *1:* 100, 110
  Hoover, J. Edgar, and, *1:* 108
  McCarthy, Joseph R., and, *1:*
    44, 117
  questioning by, *1:* 99, 107–10
  Red Scare and, *1:* 44, 99–100
  World War II and, *1:* 104–5
Human rights, *2:* 314, 315–16,
    322, 323–25, 339. *See also*
    Civil rights; Freedom
Humphrey, Hubert, *2:* 273, 312
Hungary, *2:* 194–96, 195 (ill.),
    358, 366
Hussein (king of Jordan), *2:* 204
Hussein, Saddam, *2:* 341, 365
Hydrogen bombs, *1:* 96 (ill.). *See
    also* Nuclear weapons
  definition of, *1:* 88

development of, *1:* 93–95, 171;
    2: 244
testing of, *1:* 95–96; *2:* 233,
    236, 244–45

I

"I-Feel-Like-I'm-Fixin'-to-Die
    Rag," *2:* 288
"I Have a Dream," *2:* 279–80
ICBMs. *See* Intercontinental bal-
    listic missiles (ICBMs)
IMF. *See* International Monetary
    Fund (IMF)
Imperialism. *See also* Colonialism
  Brezhnev Doctrine and, *2:* 298
  capitalism and, *2:* 208, 215
  Central Intelligence Agency
    (CIA) and, *2:* 208, 209,
    217–18, 259, 269–70, 308,
    322
  communism and, *2:* 254,
    261–62, 268, 300, 307–8
  in Cuba, *2:* 217–19, 259
  definition of, *1:* 33; *2:* 252
  democracy and, *2:* 254, 261–62,
    307–8
  in Latin America, *1:* 36; *2:*
    261–65
  Marshall Plan and, *1:* 31–32
  Molotov Plan and, *1:* 33
  Monroe Doctrine and, *1:* 186–87
  nation building and, *1:* 168,
    175–82
  Soviet Union and, *1:* 33; *2:* 298,
    300
  United States of America and,
    1: 31–32, 33; *2:* 208, 209,
    217–18, 259, 269–70, 308,
    322
  Vietnam War and, *2:* 269–70
India, *1:* 177; *2:* 336, 373
Indochina, *1:* 42, 50, 181–82; *2:*
    268–73. *See also* specific
    countries
INF. *See* Intermediate-range Nu-
    clear Force (INF) treaty
Intelligence, *1:* 133 (ill.); *2:* 223
    (ill.). *See also* Espionage; Re-
    connaissance
  Berlin Wall and, *1:* 72

Cuban Missile Crisis and, *1:* 150; *2:* 221–25, 260
definition of, *1:* 125, 127
freedom and, *1:* 108–9
Great Britain and, *1:* 127
listening stations and, *1:* 144–45
methods of, *1:* 141
nuclear weapons and, *1:* 90, 135
Reagan, Ronald, and, *1:* 159
Red Scare and, *1:* 107, 108, 115–16, 159
Soviet Union and, *1:* 160
Yeltsin, Boris, and, *1:* 160
Inter-American Committee, *2:* 262
Inter-American Development Bank, *1:* 177
Inter-American Treaty of Reciprocal Assistance, *1:* 36
Intercontinental ballistic missiles (ICBMs), *2:* 239 (ill.), 257 (ill.), 307 (ill.)
capability of, *2:* 237, 239, 244
development of, *2:* 235
operation of, *2:* 238–39
second-strike strategies and, *2:* 257–58
Strategic Arms Limitation Talks (SALT) and, *2:* 303–4, 330
Intermediate-range Nuclear Force (INF) treaty, *2:* 354–55, 372
International Monetary Fund (IMF), *1:* 13, 22
International Space Station (ISS), *2:* 199
Iran
Byrnes, James, and, *1:* 20
Carter, Jimmy, and, *2:* 334–35
containment and, *2:* 334
government of, *2:* 332–34
Great Britain and, *1:* 20
Gromyko, Andrey, and, *1:* 20
hostage crisis in, *2:* 332–35
Iran-Contra scandal and, *2:* 332–33
Iraq and, *2:* 341–42
nation building and, *1:* 178–79; *2:* 308
Nixon, Richard M., and, *2:* 308
nuclear weapons and, *2:* 373

oil and, *1:* 20, 21–22, 178; *2:* 334
Soviet Union and, *1:* 18–19, 20, 21–22
Iraq
Bush, George, and, *2:* 365
Gorbachev, Mikhail, and, *2:* 365
Iran and, *2:* 341–42
Kuwait and, *2:* 365
nuclear weapons and, *2:* 373
oil and, *2:* 204, 365
Soviet Union and, *2:* 341–42, 365
United Arab Republic (UAR) and, *2:* 204
United Nations and, *2:* 365
Iron Curtain, *1:* 20–21. *See also* Eastern Bloc
Isolationism
definition of, *1:* 2, 28
election of 1952 and, *1:* 48
of Soviet Union, *1:* 5, 22
of United States of America, *1:* 5, 6, 12, 19–20, 37, 48
Israel. *See also* Jews
Camp David Accords and, *2:* 328–30
Carter, Jimmy, and, *2:* 328–30
Egypt and, *2:* 202–3, 309–10, 328–30
espionage and, *1:* 159–60
formation of, *2:* 202, 328
October War and, *2:* 309–10
Palestine and, *2:* 328–29, 341
Reagan, Ronald, and, *1:* 159
Suez War and, *2:* 203
ISS. *See* International Space Station (ISS)
Italy, *1:* 31

J

Jackson, Henry "Scoop," *2:* 314–15, 323, 330
Jakes, Milos, *2:* 360
Japan
economy of, *1:* 42; *2:* 372
government of, *1:* 42
Korea and, *1:* 45
MacArthur, Douglas, and, *1:* 42
Potsdam Declaration and, *1:* 17
Soviet Union and, *1:* 10, 17

World War II and, *1:* 2, 8, 10,
12, 17, 39, 50, 86–88, 104–5
Jaruzelski, Wojciech, *2:* 357
JEN. *See* Junta de Energía Nuclear
(JEN)
Jews, *1:* 121–23; *2:* 315, 324,
328–30. *See also* Israel
Job Corps, *2:* 282
Joe-1, *1:* 89–90
Joe-4, *1:* 95
John Paul II (pope), *2:* 357
Johnson, Louis, *1:* 95
Johnson, Lyndon B., *2:* 261 (ill.),
272 (ill.)
Alliance for Progress and, *2:*
263
communism and, *2:* 270, 283
election of, *2:* 270
Great Society of, *2:* 254, 272,
282
Kosygin, Aleksy, and, *2:* 247
Latin America and, *2:* 263–65
nuclear weapons and, *2:* 247,
258
Panama and, *2:* 263
Vietnam War and, *2:* 270,
271–73, 282, 283, 289–90
Jordan, *1:* 161; *2:* 204
Jornada del Muerto, 1: 79
Junta de Energía Nuclear (JEN), *2:*
242–43

K

Kádár, János, *2:* 196, 358
Kassem, Abdul Karim, *2:* 204
Kazakhstan, *2:* 370, 373
Kennan, George F., *1:* 19 (ill.),
19–20, 35–36; *2:* 356
Kennedy, John F., *2:* 227 (ill.), 229
(ill.), 230 (ill.), 259 (ill.), 261
(ill.)
Alliance for Progress and, *2:*
262–63
Bay of Pigs and, *2:* 217, 218,
258–59
Berlin and, *1:* 72–73, 76–77; *2:*
259–60
brinkmanship and, *2:* 256
China and, *2:* 266
communism and, *2:* 251–54,
262, 269

Cuban Missile Crisis and, *2:*
213–14, 221–27, 228, 229,
260
death of, *2:* 254, 270
election of, *1:* 70; *2:* 212, 251
espionage and, *1:* 152
Gromyko, Andrey, and, *2:*
224–25
Hoover, J. Edgar, and, *1:* 109
Khrushchev, Nikita S., and, *1:*
70–71; *2:* 226, 228, 251–54,
259–61
McNamara, Robert S., and, *2:*
253
military and, *2:* 256
nation building and, *1:* 177
nuclear weapons and, *2:* 246,
256–58
Operation Mongoose and, *2:*
219
Peace Corps and, *2:* 255
Rusk, Dean, and, *2:* 253
second-strike strategies and, *2:*
256–58
space race and, *2:* 198–99
Vietnam War and, *2:* 269–70,
283
West Berlin and, *1:* 70–71
Kennedy, Robert F., *2:* 215, 222,
228–29, 229 (ill.)
Kent State University, *2:* 290
KGB (Soviet secret police)
Ames, Aldrich, and, *1:* 162
atomic spies and, *1:* 140
Berlin tunnel and, *1:* 146
Boyce, Christopher, and, *1:*
154–55
Cambridge Spies and, *1:*
141–42, 144
definition of, *1:* 127
Dzerzhinski, Feliks, and, *1:* 160
formation of, *1:* 132
Hanssen, Robert Philip, and, *1:*
163
Mitrokhin, Vasili, and, *1:*
163–64
Penkovsky, Oleg, and, *1:* 151,
152
Stalin, Joseph, and, *1:* 127, 132
Walker spy ring and, *1:* 156–57
Yurchenko, Vitaly, and, *1:* 158
Khomeini, Ayatollah Ruhollah, *2:*
333–35, 334 (ill.)

Khrushchev, Nikita S., *1:* 72 (ill.),
    188 (ill.); *2:* 211 (ill.), 227
    (ill.), 259 (ill.)
  Africa and, *2:* 325
  Berlin and, *1:* 69–71, 73; *2:*
    200–201, 259–60
  Camp David and, *2:* 201
  capitalism and, *1:* 188
  Castro Ruz, Fidel, and, *2:* 217
  Cold War and, *1:* 52
  on communism, *2:* 191
  Communist Party and, *1:* 170,
    188; *2:* 241, 254–55, 260
  Cuban Missile Crisis and, *2:*
    219–20, 226, 227, 228, 229,
    260
  culture and, *2:* 292–93
  Eastern Bloc and, *2:* 193–96
  economy and, *2:* 292
  Eisenhower, Dwight D., and, *1:*
    185–88; *2:* 193, 200–201,
    205, 210–12, 240
  election of, *1:* 52; *2:* 196–97
  espionage and, *2:* 240
  Hungary and, *2:* 195–96
  Kennedy, John F., and, *1:*
    70–71; *2:* 226, 228, 251–54,
    259–61
  Macmillan, Harold, and, *2:* 191
  Mao Zedong and, *2:* 265–66
  nation building and, *1:* 177; *2:*
    325
  nuclear energy and, *2:* 241
  nuclear weapons and, *1:* 70,
    174–75; *2:* 200–201
  Penkovsky, Oleg, and, *1:* 151
  Poland and, *2:* 193–94
  reconnaissance and, *1:* 150
  removal of, *2:* 254–55
  Stalin, Joseph, and, *1:* 188; *2:*
    192–93, 265–66, 292
  strength and, *1:* 70
  Third World and, *2:* 210
  threats and, *1:* 69–71
  U-2 aircraft and, *2:* 211–12
  Ulbricht, Walter, and, *1:* 71, 73
  United Nations and, *2:* 191, 210
Kim Il Sung, *1:* 45, 46
King, Martin Luther, Jr., *1:* 109; *2:*
    277, 279–81, 282 (ill.), 282
Kirkpatrick, Jeane, *2:* 339, 341
Kissinger, Henry, *2:* 303 (ill.)
  Bush, George, and, *2:* 356

Chile and, *2:* 308
China and, *2:* 300–301, 302
détente and, *2:* 310, 311, 315
Ford, Gerald, and, *2:* 314
nuclear weapons and, *2:* 305
Palestine and, *2:* 328
Soviet Union and, *2:* 302–3, 304
Vietnam War and, *2:* 312
Zhou Enlai and, *2:* 301
Kohl, Helmut, *2:* 356, 364
Korea, *1:* 45–46. *See also* Korean
    War; North Korea; South
    Korea
Korean Airlines tragedy, *2:* 343
Korean War, *1:* 47 (ill.), 50 (ill.)
  beginning of, *1:* 28, 46
  China and, *1:* 46, 47, 48
  conduct of, *1:* 45–48
  death in, *1:* 48; *2:* 372
  definition of, *1:* 28
  end of, *1:* 48, 169
  espionage and, *1:* 143
  implications of, *1:* 48–52
  nuclear weapons and, *1:* 47, 48
Kosygin, Aleksy N., *2:* 247,
    255–56
Ku Klux Klan, *1:* 109
Kubrick, Stanley, *2:* 236
Kung, H. H., *1:* 40 (ill.)
Kurchatov, Igor, *1:* 81, 89–90, 91;
    2: 244–45
Kurchatov, Marina, *1:* 90
Kuwait, *2:* 365

L

Labor, *1:* 6, 104, 108; *2:* 193–94,
    357–58
Labor camps, *1:* 120–21
Labour Party, *1:* 15
Laika, *2:* 196
Lamphere, Robert, *1:* 135,
    136–37, 138 (ill.)
Laos, *1:* 181–82
Latin America
  Alliance for Progress and, *2:*
    252, 262–63
  Carter, Jimmy, and, *2:* 324
  composition of, *2:* 193, 261, 324
  democracy and, *2:* 262, 263, 339
  dictatorship and, *2:* 308, 324,
    330–31, 339–40

Good Neighbor policy in, *2:* 265

human rights and, *2:* 324

imperialism in, *1:* 36; *2:* 261–65

Johnson, Lyndon B., and, *2:* 263–65

military and, *2:* 263

Monroe Doctrine and, *1:* 187

nation building and, *1:* 179–80; *2:* 261–65, 339–41

nuclear weapons and, *2:* 248

Reagan, Ronald, and, *2:* 339–41

Roosevelt, Franklin D., and, *2:* 265

Latin American Nuclear-Free Zone Treaty, *2:* 248, 258, 265

Latvia, *2:* 369

Leahy, William, *1:* 25

Lebanon, *2:* 204

Lee, Andrew Daulton, *1:* 154–55

LeMay, Curtis E., *1:* 93, 93 (ill.); *2:* 237–38

Lenin, Vladimir I., *1:* 4 (ill.), 7 (ill.), 102 (ill.)

  Bolshevik Revolution and, *1:* 3, 6

  Communist Party and, *1:* 3, 101

  death of, *1:* 7

  government of, *1:* 7

  Marxism and, *1:* 6

  tomb of, *2:* 355

Leningraders, *1:* 121

Liberty. *See* Freedom

Lilienthal, David, *1:* 93–94, 94 (ill.), 95

Limited Test-Ban Treaty of 1963, *2:* 234, 244, 247, 261

Lin Sen, *1:* 40 (ill.)

Lippmann, Walter, *1:* 3

Listening devices, *1:* 137

Listening stations, *1:* 144–45

Lithuania, *2:* 362, 367, 369

Little Boy, *1:* 85, 86 (ill.), 86–87, 88

Lock picks, *1:* 136

Lockheed Corporation, *1:* 147

Long Peace, *2:* 374

"Long Telegram," *1:* 19–20

Los Alamos National Laboratory, *1:* 85 (ill.)

  hydrogen bombs and, *1:* 95

  management of, *1:* 92

  Manhattan Project and, *1:* 83–85, 87, 90

Los Arzamas, *1:* 89–90

Loyalty programs

  civil rights and, *1:* 107

  Red Scare and, *1:* 104, 107, 108, 112, 115, 171

  Stalin, Joseph, and, *1:* 120

Lucas, Scott, *1:* 117

Lumumba, Patrice, *1:* 176; *2:* 193, 207, 208

Luxembourg, *1:* 37

M

MacArthur, Douglas, *1:* 29, 42, 46–47, 49 (ill.)

Maclean, Donald, *1:* 128, 140, 142–43, 143 (ill.)

Macmillan, Harold, *1:* 175 (ill.); *2:* 191

MAD. *See* Mutual assured destruction (MAD)

Malcolm X, *2:* 281

Malenkov, Georgy M., *1:* 52, 169, 170 (ill.), 170–71

"Man of the Year" award, *2:* 361

Manhattan Project

  definition of, *1:* 80

  development by, *1:* 9, 79–80, 83–84, 87, 135; *2:* 244

  espionage and, *1:* 88–89, 90–91, 115, 128, 138, 139

  testing by, *1:* 13–14, 80–81, 85–86, 87

Mao Zedong, *1:* 41 (ill.); *2:* 267 (ill.), 303 (ill.)

  children of, *1:* 48

  civil war and, *1:* 39–42; *2:* 327

  Cultural Revolution of, *2:* 266–67, 276, 277, 293–95, 295 (ill.)

  Czechoslovakia and, *2:* 300

  death of, *2:* 327

  Khrushchev, Nikita S., and, *2:* 265–66

  Kissinger, Henry, and, *2:* 301, 302

  Nixon, Richard M., and, *2:* 301

  nuclear weapons and, *2:* 206

  ping-pong and, *2:* 302

  Red Scare and, *1:* 111

Stalin, Joseph, and, *1:* 40
Truman, Harry S., and, *1:* 40, 42
March on Washington, *2:* 279–80, 280 (ill.)
Marshall, George C.
  China and, *1:* 40–41
  Marshall Plan and, *1:* 31
  McCarthy, Joseph R., and, *1:* 44, 117
  Red Scare and, *1:* 44
  Truman Doctrine and, *1:* 23
Marshall Plan, *1:* 28, 31–32, 34, 67
Martin, Arthur, *1:* 144
Marx, Karl, *1:* 6
Marxism, *1:* 6
Masters of Deceit, 1: 108
Mazowiecki, Tadeusz, *2:* 358
McCarthy Committee, *1:* 118
McCarthy, Joseph R., *1:* 117 (ill.), 119 (ill.)
  censure of, *1:* 118, 172
  Central Intelligence Agency (CIA) and, *1:* 118
  death of, *1:* 118
  Eisenhower, Dwight D., and, *1:* 118
  elections of, *1:* 116, 118
  House Un-American Activities Committee (HUAC) and, *1:* 44, 117
  Marshall, George C., and, *1:* 44, 117
  Red Scare and, *1:* 43–44, 101, 106, 116–19, 171–72
  Truman, Harry S., and, *1:* 117
McCarthyism, *1:* 44, 99–100, 101, 116–20, 172. *See also* Red Scare
McCloy, John J., *1:* 22
McCord, James W., Jr., *2:* 310
McCormick, Robert, *1:* 106
McDonald, County Joe, *2:* 288, 288 (ill.)
McFarlane, Robert, *2:* 332–33
McNamara, Robert S., *2:* 222, 253, 272 (ill.), 273
McNeil, Hector, *1:* 143
Media
  espionage and, *1:* 143
  Federal Bureau of Investigation (FBI) and, *1:* 108

Hoover, J. Edgar, and, *1:* 108
human rights and, *2:* 323
Red Scare and, *1:* 100, 108, 110, 118
Medicare, *2:* 282
Message carriers, *1:* 136
Middle East, *2:* 366 (ill.). *See also* specific countries
  Camp David Accords and, *2:* 328–30
  colonialism and, *2:* 202
  composition of, *2:* 201
  containment and, *2:* 202
  Eisenhower Doctrine and, *2:* 192, 203–5
  Great Britain and, *2:* 202
  nation building and, *1:* 178–79; *2:* 202–5
  oil and, *2:* 201–2, 205
  Reagan, Ronald, and, *2:* 341–42
  Soviet Union and, *2:* 204–5
Military. *See also* specific branches
  asymmetrical response and, *1:* 173–74
  buildup of, *1:* 144; *2:* 336
  Carter, Jimmy, and, *2:* 336
  of China, *1:* 52
  containment and, *1:* 36, 44–45, 48–49, 50
  Conventional Force Talks in Europe and, *2:* 355
  Conventional Forces in Europe (CFE) treaty and, *2:* 365–66
  Cuban Missile Crisis and, *2:* 226–27
  defense alliances and, *1:* 176
  draft, *2:* 284–85, 336
  economy and, *1:* 173–74; *2:* 275, 277–78, 290
  espionage and, *1:* 131
  Gorbachev, Mikhail, *2:* 355–56
  Kennedy, John F., and, *2:* 256
  Latin America and, *2:* 263
  North Atlantic Treaty Organization (NATO) and, *1:* 37–38; *2:* 365–66
  Reagan, Ronald, and, *2:* 338–39
  Red Scare and, *1:* 115–16
  of Soviet Union, *1:* 50–52; *2:* 355–56
  Stalin, Joseph, and, *1:* 50–52
  Warsaw Pact and, *2:* 365–66
  in West Berlin, *1:* 69–71

of West Germany, *1:* 185
Military-industrial complexes, *2:* 275, 276, 277–78, 286, 290
Military Intelligence, Department 5, *1:* 127, 131, 142
Military Intelligence, Department 6
  definition of, *1:* 127
  espionage and, *1:* 136–37, 142, 143, 145–46, 152
  function of, *1:* 131
MIRVs. *See* Multiple independently targetable reentry vehicles (MIRVs)
Missiles, *2:* 223 (ill.), 239 (ill.), 257 (ill.), 307 (ill.). *See also* Cuban Missile Crisis
  antiballistic missiles, *2:* 247, 258, 303
  cruise missiles, *2:* 330
  early warning systems and, *2:* 239 (ill.), 240
  intercontinental ballistic missiles (ICBMs), *2:* 235, 237, 238–39, 239 (ill.), 244, 257 (ill.), 257–58, 303–4, 307 (ill.), 330
  multiple independently targetable reentry vehicles (MIRVs), *2:* 303, 304
  nuclear weapons and, *2:* 196–99, 235–37, 238–39, 244
  race for, *2:* 196–99
  reconnaissance and, *2:* 197–98
  second-strike strategies and, *2:* 257–58
  Strategic Defense Initiative (SDI) and, *2:* 342, 344, 352, 354
  submarines and, *2:* 239–40, 244
Mitrokhin, Vasili, *1:* 163–64
Mitterand, François, *2:* 356
Moldavia, *1:* 7
Moles. *See also* Espionage
  Ames, Aldrich, *1:* 162
  atomic spies and, *1:* 136–37
  Cambridge Spies and, *1:* 140–44
  Central Intelligence Agency (CIA) and, *1:* 154
  definition of, *1:* 125–26, 127
  detecting, *1:* 153–54
  Gordievsky, Oleg, *1:* 157

Hanssen, Robert Philip, *1:* 162–63
  human element of, *1:* 150
  Mitrokhin, Vasili, *1:* 163–64
  Penkovsky, Oleg, *1:* 151–52
  Sombolay, Albert, *1:* 161
  VENONA and, *1:* 133–35
  Whalen, William Henry, *1:* 153
  Wu-Tai Chin, Larry, *1:* 158–59
  Yurchenko, Vitaly, *1:* 158
Molotov Plan, *1:* 28, 32–34
Molotov, Vyacheslav M., *1:* 11, 15, 33
Monarchy, *1:* 6
Mondale, Walter, *2:* 345
Money, *1:* 62
Monroe Doctrine, *1:* 36, 186–87, 187 (ill.)
Monroe, James, *1:* 186–87
Moody, Juanita, *2:* 225
Moon, *2:* 199
Mosaddeq, Mohammed, *1:* 169, 178
Movies, *1:* 100, 108, 110; *2:* 236
Mujahedeen, *2:* 335, 336, 340
Multiple independently targetable reentry vehicles (MIRVs), *2:* 303, 304
Murrow, Edward R., *1:* 118
Music, *2:* 287–88
Mutual assured destruction (MAD), *2:* 234–35, 236, 305, 342–43, 374

N

Nagasaki, *1:* 17, 18 (ill.), 87–88, 135
Nagy, Imre, *2:* 194, 196
Napalm, *2:* 283–84, 284 (ill.)
NASA. *See* National Aeronautics and Space Administration (NASA)
Nasser, Gamal Abdel, *2:* 193, 202–3, 204 (ill.), 204–5
Nation building
  Africa and, *2:* 206–8, 325–27
  Angola and, *2:* 308
  Brezhnev, Leonid, and, *2:* 325–27
  Chile and, *2:* 308
  colonialism and, *1:* 176–78

definition of, *1:* 168
Eisenhower, Dwight D., and, *1:* 177, 178–80
Iran and, *1:* 178–79; *2:* 308
Kennedy, John F., and, *1:* 177
Khrushchev, Nikita S., and, *1:* 177; *2:* 325
Latin America and, *1:* 179–80; *2:* 261–65, 339–41
Middle East and, *1:* 178–79; *2:* 202–5
Nicaragua and, *1:* 180
Paraguay and, *1:* 180
Reagan, Ronald, and, *2:* 339–41
Soviet Union and, *1:* 180; *2:* 202, 203, 254, 307–8, 325–27
Third World and, *1:* 175–82; *2:* 254, 307–8, 325–27
National Academy of Sciences, *1:* 82–83
National Aeronautics and Space Administration (NASA), *2:* 197, 198–99
National Defense Education Act, *2:* 197
National Education Association, *1:* 115
National Endowment for Democracy, *2:* 339
National Security Act, *1:* 28, 34–35, 130
National Security Agency (NSA)
  Cuban Missile Crisis and, *2:* 221, 224
  definition of, *1:* 127; *2:* 214
  espionage and, *1:* 131
  formation of, *1:* 131
  Hiss, Alger, and, *1:* 114
  VENONA and, *1:* 132
National Security Council (NSC)
  containment and, *1:* 28, 32, 44–45
  Cuban Missile Crisis and, *2:* 221–25
  formation of, *1:* 28, 34, 130–31
  Iran-Contra scandal and, *2:* 332–33
  NSC-20, *1:* 32
  NSC-30, *1:* 32
  NSC-68, *1:* 28, 44–45, 46, 48, 115–16, 173
Nationalism, *1:* 176–78. *See also* Nation building

Nationalists, *1:* 38–42, 50. *See also* Nation building
NATO. *See* North Atlantic Treaty Organization (NATO)
Nazi-Soviet Non-Aggression Pact, *1:* 6–8, 10
Nazism, *1:* 15, 81
Netherlands, *1:* 37
New Deal, *1:* 103–4
New Look, *1:* 173–75, 178
New Zealand, *1:* 50
Newton, Huey, *2:* 281
Ngo Dinh Diem, *1:* 169, 182; *2:* 253, 269–70, 283
Nicaragua, *1:* 180; *2:* 330–33, 355
9/11. *See* September 11, 2001, terrorist attacks
Ninjas, *1:* 141
Nitze, Paul H., *1:* 44–45
Nixon Doctrine, *2:* 311–12
Nixon, Pat, *2:* 301
Nixon, Richard M., *2:* 305 (ill.), 311 (ill.)
  Brezhnev, Leonid, and, *2:* 273, 304, 307
  Chile and, *2:* 308
  China and, *2:* 300–302, 311, 312
  communism and, *2:* 251, 311–12
  détente and, *2:* 310, 311, 314
  elections of, *2:* 212, 251, 273, 312
  Iran and, *2:* 308
  Mao Zedong and, *2:* 301
  military draft and, *2:* 336
  Nixon Doctrine and, *2:* 311–12
  nuclear weapons and, *2:* 305
  Pahlavi, Mohammed Reza, and, *2:* 308
  Red Scare and, *1:* 44, 109, 113, 114
  Silent Majority and, *2:* 276, 288–89
  Strategic Arms Limitation Talks (SALT) and, *2:* 304
  Taiwan and, *2:* 301
  Vietnam War and, *2:* 276, 288–89, 290, 301, 311, 312–13
  Watergate scandal and, *2:* 298, 299, 310
  Zhou Enlai and, *2:* 301

Nobel Peace Prize, *2:* 361

North American Air Defense Command (NORAD), *2:* 240

North Atlantic Treaty, *1:* 38, 39 (ill.)

North Atlantic Treaty Organization (NATO)
Bush, George, and, *2:* 363–64
composition of, *1:* 38, 68, 171
Conference on Security and Cooperation in Europe (CSCE) and, *2:* 365–66
containment and, *1:* 28, 168; *2:* 348
Conventional Force Talks in Europe and, *2:* 355
definition of, *1:* 28, 168; *2:* 348
disbanding of, *1:* 185–86; *2:* 363
formation of, *1:* 37–38
France and, *2:* 203, 306
Germany and, *2:* 363–64
Gorbachev, Mikhail, and, *2:* 363–64
growth of, *1:* 50
military and, *1:* 37–38; *2:* 365–66
nuclear weapons and, *1:* 174; *2:* 199, 200, 336–37, 356–57, 364, 373
Russia and, *2:* 370
Soviet Union and, *1:* 173; *2:* 363–64
strength of, *1:* 185
Truman, Harry S., and, *1:* 37–38
Warsaw Pact and, *1:* 185; *2:* 364
West Germany and, *1:* 68, 173
Yeltsin, Boris, and, *2:* 370

North Korea, *1:* 45, 46–48, 50 (ill.); *2:* 373

North, Oliver, *2:* 332–33

Novikov, Nikolai, *1:* 22

NSA. *See* National Security Agency (NSA)

NSC. *See* National Security Council (NSC)

Nuclear and Space Arms Talks (NST), *2:* 345

Nuclear energy, *2:* 241

Nuclear Nonproliferation Treaty, *2:* 248, 258

Nuclear weapons, *1:* 18 (ill.), 82 (ill.), 86 (ill.), 91 (ill.), 96 (ill.); *2:* 243 (ill.), 307 (ill.). *See also* Atomic bombs; Hydrogen bombs
accidents and, *2:* 242–43
Adenauer, Konrad, and, *1:* 171
asymmetrical response and, *1:* 173–75
balance of, *1:* 169; *2:* 374
Berlin and, *1:* 62, 64–65, 70
Brezhnev, Leonid, and, *2:* 256–58, 304, 305, 323, 330, 336–37
brinkmanship and, *1:* 167, 168, 169, 184
Bush, George, and, *2:* 356–57, 362, 368, 369–70, 372
Carter, Jimmy, and, *2:* 315, 323, 330, 336, 337
China and, *1:* 185; *2:* 206, 246–47, 258, 266, 300, 373
Churchill, Winston, and, *1:* 171
Cold War and, *2:* 233–35
Commonwealth of Independent States (CIS) and, *2:* 370
containment and, *1:* 32, 92, 93
cost of, *2:* 372
countries with, *2:* 373
Cuba and, *2:* 219–20, 248, 265
deterrent effect of, *1:* 169, 175; *2:* 234–35, 256, 374
development of, *1:* 9, 80–84, 87, 88–91, 92–95, 135, 171; *2:* 244
Dulles, John Foster, and, *1:* 171
early warning systems and, *2:* 239 (ill.), 240
Eisenhower, Dwight D., and, *1:* 70, 170–71; *2:* 200–201
espionage and, *1:* 9, 14, 19, 43, 88–89, 90–91, 108, 115, 128, 135–40, 143; *2:* 197–98
France and, *2:* 247, 373
Germany and, *1:* 81–82, 85; *2:* 200–201, 364
Gorbachev, Mikhail, and, *2:* 351, 352–55, 356–57, 364, 368, 369–70, 372
Great Britain and, *1:* 138; *2:* 245–46, 373
Hitler, Adolf, and, *1:* 81–82
hot line for, *2:* 230, 241–44
India and, *2:* 373

intelligence and, *1:* 90, 135

Intermediate-range Nuclear Force (INF) treaty and, *2:* 354–55, 372

Iran and, *2:* 373

Iraq and, *2:* 373

Johnson, Lyndon B., and, *2:* 247, 258

Kennedy, John F., and, *2:* 246, 256–58

Khrushchev, Nikita S., and, *1:* 70, 174–75; *2:* 200–201

Kissinger, Henry, and, *2:* 305

Korean War and, *1:* 47, 48

Kosygin, Aleksy, and, *2:* 247

Latin America and, *2:* 248

Malenkov, Georgy M., and, *1:* 170–71

Manhattan Project and, *1:* 9, 13–14, 79–81, 83–86, 87, 88–89, 90–91, 115, 128, 135, 138, 139; *2:* 244

Mao Zedong and, *2:* 206

missiles and, *2:* 196–99, 235–37, 238–39, 244

mutual assured destruction (MAD) and, *2:* 234–35, 236, 305, 342–43, 374

National Academy of Sciences and, *1:* 82–83

negotiations concerning, *1:* 19, 95, 170–71, 185, 186–87; *2:* 199–201, 210, 211–12, 230, 244, 247–48, 258, 260–61, 265, 273, 297–98, 302–5, 323, 328, 330, 338, 342, 344–45, 351, 352–55, 356–57, 368

Nixon, Richard M., and, *2:* 305

North Atlantic Treaty Organization (NATO) and, *1:* 174; *2:* 199, 200, 336–37, 356–57, 364, 373

North Korea and, *2:* 373

Nuclear and Space Arms Talks and, *2:* 345

October War and, *2:* 309–10

opposition to, *2:* 243, 244–46

Pakistan and, *2:* 373

race for, *1:* 22, 24, 43, 88–96, 144, 168, 169, 173–75, 185; *2:* 199, 233–38, 244, 246–47,

256–58, 275, 298, 320–21, 336–39, 342–45

Reagan, Ronald, and, *2:* 319, 320–21, 338, 342–45, 352–55, 372

Roosevelt, Franklin D., and, *1:* 9, 81–82, 83, 94; *2:* 244

Russia and, *2:* 370, 373

second-strike strategies and, *2:* 256–58

Shevardnadze, Eduard, and, *2:* 355

Shultz, George, and, *2:* 344

South Africa and, *2:* 373

Soviet Union and, *1:* 22, 43, 70, 88–91, 95–96, 115, 135–40, 174–75; *2:* 200–201, 235, 236–37, 240–41, 244–45, 247, 256–58, 303–4, 305, 323, 330, 336–39, 349, 362, 364, 369–70, 372

Stalin, Joseph, and, *1:* 9, 14, 88–89

stockpiles of, *1:* 93

Strategic Arms Limitation Talks (SALT) and, *2:* 248, 297–98, 302–5, 320, 323, 330, 335, 336, 338, 353

Strategic Arms Reduction Talks (START) and, *2:* 352, 357, 372

Strategic Defense Initiative (SDI) and, *2:* 342–45, 352, 354

Strategic Triad and, *2:* 234, 235, 238–40

strength of, *1:* 79, 88, 95; *2:* 219, 240–41

test bans and, *2:* 199–201, 210, 212, 230, 234, 244, 261

testing of, *1:* 13–14, 43, 79–80, 85–86, 87, 88, 90, 91, 95–96, 115, 135; *2:* 233, 236, 240–41, 244–45, 260

threats and, *1:* 32, 64–65, 184; *2:* 205, 256, 338

treaties concerning, *2:* 234, 244, 247–48, 258, 261, 265, 273, 297–98, 302–5, 330, 335, 336, 338, 344, 353, 354–55, 368, 372

Truman, Harry S., and, *1:* 13–14, 43, 86, 88, 91, 92–95, 115–16

Ukraine and, *2:* 370, 373

U.S. Air Force and, *1:* 174; *2:* 235, 237–38

U.S. Congress and, *2:* 342

U.S. Navy and, *2:* 239–40

use of, *1:* 17, 18 (ill.), 86–88, 135; *2:* 219, 241

Vietnam War and, *2:* 270, 290

World War II and, *1:* 17, 18 (ill.), 80–82, 85–88, 135; *2:* 219, 241

Yeltsin, Boris, *2:* 370

O

OAS. *See* Organization of American States (OAS)

October War, *2:* 309 (ill.), 309–10

Office of Scientific Research and Development (OSRD), *1:* 83

Office of Strategic Services (OSS), *1:* 130

Ogonek, 2: 293

Ogorodnik, Aleksandr Dmitrievich, *1:* 154

Oil
Iran and, *1:* 20, 21–22, 178; *2:* 334
Iraq and, *2:* 204, 365
Middle East and, *2:* 201–2, 205
Suez War and, *2:* 203

Olympics, *2:* 336

Open Skies, *1:* 186–87

Operation Desert Shield/Storm, *2:* 365

Operation Mongoose, *2:* 219

Operation Plain Fare, *1:* 56, 64

Operation Rescue, *2:* 332–33

Operation Rolling Thunder, *2:* 270

Operation Vittles, *1:* 56, 64

Oppenheimer, J. Robert, *1:* 84 (ill.)
awards of, *1:* 171
firing of, *1:* 171
hydrogen bombs and, *1:* 94, 171; *2:* 244
Manhattan Project and, *1:* 83, 84, 89

Organization of American States (OAS), *1:* 36; *2:* 226, 265, 330–31

Ortega, Daniel, *2:* 332, 333 (ill.)

OSRD. *See* Office of Scientific Research and Development (OSRD)

OSS. *See* Office of Strategic Services (OSS)

Ostopolitik, 2: 305–6

Oswald, Lee Harvey, *2:* 254

Outer Space Treaty, *2:* 248, 258, 344

P

Pahlavi, Mohammed Reza, *1:* 178; *2:* 308, 332–34

Pakistan, *2:* 336, 373

Palestine, *2:* 328–29, 341

Palestine Liberation Organization (PLO), *2:* 328–29

Palmer, A. Mitchell, *1:* 102–3, 103 (ill.)

Palmer Raids, *1:* 103

Palomares Incident, *2:* 242, 243, 243 (ill.)

Pan Am bombing, *2:* 376

Panama, *2:* 262–63, 264 (ill.)

Paraguay, *1:* 180

Peace, *2:* 246 (ill.)
Cold War and, *2:* 374
counterculture and, *2:* 287
Europe and, *2:* 364–67
movements for, *2:* 245–46
nuclear energy and, *2:* 241
symbol for, *2:* 245, 246
Vietnam War and, *2:* 271–73, 312–13
World War II and, *2:* 364

Peace Corps, *2:* 252, 255

Pearl Harbor, *1:* 8, 104–5

Pelton, Ronald, *1:* 158

Penkovsky, Oleg, *1:* 151–52, 152 (ill.)

People's Republic of China (PRC), *1:* 41–42. *See also* China; Republic of China (ROC); Taiwan

Perestroika, *2:* 348, 351, 358, 361

Permanent Subcommittee on Investigations. *See* McCarthy Committee

Persian Gulf War, *1:* 161

Philby, Kim, *1:* 128, 140–41, 142, 143, 144

Photography, *1:* 137 (ill.)
  Cuban Missile Crisis and, *2:* 222, 225
  espionage and, *1:* 136, 137 (ill.), 147–50; *2:* 198, 222

Pinay, Antoine, *1:* 175 (ill.)

Ping-pong, *2:* 301, 302

Pinochet Ugarte, Augusto, *2:* 308

PLO. *See* Palestine Liberation Organization (PLO)

Poetry, *2:* 292, 293

Poindexter, John, *2:* 332–33

Poland, *2:* 194 (ill.)
  communism in, *1:* 57
  Communist Party in, *1:* 11, 12–13; *2:* 357–58
  democracy and, *2:* 357–58
  elections in, *2:* 357–58
  freedom in, *2:* 193–94
  Gorbachev, Mikhail, and, *2:* 358
  Khrushchev, Nikita S., and, *2:* 193–94
  labor in, *2:* 193–94, 357–58
  Ostopolitik and, *2:* 306
  riots in, *2:* 193–94
  Soviet Union and, *1:* 9, 10, 11, 12–13, 57; *2:* 358
  Stalin, Joseph, and, *1:* 9, 11
  World War II and, *1:* 7, 9–10, 11

Politics, *1:* 36

Pollard, Jonathan Jay, *1:* 159–60

Portugal, *2:* 206

Potsdam Conference, *1:* 13–17, 14 (ill.), 16 (ill.), 86, 143

Potsdam Declaration, *1:* 17

Power, Thomas, *2:* 240

Powers, Francis Gary, *1:* 149–50; *2:* 211, 240

Prague Spring, *2:* 252, 267–68

A Precocious Autobiography, *2:* 293

Prevention of Nuclear War, *2:* 307

Project Apollo, *2:* 199

Project Vanguard, *2:* 198

Project Y, *1:* 83–84

Propaganda
  Berlin airlift and, *1:* 66

Federal Bureau of Investigation (FBI) and, *1:* 108
  human rights and, *2:* 323
  racism and, *2:* 282–83
  Sputnik I and, *2:* 196
  as weapon, *1:* 2, 28, 56, 80, 100, 126, 127, 168; *2:* 192, 234, 252, 276, 298, 320, 348

Property
  capitalism and, *1:* 4, 27, 28, 56, 58, 101, 126, 128, 168, 169; *2:* 192, 214, 216, 298, 299, 320, 348
  communism and, *1:* 2, 3, 7, 27–29, 56, 57, 80, 99, 100, 104, 126, 128, 167, 168; *2:* 192, 214, 215, 234, 251, 252, 276, 298, 299, 319–20, 347, 348
  Marxism and, *1:* 6

Putin, Vladimir, *2:* 373

Q

Quarantine, *2:* 214, 225–26, 227–29, 260

R

Racism, *2:* 275–76, 278–83, 279 (ill.), 285. *See also* Ethnic conflict

Radio, *1:* 110, 118, 136, 143; *2:* 323

Radio Free Europe, *2:* 323

Radio Liberty, *2:* 323

Radio transmitters, *1:* 136

Rankin, John E., *1:* 107

Ray, James Earl, *2:* 282

Reagan Doctrine, *2:* 339

Reagan, Ronald, *2:* 353 (ill.), 354 (ill.)
  Afghanistan and, *2:* 355
  Bush, George, and, *2:* 356
  communism and, *2:* 338
  containment and, *2:* 340–41
  détente and, *2:* 315, 338
  dictatorship and, *2:* 339–40
  El Salvador and, *2:* 339

election of, *2:* 337–38, 344–45, 347–48
espionage and, *1:* 157
foreign affairs experience of, *2:* 338
Gorbachev, Mikhail, and, *2:* 352–56, 372
Grenada and, *2:* 340–41
human rights and, *2:* 339
Iran-Contra scandal and, *2:* 332–33
Israel and, *1:* 159
Korean Airlines tragedy and, *2:* 343
Latin America and, *2:* 339–41
Middle East and, *2:* 341–42
military and, *2:* 338–39
nation building and, *2:* 339–41
National Endowment for Democracy and, *2:* 339
Nicaragua and, *2:* 332–33, 355
Nuclear and Space Arms Talks and, *2:* 345
nuclear weapons and, *2:* 319, 320–21, 338, 342–45, 352–55, 372
Ortega, Daniel, and, *2:* 332
Reagan Doctrine and, *2:* 339
Red Scare and, *2:* 338
Soviet Union and, *2:* 342
Strategic Arms Limitation Talks (SALT) and, *2:* 338, 353
Strategic Arms Reduction Talks (START) and, *2:* 352
Strategic Defense Initiative (SDI) and, *2:* 342–45, 352, 354
United Nations and, *2:* 341, 345
Reconnaissance, *1:* 147 (ill.), 148 (ill.), 149 (ill.). *See also* Espionage; Intelligence
Bay of Pigs and, *1:* 150
Central Intelligence Agency (CIA) and, *1:* 147, 150
Cuban Missile Crisis and, *1:* 150; *2:* 222, 223 (ill.), 225
definition of, *1:* 127
Eisenhower, Dwight D., and, *1:* 148, 150; *2:* 211–12
espionage and, *1:* 147–50
Khrushchev, Nikita S., and, *1:* 150

missiles and, *2:* 197–98
satellites and, *1:* 150
U-2 aircraft and, *1:* 147–50; *2:* 211, 240
Red Guard, *2:* 266, 267 (ill.), 294, 295, 295 (ill.)
Red Scare. *See also* McCarthyism
African Americans and, *1:* 115
Berlin airlift and, *1:* 111
Bolshevik Revolution and, *1:* 101–3
Central Intelligence Agency (CIA) and, *1:* 118
China and, *1:* 111
civil rights and, *1:* 110, 113, 115, 172
Cold War and, *1:* 114
costs of, *2:* 372
definition of, *1:* 100
democracy and, *1:* 108–9
Democratic Party and, *1:* 106–7
elections and, *1:* 106
espionage and, *1:* 44, 107, 112, 113–14
fear and, *1:* 11, 105
Federal Bureau of Investigation (FBI) and, *1:* 100, 107, 108
Fifth Amendment and, *1:* 110, 113
freedom and, *1:* 103, 104–5, 107–12
Hiss, Alger, and, *1:* 113
Hollywood Ten and, *1:* 100, 110, 111 (ill.)
Hoover, J. Edgar, and, *1:* 103, 107, 108, 111
House Un-American Activities Committee (HUAC) and, *1:* 44, 99–100
intelligence and, *1:* 107, 108, 115–16, 159
labor and, *1:* 108
loyalty programs and, *1:* 104, 107, 108, 112, 115, 171
McCarthy, Joseph R., and, *1:* 43–44, 101, 106, 116–19, 171–72
McCarthyism and, *1:* 116–20
media and, *1:* 100, 108, 110, 118
military and, *1:* 115–16
movies and, *1:* 100, 108, 110

Nixon, Richard M., and, *1:* 44,
  109, 113, 114
overview of, *1:* 43–44
Palmer, A. Mitchell, and, *1:*
  102–3
radio and, *1:* 110, 118
Reagan, Ronald, and, *2:* 338
Roosevelt, Franklin D., and, *1:*
  108
Smith Act and, *1:* 104, 107, 112
subversives and, *1:* 104, 107
television and, *1:* 110
Truman, Harry S., and, *1:* 106,
  107, 108, 117
Truman Doctrine and, *1:* 107
U.S. Army and, *1:* 118, 172
U.S. Congress and, *1:* 102–3,
  104, 106
U.S. State Department and, *1:*
  113, 117, 118
Refugees, *1:* 68–69, 71, 73
Reparations, *1:* 15–17, 57, 58
Republic of China (ROC), *1:*
  41–42, 176; *2:* 327. *See also*
  China; People's Republic of
  China (PRC); Taiwan
Republic of Korea. *See* South
  Korea
Republic of Vietnam, *1:* 181
Republican Party, *1:* 48
Reserve Officers' Training Corps
  (ROTC), *2:* 285
Reuter, Ernst, *1:* 63
Rhee, Syngman, *1:* 45
Rio Pact, *1:* 36
Robinson, Jackie, *1:* 115
Romania, *1:* 18; *2:* 360
Roosevelt, Eleanor, *2:* 315
Roosevelt, Franklin D., *1:* 30 (ill.)
  Big Three and, *1:* 2, 9–10, 29
  character of, *1:* 25
  death of, *1:* 10, 86
  economy and, *1:* 5, 12–13,
    103–4
  Einstein, Albert, and, *2:* 244
  espionage and, *1:* 140, 142
  Great Depression and, *1:* 5,
    103–4
  Hoover, J. Edgar, and, *1:* 108
  isolationism and, *1:* 6, 12
  Latin America and, *2:* 265
  nuclear weapons and, *1:* 9,
    81–82, 83, 94; *2:* 244

Red Scare and, *1:* 108
Soviet Union and, *1:* 5
United Nations and, *1:* 12
Yalta agreements and, *1:* 2, 10,
  105
Roosevelt, Theodore, *1:* 187 (ill.)
Rosario Casas, Maria del, *1:* 162
Rosenberg, Ethel, *1:* 91, 108, 139
  (ill.), 139–40
Rosenberg, Julius, *1:* 91, 108, 139
  (ill.), 139–40
ROTC. *See* Reserve Officers' Train-
  ing Corps (ROTC)
Royal Air Force, *1:* 62–66
Rusk, Dean, *2:* 222, 228, 253, 258
Russell, Bertrand, *2:* 245
Russia, *2:* 371 (ill.), 374 (ill.). *See
  also* Russian Federation; Sovi-
  et Union
  Bolshevik Revolution and, *1:* 2,
    3–5, 6–7, 100–101, 132
  capitalism and, *2:* 373
  Chechnya and, *2:* 375
  Communist Party in, *1:* 3, 101;
    2: 369, 373
  democracy and, *2:* 373
  economy of, *2:* 373
  elections in, *2:* 373
  greatness of, *1:* 1
  monarchy in, *1:* 6
  Monroe Doctrine and, *1:*
    186–87
  North Atlantic Treaty Organiza-
    tion (NATO) and, *2:* 370
  nuclear weapons and, *2:* 370,
    373
  World War I and, *1:* 6
Russian Federation, *2:* 370, 375
Russian Foreign Intelligence Ser-
  vice (SVR), *1:* 132, 160
Russian Revolution of 1917. *See*
  Bolshevik Revolution

S

SAC. *See* Strategic Air Command
  (SAC)
Sadat, Anwar, *2:* 329, 329 (ill.)
Sakharov, Andrey, *2:* 245 (ill.)
  Carter, Jimmy, and, *2:* 315, 324
  exile of, *2:* 349, 351

hydrogen bombs and, *1:* 95; *2:* 233, 244–45

SALT. *See* Strategic Arms Limitation Talks (SALT)

Sandinista National Liberation Front, *2:* 330–32

Satellites, *1:* 150, 154–55; *2:* 196, 198, 275

Screen Actors Guild, *2:* 338

SDI. *See* Strategic Defense Initiative (SDI)

Seaborg, Glenn T., *1:* 87

Seale, Bobby, *2:* 281

Second-strike strategies, *2:* 256–58

Secret Intelligence Service (SIS), *1:* 131

Segregation, *2:* 278–79, 279 (ill.), 281. *See also* Racism

Sellers, Peter, *2:* 236, 236 (ill.)

Separatism, *2:* 281

September 11, 2001, terrorist attacks, *2:* 376

Serber, Robert, *1:* 84

Shadows, *1:* 141

Shepard, Alan B., Jr., *2:* 198

Shevardnadze, Eduard, *2:* 349, 351, 355, 367

Shriver, R. Sargent, *2:* 255

Shultz, George, *2:* 332–33, 344, 352

Signals intelligence (SIGINT), *2:* 224, 225. *See also* Listening stations

Silent Majority, *2:* 276, 288–89

Sino-Soviet Treaty, *1:* 42, 184

SIS. *See* Secret Intelligence Service (SIS)

Smith Act, *1:* 104, 107, 112

Social Democratic Labor Party, *1:* 6

Solidarity, *2:* 357–58

Solomatin, Boris Aleksandrovich, *1:* 157

Solzhenitsyn, Aleksandr, *2:* 293, 349

Somalia, *2:* 325–26

Sombolay, Albert, *1:* 161

Somoza, Anastasio (father), *1:* 180

Somoza, Anastasio (son), *1:* 180; *2:* 330–31

"The Sources of Soviet Conduct," *1:* 35–36

South Africa, *2:* 373

South Korea, *1:* 45, 46–48, 50 (ill.), 176; *2:* 324

Southeast Asia Treaty Organization (SEATO), *1:* 168, 182, 183 (ill.)

Soviet Union, *2:* 350 (ill.). *See also* Russia

Afghanistan and, *2:* 335–36, 337, 351, 355–56

Angola and, *2:* 326–27

Berlin and, *1:* 61–62, 65–66, 111

Big Three and, *1:* 2, 9–10

Bretton Woods Conference and, *1:* 12

Brezhnev Doctrine and, *2:* 298, 300

Bush, George, and, *2:* 369–70

capitalism and, *2:* 304, 352, 361, 367–68

Carter, Jimmy, and, *2:* 335–36

China and, *1:* 40–42, 52, 111, 184–85; *2:* 205–6, 265–66, 300–301, 301–2, 327, 356

communism in, *1:* 27–29; *2:* 299

Communist Party in, *1:* 120, 121, 170, 188; *2:* 241, 254–55, 260, 338, 347, 348–49, 360–62, 367–69, 372

composition of, *1:* 1, 7

Congo and, *2:* 208

Congress of People's Deputies in, *2:* 360–61

constitution of, *2:* 360

coup attempt in, *2:* 368–69

Cuba and, *2:* 209–10, 216, 217, 219–21, 258, 273, 310

Cuban Missile Crisis and, *2:* 219–20, 226, 227, 228, 229, 260

culture in, *2:* 292–93, 338

Czechoslovakia and, *1:* 34; *2:* 268

democracy and, *2:* 347, 360–61, 367–68

de-Stalinization of, *2:* 192–93, 265–66

détente and, *2:* 297–98, 304–5, 310, 311

East Berlin and, *1:* 69–71

East Germany and, *1:* 68, 69–71; *2:* 358–59

Eastern Bloc and, *2:* 193–96, 349

economy of, *1:* 17, 174–75; *2:* 277, 278, 290–92, 303, 304, 337, 338, 343, 347–52, 361, 362, 367–68

Egypt and, *2:* 202, 203

Eisenhower Doctrine and, *2:* 204–5

elections in, *1:* 52; *2:* 255–56, 360–61

end of, *2:* 367–72

espionage and, *1:* 9, 14, 19, 43, 60, 88–89, 90–91, 127, 132, 136–45, 146, 148–50, 151, 152, 153, 154–58, 160, 162, 163–64

Ethiopia and, *2:* 325–26

ethnic conflict in, *2:* 315, 324, 374–76

formation of, *1:* 4–5, 7

freedom in, *2:* 292, 348, 351, 357, 367

freedom of religion and, *2:* 357

Germany and, *1:* 6–8, 29, 57; *2:* 363–64

glasnost in, *2:* 348, 351, 357, 367

Grand Alliance and, *1:* 8–9

Great Britain and, *1:* 18–19

Great Terror in, *1:* 120–23, 188; *2:* 192–93

Greece and, *1:* 23

Ho Chi Minh and, *1:* 42

human rights and, *2:* 323–24, 325

imperialism and, *1:* 33; *2:* 298, 300

India and, *2:* 336

intelligence and, *1:* 160

International Monetary Fund (IMF) and, *1:* 22

Iran and, *1:* 18–19, 20, 21–22

Iraq and, *2:* 341–42, 365

isolationism and, *1:* 5, 22

Japan and, *1:* 10, 17

Jews and, *2:* 315, 324

Kissinger, Henry, and, *2:* 302–3, 304

Korea and, *1:* 45–46

Korean Airlines tragedy and, *2:* 343

Korean War and, *1:* 46

labor camps in, *1:* 120–21

Marshall Plan and, *1:* 31–32

Middle East and, *2:* 204–5

military and, *1:* 50–52; *2:* 355–56

military-industrial complexes in, *2:* 277, 278

Molotov Plan and, *1:* 32–34

most-favored-nation trade status of, *2:* 336, 362

nation building and, *1:* 180; *2:* 202, 203, 254, 307–8, 325–27

Nazi-Soviet Non-Aggression Pact and, *1:* 6–8, 10

Nicaragua and, *2:* 331

North Atlantic Treaty Organization (NATO) and, *1:* 173; *2:* 363–64

nuclear weapons and, *1:* 22, 43, 70, 88–91, 95–96, 115, 135–40, 174–75; *2:* 200–201, 235, 236–37, 240–41, 244–45, 247, 256–58, 303–4, 305, 323, 330, 336–39, 349, 362, 364, 369–70, 372

October War and, *2:* 309–10

perestroika in, *2:* 348, 351, 358, 361

Poland and, *1:* 9, 10, 11, 12–13, 57; *2:* 358

Potsdam Conference and, *1:* 13–17

racism and, *2:* 282–83

Reagan, Ronald, and, *2:* 342

reparations and, *1:* 15–17, 57

republics of, *2:* 361–62

Roosevelt, Franklin D., and, *1:* 5

Soviet Central Committee in, *1:* 121

strength and, *1:* 70

Suez War and, *2:* 203

as superpower, *1:* 1, 27, 37, 128

Third World and, *2:* 210, 254, 321–22, 349, 351

Truman Doctrine and, *1:* 2

Turkey and, *1:* 18–19, 23

Ukraine and, *1:* 7

Ulbricht, Walter, and, *1:* 71

Vietnam and, *1:* 42; *2:* 328

Vietnam War and, *2:* 270, 290

West Berlin and, *1:* 69–71

West Germany and, *1:* 60–62,
  65–66; *2:* 206
World Bank and, *1:* 22
World War II and, *1:* 3, 7–8,
  8–14, 15–17, 17–18, 29–30;
  2: 364
Yalta agreements and, *1:* 9, 10,
  11, 12
Yugoslavia and, *1:* 51
Space race, *2:* 196, 198–99, 314
Spain, *2:* 242–43
Spies. *See* Espionage; Moles
Sputnik I, 2: 196, 197 (ill.), 198
Spying. *See* Espionage
Stalin, Joseph, *1:* 10 (ill.), 14 (ill.),
  30 (ill.), 122 (ill.)
  Baltic States and, *2:* 362
  Big Three and, *1:* 2, 9–10, 29
  Bolshevik Revolution and, *1:* 5
  character of, *1:* 25
  China and, *1:* 40, 42
  Cold War and, *1:* 25, 52
  Communist Party and, *1:* 120,
    121
  death of, *1:* 52, 123, 144, 169,
    170
  espionage and, *1:* 140, 142–43
  freedom and, *1:* 100, 120
  Great Terror of, *1:* 120–23, 188;
    2: 192–93
  Iron Curtain and, *1:* 21
  isolationism and, *1:* 22
  Jews and, *1:* 121–23
  KGB (Soviet secret police) and,
    1: 127, 132
  Khrushchev, Nikita S., and, *1:*
    188; *2:* 192–93, 265–66, 292
  loyalty programs and, *1:* 120
  Maclean, Donald, and, *1:*
    142–43
  Mao Zedong and, *1:* 40
  Marshall Plan and, *1:* 34
  military and, *1:* 50–52
  Nazi-Soviet Non-Aggression
    Pact and, *1:* 6–7, 10
  nuclear weapons and, *1:* 9, 14,
    88–89
  Philby, Kim, and, *1:* 143
  Poland and, *1:* 9, 11
  Potsdam Conference and, *1:*
    14–17
  Truman, Harry S., and, *1:* 86
  "Two Camps" speech of, *1:* 19

United Nations and, *1:* 12
Yalta agreements and, *1:* 2, 11,
  105
Yugoslavia and, *1:* 51, 121
Star Wars. *See* Strategic Defense
  Initiative (SDI)
START. *See* Strategic Arms Reduc-
  tion Talks (START)
Stevenson, Adlai, *1:* 48
Strategic Air Command (SAC)
  Bush, George, and, *2:* 369
  Cuban Missile Crisis and, *2:*
    225
  definition of, *1:* 80; *2:* 234
  early warning systems and, *2:*
    240
  formation of, *1:* 92
  nuclear accidents and, *2:* 243
  nuclear weapons and, *2:*
    237–38, 239
Strategic arms, *2:* 234, 235
Strategic Arms Limitation Talks
  (SALT), *2:* 307 (ill.), 331 (ill.)
  Brezhnev, Leonid, and, *2:* 304,
    323, 330
  Carter, Jimmy, and, *2:* 323, 330,
    336
  definition of, *2:* 298, 320
  description of, *2:* 302–5
  détente and, *2:* 297–98, 304–5
  location of, *2:* 248
  Nixon, Richard M., and, *2:* 304
  Reagan, Ronald, and, *2:* 338, 353
  U.S. Congress and, *2:* 330, 335,
    336
Strategic Arms Reduction Talks
  (START), *2:* 352, 357, 372
Strategic Defense Initiative (SDI),
  2: 342–45, 352, 353 (ill.), 354
Strategic Triad, *2:* 234, 235,
  238–40
Strength
  containment and, *1:* 93
  Khrushchev, Nikita S., and, *1:* 70
  of North Atlantic Treaty Orga-
    nization (NATO), *1:* 185
  of nuclear weapons, *1:* 79, 88,
    95; *2:* 219, 240–41
  Truman, Harry S., and, *1:* 22–23
Stroessner, Alfredo, *1:* 180
Submarines, *2:* 243 (ill.)
  cost of, *2:* 372
  Cuba and, *2:* 310

missiles and, *2:* 239–40, 244

nuclear powered, *2:* 237

Subversives, *1:* 104, 107

Suez War, *2:* 203, 203 (ill.)

Summer of love, *2:* 287

SVR (Russian Foreign Intelligence Service), *1:* 132

Syria, *2:* 204, 309–10

Szilard, Leo, *1:* 81

T

Tactical Air Command (TAC), *2:* 225

Tactical arms, *2:* 234, 235

Taft, Robert A., *1:* 48

Taiwan. *See also* China; People's Republic of China (PRC); Republic of China (ROC)

China and, *1:* 50, 183–85; *2:* 205, 266, 301

Communist Party and, *1:* 184–85

Eisenhower, Dwight D., and, *1:* 184

formation of, *1:* 41

Nationalists in, *1:* 50

Nixon, Richard M., and, *2:* 301

Truman, Harry S., and, *1:* 50

Taiwan Resolution, *1:* 184

Taylor, Maxwell, *2:* 222

Teachers, *1:* 115

Teach-ins, *2:* 284, 285

Tehran Conference, *1:* 143

Television, *1:* 110

Teller, Edward, *1:* 81, 94; *2:* 353 (ill.)

Terrorism, *2:* 376

Tet Offensive, *2:* 271–72

Thatcher, Margaret, *1:* 144; *2:* 352

Thermonuclear bombs, *1:* 88. *See also* Nuclear weapons

Third World

in Africa, *2:* 206

Carter, Jimmy, and, *2:* 325

communism and, *1:* 176–78; *2:* 193

definition of, *1:* 168; *2:* 193, 252, 307, 321–22, 349

economy and, *2:* 252, 254, 307

Four Point Program and, *1:* 49–50

Khrushchev, Nikita S., and, *2:* 210

nation building and, *1:* 175–82; *2:* 254, 307–8, 325–27

Peace Corps and, *2:* 255

Soviet Union and, *2:* 210, 254, 321–22, 349, 351

United Nations and, *2:* 210

Threats

asymmetrical response and, *1:* 173–75

Berlin airlift and, *1:* 64–65

Cuban Missile Crisis and, *2:* 226, 227

Khrushchev, Nikita S., and, *1:* 69–71

nuclear weapons and, *1:* 32, 64–65, 184; *2:* 205, 256, 338

as weapon, *1:* 2, 28, 56, 80, 100, 126, 127, 168; *2:* 192, 234, 252, 276, 298, 320, 348

Thule Accident, *2:* 243

Tiananmen Square, *2:* 295 (ill.), 362

Time, 2: 361

Tito, Josip Broz, *1:* 51, 51 (ill.), 121, 188

Tocqueville, Alexis de, *1:* 1

Tradecraft, *1:* 136–37, 137 (ill.), 141

Transportation, *1:* 68–69, 70, 71

Treaty on the Final Settlement with Respect to Germany, *2:* 364

Trilateral Commission, *2:* 321

Trinity, *1:* 79, 82 (ill.), 85, 87

Trotsky, Leon, *1:* 4 (ill.)

Truman Doctrine, *1:* 2, 23–24, 107

Truman, Harry S., *1:* 14 (ill.), 16 (ill.)

Attlee, Clement, and, *1:* 86

character of, *1:* 25

China and, *1:* 40, 42

Cold War and, *1:* 24, 25, 52

containment and, *1:* 29–30, 168–69, 173–74

espionage and, *1:* 140, 142

Executive Order 9835, *1:* 107

Indochina and, *1:* 50

Iron Curtain and, *1:* 20–21

Korean War and, *1:* 46, 47, 48

Mao Zedong and, *1:* 40, 42

Marshall Plan and, *1:* 32

McCarthy, Joseph R., and, *1:* 117

National Security Act and, *1:* 34

North Atlantic Treaty Organization (NATO) and, *1:* 37–38

NSC-68 and, *1:* 45, 46, 173

nuclear weapons and, *1:* 13–14, 43, 86, 88, 91, 92–95, 115–16

Office of Strategic Services (OSS) and, *1:* 130

Potsdam Conference and, *1:* 13–17

Red Scare and, *1:* 106, 107, 108, 117

Smith Act and, *1:* 107

Stalin, Joseph, and, *1:* 86

strength and, *1:* 22–23

Taiwan and, *1:* 50

Truman Doctrine and, *1:* 2, 23–24, 107

Vietnam and, *1:* 42

World War II and, *1:* 10–11, 18, 86

Yalta agreements and, *1:* 11

Yugoslavia and, *1:* 51

TRW, *1:* 154–55

Turkey

Cuban Missile Crisis and, *2:* 228, 229–30, 260

Great Britain and, *1:* 23

Soviet Union and, *1:* 18–19, 23

Truman Doctrine and, *1:* 2

"Two Camps" speech, *1:* 19

Tydings, Millard, *1:* 117

U

U-2 aircraft, *1:* 147 (ill.)

Cuban Missile Crisis and, *2:* 225, 228

definition of, *1:* 127

espionage and, *1:* 127, 147–50; *2:* 211, 240, 310

missiles and, *2:* 198

Powers, Francis Gary, and, *1:* 149–50; *2:* 211, 240

U.S. Air Force and, *1:* 147

UAR. *See* United Arab Republic (UAR)

Ukraine, *1:* 7; *2:* 369, 370, 373

Ulbricht, Walter, *1:* 57, 68, 71, 72 (ill.), 73

UNESCO. *See* United Nations Educational, Scientific, and Cultural Organization (UNESCO)

Union of Soviet Socialist Republics (USSR). *See* Soviet Union

United Arab Republic (UAR), *2:* 204

United Fruit Company, *1:* 179, 180

United Nations

Atomic Energy Commission, *1:* 18, 22

Bevin, Ernest, and, *1:* 18–19

charter of, *1:* 12, 13

China and, *2:* 266, 327

composition of, *2:* 210

Congo and, *2:* 207–8

Cuban Missile Crisis and, *2:* 226, 227

definition of, *1:* 2

formation of, *1:* 10, 12

function of, *1:* 12–13, 113; *2:* 191

Gorbachev, Mikhail, and, *2:* 355, 365

human rights and, *2:* 315

Iraq and, *2:* 365

Khrushchev, Nikita S., and, *2:* 191, 210

Korean War and, *1:* 46–48

members of, *1:* 13

Reagan, Ronald, and, *2:* 341, 345

Roosevelt, Franklin D., and, *1:* 12

Security Council, *1:* 12, 20, 46

Stalin, Joseph, and, *1:* 12

Suez War and, *2:* 203

Third World and, *2:* 210

UNESCO, *2:* 341

voting in, *1:* 11, 12

Yalta Conference and, *1:* 12

United Nations Educational, Scientific, and Cultural Organization (UNESCO), *2:* 341

United Nations Security Council, *1:* 12, 20, 46

United States of America. *See also* specific presidents, officials, and offices

dictatorship and, *2:* 268, 275–77, 279, 280–81

economy of, *1:* 17; *2:* 304, 338–39, 362, 372–73
greatness of, *1:* 1
imperialism and, *1:* 31–32, 33; *2:* 208, 209, 217–18, 259, 269–70, 308, 322
isolationism and, *1:* 5, 6, 12, 19–20, 37, 48
population of, *1:* 17
strength and, *1:* 22–23
as superpower, *1:* 1, 17, 27, 28, 128
World War I and, *1:* 5
World War II and, *1:* 3, 8–18, 29–30; *2:* 364
Uranium Committee, *1:* 82
U.S. Air Force, *2:* 237 (ill.)
Berlin airlift and, *1:* 62–66
Cuban Missile Crisis and, *2:* 225
nuclear accidents and, *2:* 242–43
nuclear weapons and, *1:* 174; *2:* 235, 237–38
U-2 aircraft and, *1:* 147
U.S. Army, *1:* 118, 145–46, 153, 161, 172
U.S. Army Signals Intelligence Service, *1:* 127, 131, 132–35
U.S. Congress. *See also* House Un-American Activities Committee (HUAC)
Alliance for Progress and, *2:* 263
Atomic Energy Commission and, *1:* 80, 92
Dominican Republic and, *2:* 265
Eisenhower Doctrine and, *2:* 203–4
Four Point Program and, *1:* 49–50
Gulf of Tonkin Resolution and, *2:* 270
Hatch Act and, *1:* 104
Intermediate-range Nuclear Force (INF) treaty and, *2:* 354–55
Iran-Contra scandal and, *2:* 332, 333
Marshall Plan and, *1:* 32
National Defense Education Act and, *2:* 197

National Security Act and, *1:* 34
Nicaragua and, *2:* 332
NSC-68 and, *1:* 45
nuclear weapons and, *2:* 342
Peace Corps and, *2:* 255
Red Scare and, *1:* 102–3, 104, 106
Smith Act and, *1:* 104
Strategic Arms Limitation Talks (SALT) and, *2:* 330, 335, 336
Taiwan and, *1:* 184; *2:* 266
Vietnam War and, *2:* 312
U.S. Department of Defense, *1:* 35; *2:* 198, 285
U.S. Navy, *1:* 155–57; *2:* 210, 239–40
U.S. State Department, *1:* 113, 117, 118
U.S. Supreme Court, *2:* 278
USS *Missouri,* *1:* 17, 21 (ill.)
U.S.S.R. *See* Soviet Union

V

Vance, Cyrus, *2:* 321, 322 (ill.), 323, 325, 335
VENONA, *1:* 133 (ill.)
atomic spies and, *1:* 138
Cambridge Spies and, *1:* 140
definition of, *1:* 127
overview of, *1:* 132–35
Philby, Kim, and, *1:* 143
Vietcong, *2:* 252, 269, 270, 276, 283
Vietnam, *2:* 285 (ill.)
Cambodia and, *2:* 327, 328
China and, *1:* 42; *2:* 328
communism in, *1:* 42
division of, *1:* 181–82; *2:* 283
Eisenhower, Dwight D., and, *1:* 181–82; *2:* 283
elections in, *1:* 182
France and, *1:* 42, 181–82; *2:* 283
Ho Chi Minh and, *1:* 42
Soviet Union and, *1:* 42; *2:* 328
Truman, Harry S., and, *1:* 42
Vietnam War, *2:* 271 (ill.), 284 (ill.), 285 (ill.), 286 (ill.), 289 (ill.)
causes of, *2:* 268–69

chemical warfare and, *2:* 283–84, 290
China and, *2:* 270–71, 290, 301
Christmas bombing in, *2:* 313
communism and, *2:* 283, 284, 290
conduct of, *2:* 269–73
counterculture and, *2:* 286–88
death in, *2:* 271, 273, 283–84, 290, 313, 372
détente and, *2:* 312
end of, *2:* 312–13
Gulf of Tonkin and, *2:* 270
Hoover, J. Edgar, and, *1:* 109
Johnson, Lyndon B., and, *2:* 270, 271–73, 282, 283, 289–90
Kennedy, John F., and, *2:* 269–70, 283
King, Martin Luther, Jr., and, *2:* 282
Kissinger, Henry, and, *2:* 312
military draft and, *2:* 284–85
military-industrial complexes and, *2:* 286
Nixon, Richard M., and, *2:* 276, 288–89, 290, 301, 311, 312–13
nuclear weapons and, *2:* 270, 290
Operation Rolling Thunder, *2:* 270
opposition to, *2:* 268, 271, 272–73, 275–76, 276–77, 283–88, 286 (ill.), 289 (ill.), 289–90, 312, 313
peace and, *2:* 271–73, 312–13
Silent Majority and, *2:* 276, 288–89
Soviet Union and, *2:* 270, 290
support for, *2:* 288–89
teach-ins and, *2:* 284, 285
Tet Offensive, *2:* 271–72
U.S. Congress and, *2:* 312
Vietcong and, *2:* 252, 269, 270, 276, 283
Vietnamization, *2:* 312–13
Voice of America, *1:* 118; *2:* 323
Voorhis, Jerry, *1:* 44, 109
Voting. *See* Elections
Voting Rights Act of 1965, *2:* 254, 282

W

Walesa, Lech, *2:* 358
Walker, Arthur, *1:* 156
Walker, Barbara, *1:* 156
Walker, John A., Jr., *1:* 156–57
Walker, Michael, *1:* 156
Wall of Shame. *See* Berlin Wall
Wallace, Henry A., *1:* 23
Warsaw Pact, *1:* 172 (ill.)
  Conference on Security and Cooperation in Europe (CSCE) and, *2:* 365–66
  Conventional Force Talks in Europe and, *2:* 355
  Czechoslovakia and, *2:* 268
  definition of, *1:* 168; *2:* 348
  disbanding of, *2:* 363, 366–67
  formation of, *1:* 173
  Hungary and, *2:* 194–95, 366
  military and, *2:* 365–66
  North Atlantic Treaty Organization (NATO) and, *1:* 185; *2:* 364
Watergate scandal, *2:* 298, 299, 310–11
Wauck, Bonnie, *1:* 162, 163
Weapons. *See also* Missiles; Nuclear weapons
  chemical, *2:* 283–84, 290
  hidden, *1:* 136
  strategic arms, *2:* 234, 235
  tactical arms, *2:* 234, 235
  words as, *1:* 2, 28, 56, 80, 100, 126, 127, 168; *2:* 192, 234, 252, 276, 298, 320, 348
Weinberger, Caspar, *2:* 332–33
Welch, Joseph N., *1:* 118
West Berlin, *1:* 73 (ill.), 75 (ill.), 76 (ill.)
  blockades of, *1:* 37, 56, 62–66, 64 (ill.), 67 (ill.), 111
  détente and, *2:* 306
  Eisenhower, Dwight D., and, *1:* 70
  Kennedy, John F., and, *1:* 70–71
  military and, *1:* 69–71
  Soviet Union and, *1:* 69–71
West Germany, *1:* 33 (ill.), 60 (ill.)
  economy of, *1:* 62–66, 67–68, 68–69
  elections in, *1:* 67, 173
  espionage and, *1:* 60

formation of, *1:* 30–31, 38, 55, 60–61, 66–68, 173
government of, *1:* 66–67
Marshall Plan and, *1:* 67
military of, *1:* 185
North Atlantic Treaty Organization (NATO) and, *1:* 68, 173
Ostopolitik and, *2:* 305–6
Soviet Union and, *1:* 60–62, 65–66; *2:* 206
Western European Union (WEU), *1:* 37
Westmoreland, William C., *2:* 271
WEU. *See* Western European Union (WEU)
Whalen, William Henry, *1:* 153
Whitworth, Jerry A., *1:* 156
Wigner, Eugene, *1:* 81
Wilson, Woodrow, *1:* 4–5
Woodstock Festival, *2:* 287–88
World Bank, *1:* 13, 22
World Court, *2:* 332
World War I, *1:* 5, 6, 126–27, 149
World War II
  Allies and, *1:* 2, 8–18, 48, 55, 105; *2:* 364
  Attlee, Clement, and, *1:* 86
  battles of, *1:* 7–8, 9, 12, 17, 104–5
  beginning of, *1:* 7–8
  Berlin and, *1:* 57
  Big Three and, *1:* 2, 9–18, 14 (ill.), 29, 30 (ill.)
  Bulgaria and, *1:* 18
  China and, *1:* 12, 39
  ciphers and, *1:* 131
  Council of Foreign Ministers and, *1:* 17–18
  death in, *1:* 17, 87
  end of, *1:* 105; *2:* 364
  espionage and, *1:* 127, 131, 140, 142–43, 149; *2:* 224
  Four-power Allied Control Council and, *1:* 15
  France and, *1:* 3; *2:* 364
  Germany and, *1:* 2, 3, 7–8, 8–9, 10, 11, 15–17, 29, 55, 56–57, 58–59; *2:* 364
  Great Britain and, *1:* 2, 3, 8–11, 12, 13, 15, 17, 86; *2:* 364
  House Un-American Activities Committee (HUAC) and, *1:* 104–5

Japan and, *1:* 2, 8, 10, 12, 17, 39, 50, 86–88, 104–5
nuclear weapons and, *1:* 17, 18 (ill.), 80–82, 85–88, 135; *2:* 219, 241
peace treaty of, *2:* 364
Poland and, *1:* 7, 9–10, 11
Potsdam Conference, *1:* 13–17, 14 (ill.), 16 (ill.), 86, 143
reparations and, *1:* 15–17, 57, 58
Romania and, *1:* 18
Soviet Union and, *1:* 3, 7–8, 8–14, 15–17, 17–18, 29–30; *2:* 364
Tehran Conference, *1:* 143
Truman, Harry S., and, *1:* 10–11, 18, 86
United States of America and, *1:* 3, 8–18, 29–30; *2:* 364
Yalta Conference and, *1:* 2, 9, 10, 11, 12, 105, 143
Wu-Tai Chin, Larry, *1:* 158–59
Wynne, Greville, *1:* 151, 152

Y

Yalta Conference
  agreements of, *1:* 10, 11, 105
  definition of, *1:* 2
  espionage and, *1:* 143
  location of, *1:* 9
  United Nations and, *1:* 12
Yasgur, Max, *2:* 287
Yeltsin, Boris, *2:* 367 (ill.)
  Bush, George, and, *2:* 369
  capitalism and, *2:* 367–68
  Commonwealth of Independent States (CIS) and, *2:* 370
  Communist Party and, *2:* 369
  coup attempt and, *2:* 368
  democracy and, *2:* 367–68
  economy and, *2:* 373
  election of, *2:* 360–61, 373
  Gorbachev, Mikhail, and, *2:* 367–68, 373
  intelligence and, *1:* 160
  North Atlantic Treaty Organization (NATO) and, *2:* 370
  nuclear weapons and, *2:* 370
  resignation of, *2:* 373
Yemen, *2:* 204

Yevtushenko, Yevgeny, *2:* 292,
  293, 293 (ill.)
Yom Kippur War. *See* October War
Yugoslavia, *1:* 51, 121; *2:* 375
Yurchenko, Vitaly, *1:* 158, 158 (ill.)

Z

Zaire. *See* Congo
Zel'dovich, Yakov, *1:* 95
Zhou Enlai, *2:* 300, 301